W9-AEN-029

Back (left to right): Ruth M. Heaton, Penelope L. Peterson, Sarah J. McCarthey, Joan E. Talbert, David K. Cohen, Suzanne M. Wilson

Front (left to right): Deborah L. Ball, Milbrey W. McLaughlin, Magdalene Lampert, Carol A. Barnes

TEACHING
for
UNDERSTANDING

David K. Cohen
Milbrey W. McLaughlin
Joan E. Talbert

Editors

TEACHING
for
UNDERSTANDING

CHALLENGES for
POLICY and PRACTICE

Jossey-Bass Publishers · San Francisco

Substantial discounts on bulk quantities of Jossey-Bass books are available to corporations, professional associations, and other organizations. For details and discount information, contact the special sales department at Jossey-Bass Inc., Publishers. (415) 433-1740; Fax (415) 433-0499.

For sales outside the United States, contact Maxwell Macmillan International Publishing Group, 866 Third Avenue, New York, New York 10022.

Manufactured in the United States of America

The paper used in this book is acid-free and meets the State of California requirements for recycled paper (50 percent recycled waste, including 10 percent postconsumer waste), which are the strictest guidelines for recycled paper currently in use in the United States.

10% POST CONSUMER WASTE

The ink in this book is either soy- or vegetable-based and during the printing process emits fewer than half the volatile organic compounds (VOCs) emitted by petroleum-based ink.

Library of Congress Cataloging-in-Publication Data

Teaching for understanding : challenges for policy and practice /
David K. Cohen, Milbrey W. McLaughlin, Joan E. Talbert, editors. —
1st ed.
    p.   cm.—(The Jossey-Bass education series)
    Includes bibliographical references (p.   ) and index.
    ISBN 1-55542-515-1
    1. Teaching. 2. Teachers—Training of. 3. Education—Aims and
objectives. I. Cohen, David K., date. II. McLaughlin, Milbrey
Wallin. III. Talbert, Joan E. IV. Series.
LB1025.3.T436   1993
371.1′02—dc20   92-35498
                                                                CIP

FIRST EDITION
HB Printing   10 9 8 7 6 5 4 3 2 1   *Code 9313*

The Jossey-Bass
Education Series

Contents

ix

Preface

Education reform goals challenge America's schools and teachers to move away from transmitting knowledge and facts to promoting students' deeper understanding of academic subjects—understanding based in active engagement with subject area concepts. This vision of teaching and learning, called *teaching for understanding* to distinguish it from traditional modes of instruction, would promote students' critical thinking skills and authentic learning.

Teaching for understanding entails new educational standards that challenge existing conventions of practice, research, and policy. Classrooms where teachers and students develop knowledge collaboratively, where "facts" are challenged continually in discourse, and where teachers as well as their students engage in learning and inquiry, depart from orthodox pedagogy where teachers are in control and students are receivers of knowledge. These visions of practice elude research framed in terms of traditional social science models because such inquiry is insensitive to the dynamic, complex interactions of the classroom and the critical role of "up-close" context.

Reforms seeking to promote teaching for understanding likewise encounter the incongruence between policies that attempt to "transmit" or direct and education strategies that assume adaptation, learning, and situational meaning. Even a cursory look at the education policy system shows that coexisting with the enthusiasm of reformers about teaching for understanding and its promise for enhancing the productivity of both teachers and students is uncertainty about how to implement such reforms. Visions of teaching for understanding entail new roles for all actors in the education policy system—teachers, parents, administrators, teacher educators, students, and researchers—but the nature of these new roles remains unclear. The new orientation among these actors would require changed policies and support systems for teachers—new forms of support for professional growth and change, new concepts of accountability and supervision, for example—but these transformations are still undefined.

We do not claim to definitively answer the complex and difficult questions raised by this new agenda for education reform. Rather, our aim is to draw on our diverse experience as teachers, education researchers, and policy analysts to suggest what teaching for understanding looks like in classrooms, to explore how people learn to do it, to frame issues for further research and appropriate policy-making. *Teaching for Understanding* reflects our realization that each of us holds a different but essential perspective on the promise and challenges of the new standard for teaching and learning in American schools of the twenty-first century. Enacting the vision requires discourse, insight, and understanding among the various constituencies of American education. This book initiates a discourse among the worlds of practice, research, and policy that will be critical to building a new community of education practice.

Overview of the Contents

Chapter One outlines what teachers need to know and be able to do in order to promote deeper student understanding of subject matter. Drawing upon a rapidly expanding research literature, Milbrey W. McLaughlin and Joan E. Talbert highlight the demands for teachers' knowledge of subject matter, pedagogical content knowledge, knowledge of the learner, and new management strategies entailed in this move from a teacher-dominated, transmission mode of instruction. We emphasize that the new vision of practice calls for substantial learning on the part of teachers—the sort of learning that takes a great deal of time, courage, and support—and for new research and policy strategies to enable this kind of professional growth.

Chapters Two to Four illuminate the kinds of classroom decisions entailed in teaching for understanding. The authors of these chapters narrate the process, uncertainties, and demands inherent in this mode of teaching and the collegial support that enabled and sustained the process. Administrators, policymakers, researchers, and teachers can learn much from these chapters about the complex reality of the new education practice.

Deborah L. Ball and Sylvia S. Rundquist (Chapter Two) focus on collaboration as a context for learning to teach for understanding. Ball, a professor at Michigan State University, worked with Rundquist, a third-grade teacher, to investigate what it may take to teach mathematics for understanding. Their chapter depicts the complex, multidimensional relationship of the collaborators and the joint learning that occurred. Ball learned about the concrete problems and dilemmas inherent in such teaching; Rundquist learned about new ways to think about her role as classroom teacher. Teachers and teacher educators will find in this chapter insight about both collaboration and teaching for understanding in elementary classrooms. Teacher educators will find rich illustration of collaborative roles for school of education faculty that enrich all parties.

Ruth M. Heaton and Magdalene Lampert (Chapter Three) move the discussion explicitly to the context of teacher education and explore the role of collaboration and mentoring in enabling teacher educators to learn to teach for understanding themselves and to learn how to teach new teachers to do so. While this chapter focuses on teaching for understanding from the perspective of teacher educators, Heaton's experience as a Michigan State University graduate student working with Lampert, a professor and mathematics education expert, parallels that of Rundquist and of Carol Miller and Carol Yerkes (Chapter Four) in terms of the meaningful personal and professional challenges in "relearning," the high levels of trust and courage required, and the time such learning and teaching demand. This chapter will be of particular interest to teacher educators seeking concrete illustration of innovative graduate training programs and ways to think about the construction of practice within their curricula.

In Chapter Four, Suzanne M. Wilson, a professor at Michigan State University, with Carol Miller and Carol Yerkes, teachers in a nearby elementary school, reflects on the evolution of their learning to teach for understanding and the necessarily individual nature of the enterprise. Drawing upon their experiences collaborating on social studies teaching over three years, Wilson captures the situational quality of learning for all involved. Learning for all collaborators was conditioned by previous understandings and assumptions, personal styles, professional communities, and institutional commitments. A central theme of this account is the importance of acknowledging and supporting different rates and styles of learning for teachers, just as teaching for understanding assumes for students. Wilson, Miller, and Yerkes also illustrate the importance of professional community and the norms and values associated with it as critical context for collaboration. The norms of discourse—ways of seeing, representing, thinking, and talking—and interaction in Wilson's university environment were foreign to the norms of the elementary school, where argument often was perceived as divisive and confrontation was to be avoided. Administrators will see much in this account about the ways in which usual conceptions of management, "quality control," and school organization influence teachers' willingness to change, or more particularly, to admit ignorance or need to learn. Teacher educators will also gain appreciation for the individual nature of learning and change for teachers and the importance of support systems based in the school workplace.

Collectively, Chapters Two through Four describe collaborations and engagements in teaching and learning that are enormously intense, personal, and demanding of patience and perseverence. These up-close accounts illuminate the classroom aspects of teaching for understanding and collaboration as a context for change and detail the nature of the task, the demands it makes on the individuals involved, and, by implication, on the institutions in which they function.

Sarah J. McCarthey and Penelope L. Peterson (Chapter Five) focus a broader lens on the institutional resources that enable teachers to change their teaching and on how the school and district contexts influence those changes. "Restructuring," their cases show, does not by itself create the discourse critical to learning to teach for understanding. Their analysis considers the strategy of using a system agent to facilitate teachers' change and underscores the important role of a trusted professional colleague in enabling teachers to learn new roles and knowledge. In their study of two teachers, the one who had a coach to stimulate and guide her learning was able to move toward teaching for understanding. Lacking this kind of professional support, these changes in teachers' knowledge and beliefs did not take place.

The case analyses in Chapter Five suggest what "midrange" practice in the realm of teaching for understanding may look like. The sea change in teaching practice is inevitably gradual, if tumultuous. For most teachers, it involves moving along a continuum from traditional, transmission methods to the interactive, constructivist practices described in the other chapters on teaching. McCarthey and Peterson sketch what such midrange practices look like and consider the personal and professional factors that might contribute to different rates of learning for teachers or willingness to significantly transform practice.

Chapters Two through Five all have implications for teachers' inservice and preservice training, for administrator roles, and for ways in which policymakers and practitioners can most fruitfully frame the problem of reforms intended to promote teaching for understanding. They detail the many and unanticipated ways in which teaching for understanding makes teaching much harder because of its demand on energy, expertise, concentration, and commitment. They also suggest how these classroom-level realities signal increased complexity at all levels of the education policy system. These chapters draw attention to the particular kind of challenge learning to teach for understanding represents. As stated previously, it requires "relearning," letting go of practices of earlier structured teaching—carefully preparing lesson plans, preparing student worksheets, writing out lectures, for example—and then learning to think about and convey the subject matter in different ways. These facets of learning to teach for understanding are simultaneously risky and exhilarating, just as the changed relationships with students are both threatening and rewarding.

Unlike change efforts with clear endings or clear indicators of goals accomplished, learning to teach for understanding is by its nature an unfinished and ongoing enterprise. The new standards for teaching present a difficult challenge for practitioners or policymakers who want to know "when we've gotten there" or "when we're done," or who want a clear structure for action or programmatic authority. Teaching for understanding is orthogonal to a program adoption concept of change or a regulatory policy framework. For these reasons, the educational standard is more difficult to manage, support, assess, understand, and promote than traditional classroom practice. These chapters amply illustrate the disjunctions between existing concepts of knowledge and the ways in which teaching is managed, governed, supported, and studied.

Joan E. Talbert and Milbrey W. McLaughlin (Chapter Six) look at education research as it has been conceived and ask how well it can inform either policymakers or practitioners about the nature or conditions of teaching for understanding. They find that traditional social science models and findings fall short in helping to understand the realities of teaching of any stripe and are especially ill-suited to understanding the combination of factors that may transform practice into teaching for understanding. Traditional social science research is insensitive to the taken-for-granted, invariant conditions of teaching and to complex interactions among variables that characterize a particular teaching setting. Thus, it risks misinforming research and policy communities about key factors that promote or that inhibit teaching and learning for understanding. Research that misconstrues the reality it ought to depict can be of little effective use either in discovering or describing levers for educational change.

David K. Cohen and Carol A. Barnes (Chapters Seven and Eight) examine the policy system through a similar lens and locate the general failure of policy to influence practice in the ways reformers had hoped. The success of policies aimed to reform education turns fundamentally on the extent to which they reflect accurately the reality on which they focus. Cohen and Barnes argue, as do Talbert and McLaughlin, that teaching for understanding requires changed ways of thinking about, understanding, and solving problems of practice.

A theme running throughout all the chapters is that moving practice, research, and policy in directions that can enable and support the vision of practice called teaching for understanding requires breaking out of routines—transforming routine ways of thinking about practice, routine ways of administering schools and classrooms, routine ways of formulating education research and policy. This book takes up that task.

Acknowledgments

Our various research endeavors have provided essential experience and involvement. The National Science Foundation's support for Ball's and Lampert's work in classrooms and Michigan State University's commitment to integrating research and practice and to teacher educators' direct and ongoing involvement in classrooms has permitted Wilson, Ball, and Lampert to teach in elementary school classrooms as part of their responsibilities as Michigan State faculty. Assistance from centers supported by the Office of Educational Research and Improvement has been essential to our individual and collective work. McLaughlin and Talbert have learned about teaching "in context" and the shortcomings of traditional research approaches through their work at the Center for Research on the Context of Secondary School Teaching (CRC) at Stanford University. Cohen and Peterson have immersed themselves in classrooms and efforts to change practice with support from the Consortium for Policy Research in Education and the Center for the Learning and Teaching of Elementary Subjects at Michigan State University. CRC supported the occasion for conversation and writing that produced this book. Juliann Cummer at CRC juggled logistics, incompatible software, and geographically dispersed authors to create a manuscript that was consistent in terms of fonts, formats, and notes.

December 1992   David K. Cohen
                                                   East Lansing, Michigan

                                                   Milbrey W. McLaughlin
                                                   Joan E. Talbert
                                                   Stanford, California

The Editors

David K. Cohen is the John A. Hannah Distinguished Professor of Education and Social Policy at Michigan State University. He received his A.B. degree (1956) from Alfred University in history and political science and his Ph.D. degree (1961) from the University of Rochester in European intellectual history. Cohen's current research interests include the relations between policy and practice, the nature of teaching practice, and educational policy. His recent publications include articles in the *Review of Research in Education* (with J. Spillane) and *Educational Evaluation and Policy Analysis*.

Milbrey W. McLaughlin is professor of education and public policy at Stanford University and director of the Center for Research on the Context of Secondary School Teaching. She received her B.A. degree (1963) from Connecticut College in philosophy and her M.Ed. and Ed.D degrees (1973) from Harvard University in education and social policy. McLaughlin's primary research activities have been in the areas of policy implementation, educational change, school contexts, and community-based organizations for youth. Her books include *The Contexts of Teaching in Secondary Schools* (1990, with J. Talbert and N. Bascia), *Steady Work* (1989, with R. Elmore), and *Teacher Evaluation: Improvement, Accountability and Effective Learning* (1989, with R. S. Pfeifer). Prior to joining the Stanford faculty, McLaughlin was a policy analyst with the RAND Corporation. At RAND, she conducted, with Paul Berman, the Change Agent study and coauthored the multivolume *Federal Programs Affecting Educational Change* (1974–1978).

Joan E. Talbert is senior research scholar and associate director of the Center for Research on the Context of Secondary School Teaching at Stanford University. She received her B.A. degree (1967) from Vassar College in sociology and child study and her M.A. degree (1973) and Ph.D. degree (1978) from the University of Washington in sociology. Talbert's long-standing research interest concerns the organizational, occupational, and social-cultural foundations of individuals' careers and work orientations. Her current research analyzes diverse social and organizational contexts of high school teaching and their effects on teachers' professional identities and practice. She has published articles on teachers' career patterns, school organization, and professional communities among secondary school teachers and an edited book on the multiple, embedded contexts of teaching, *The Contexts of Teaching in Secondary Schools* (1990, with M. McLaughlin and N. Bascia).

The Contributors

Deborah L. Ball is associate professor of teacher education at Michigan State University, where she teaches prospective teachers and graduate students. She received her Ph.D. degree (1988) from Michigan State University in curriculum, teaching, and policy. Her research focuses on the practice of teaching, on teacher learning, and on efforts to effect reform practice. Since 1988 she has also been teaching mathematics to the children in Sylvia Rundquist's class.

Carol A. Barnes is a doctoral student in education policy at Michigan State University (MSU), where she works for a research center interested in the relation of policy and teaching practice. She received her B.A. degree (1971) from MSU in education. Before entering MSU's doctoral program, Barnes was a policy adviser with the Governor's Cabinet Council on Human Investment, an agency that developed education policy for Michigan's governor. She also served as director of a Michigan interdepartmental program for the Women's Commission, the First Lady, and the Department of Civil Rights and as director of a governor's task force on employment for older citizens. Prior to her state government service, Barnes was federal grants coordinator and director of community outreach for Congressman Bob Carr.

Ruth M. Heaton is a research assistant and doctoral candidate in teacher education at Michigan State University. She is also an experienced elementary school teacher. Heaton's main interests are

mathematics teaching and teacher education. In an effort to understand the changes in practice called for by the current reforms in
mathematics education and what it would be like for an experienced
teacher to try to make such changes, Heaton is studying her own
teaching of elementary mathematics. She received her B.S. degree
(1979) from the University of Minnesota in elementary education
and her M.Ed. degree (1988) from the University of Vermont.

Magdalene Lampert is a fifth-grade mathematics teacher, a teacher
educator, and a researcher on teaching. Since 1984 she has been on
the faculty at Michigan State University, where she has pioneered
new kinds of connections between scholarship and practice. Lampert received her B.S. degree (1969) from Chestnut Hill College in
mathematics, an M.Ed. degree (1971) from Temple University in
secondary curriculum and instruction, an M.Ed. degree (1973) from
Antioch University in elementary education, and her Ed.D. degree
(1981) from Harvard University. Her research interests focus on the
teaching and learning of authentic mathematics for understanding
in school classrooms. She is currently exploring the use of new
technologies for communicating with teachers, researchers, and policymakers about the nature of teaching practice.

Sarah J. McCarthey is assistant professor of language and literacy
in the Department of Curriculum and Instruction at the University
of Texas, Austin. She received her B.A. degree (1977) from Tufts
University in English, her M.A. degree (1982) from Stanford University in education, and her Ph.D. degree (1991) from Michigan
State University in teacher education. Her research interests are literacy instruction in elementary schools and the relationships between literacy, dialogue, and student learning. McCarthey, who has
published in *Journal of Reading Behavior,* received the Outstand-
ing Student Research Award from the National Reading Conference
in 1991.

Carol Miller is a third-grade teacher at Kendon Elementary School
in Lansing, Michigan, which is a professional development school
sponsored by the Michigan Partnership for a New Education. She
received her B.A. degree (1968) from Michigan State University in

elementary education and is working on her M.A. degree at Michigan State University in education. She has been teaching elementary school for twelve years. Her current interests include reconceptualizing teacher education in restructured schools in cooperation with school–university partnerships.

Penelope L. Peterson is University Distinguished Professor of Education at Michigan State University, where she is also co-director of the Institute for Research on Teaching. She received her B.S. degree (1971) from Iowa State University in psychology and philosophy and her M.A. and Ph.D. degrees (1976) from Stanford University in education. Peterson's research focuses on learning and teaching in classrooms, particularly in mathematics and literacy; learning in reform contexts; and relations among educational research, policy, and practice. Currently she is co-directing (with D. Cohen, D. Ball, and S. Wilson) a National Science Foundation research project, Teachers' Learning from Reform, and another project, Supporting State Efforts to Reform Teaching, funded by the Carnegie Corporation and Pew Charitable Trusts.

Sylvia S. Rundquist is a third-grade teacher at Spartan Village School in East Lansing, Michigan. She received her B.S. degree (1957) from Michigan State University. She is an active member of the faculty and works with prospective teachers from Michigan State University. She collaborates with Deborah L. Ball in seeking to understand alternative approaches to teaching mathematics and in creating different kinds of opportunities for others to learn about teaching.

Suzanne M. Wilson is associate professor of teacher education at Michigan State University, where she is also a senior researcher at the National Center for Research on Teacher Learning and the Center for Policy Research in Education. She received her B.A. degree (1977) from Brown University in American civilization and history, her M.S. degree (1986) from Stanford University in statistics, and her Ph.D. degree (1988) from Stanford University in educational psychology. Her major research activities include investigating questions about the professional knowledge base of teaching, teacher education, and teacher assessment.

Carol Yerkes is a third-grade teacher at Kendon Elementary School in Lansing, Michigan, which is a professional development school sponsored by the Michigan Partnership for a New Education. She received her B.A. degree (1963) from Michigan State University in elementary education and her M.A. degree (1968) from Michigan State University in education. A veteran of twenty-nine years, Yerkes has taught in several schools in the Lansing area and has participated in a number of research projects with faculty from Michigan State University. Her current interests include developing innovative and integrated curricula for elementary schools and exploring restructuring schools to facilitate children's learning.

TEACHING
for
UNDERSTANDING

1

Introduction:
New Visions of Teaching

Milbrey W. McLaughlin
Joan E. Talbert

New visions of educational practice engage the energy and attention of education reformers.[1] These visions depart substantially from conventional practice and frame an active role for students as explorers, conjecturers, and constructors of their own learning. In this new way of thinking, teachers function as guides, coaches, and facilitators of students' learning through posing questions, challenging students' thinking, and leading them in examining ideas and relationships. Advocates of this approach to practice assume that what students learn has to do fundamentally with how they learn it.

Education reformers envision classrooms where students and teachers acquire knowledge collaboratively, where orthodoxies of pedagogy and "facts" are continually challenged in classroom discourse, and where conceptual (versus rote) understanding of subject matter is the goal. This image of educational practice is often called teaching for understanding.[2]

American schools are often relatively successful in terms of basic skills achievement, but teaching for understanding aims to enhance the success of students at tasks variously described as problem solving, critical analysis, higher-order thinking, or flexible understanding of academic subject matter. With respect to outcomes of this sort, the success of the American educational system—and particularly American high schools—has been called into question. Teaching for understanding is held up as the new standard for teaching practice—a goal toward which schools and the education profession should move.[3]

This vision of practice signals a sea change in notions of teaching and learning; constructivist ideas about teachers' co-constructing knowledge with learners replace traditional views of teacher as knowledge transmitter and behavioral engineer.[4] In this view of teaching and learning, teachers' central responsibility is to create worthwhile activities and select materials that engage students' intellect and stimulate them to move beyond acquisition of facts to sense making in a subject area. Rather than reproduce facts, teachers expect their students to explain their ideas, support their conclusions, and persist when they are stumped. Teaching for understanding promises to enhance the kinds of cognitive outcomes for students that the American educational system has heretofore been notoriously ineffective at producing. Students engaged in learning for understanding will aim not only to master "facts" conventionally conceived but also to explore, imagine, reason, formulate, and solve problems: What makes something "true" in mathematics? What is evidence in history? What are the ways to think about light?

Teaching for understanding assumes substantial new learning on teachers' part; it requires change not only in what is taught but also in how it is taught. Learning how to involve students actively in the construction of knowledge, how to move beyond fact-based concepts of knowledge and learner outcomes, and how to fashion new classroom roles and relationships involves more than simply sharpening up teaching skills or teachers' professional knowledge base as conventionally conceived. Teaching for understanding requires teachers to have comprehensive and in-depth knowledge of subject matter, competence in representation and manipulation of this knowledge in instructional activities, and skill in managing classroom processes in a way that enables active student learning.[5]

Teachers with only superficial knowledge of their subject matter will have little flexibility in their pedagogical choices and preferences and thus be effectively constrained to teach "just the facts," or to leave learning up to the students. By contrast, teachers who have mastered the rich interconnections and multiple forms of knowledge found in a subject area will have the substantive control of a subject needed to develop the kinds of activities and strategies involved in teaching for understanding.

Additionally, teaching for understanding requires pedagogical content knowledge, what Shulman (1989) once called "the missing paradigm in research on teaching." This is knowledge not simply of a subject area but also of how to teach it—how to select, represent, and organize information, concepts, and procedures so that subject matter knowledge can be transformed into teaching for understanding. Lack of pedagogical knowledge in a content area can be a serious constraint on teaching for understanding. For example, "crossover" teaching, or teaching out of one's subject area, is an important factor promoting a "transmission" style of teaching.[6] Crossover teachers express discomfort not only with subject matter but also with the different pedagogies associated with different subject areas. Knowing *how* to teach in a subject area and within a particular topic area is regarded as an essential element of teaching for understanding.

Knowledge of the learner, essential to teaching for understanding, enables teachers to move beyond mere transmission. A teacher needs information about a students' existing understanding of subject matter in order to promote conceptual change and flexible comprehension of the subject. Teachers must be able to consider subject matter through the eyes of the learners; they must be able to interpret the learners' comments, questions, and activities through the lens of a particular subject.[7]

Teaching for understanding also requires new classroom management strategies. Routines and activities that promote active student learning differ fundamentally from those that accompany the transmission of information by teachers and its reproduction by students. Teachers and students have different classroom roles. Classrooms where teaching for understanding occurs are marked by cooperative relations among students, social support for trying out new ideas, and a close and interactive relationship between students and teacher. Students need to talk among themselves and with the teacher.

The teacher-dominated classrooms traditional in American

education are marked by flow of knowledge from teacher to student and impose a passive student role. The noise, unpredictability, and sheer movement characteristic of classrooms where teaching for understanding takes place contrast fundamentally with teacher-dominated techniques of lecture or individual student seat work typical of transmission-style teaching. Managing these new student roles presents a daunting challenge for many teachers and contradicts principles of practice conveyed in teacher education programs and assessed in teacher evaluation schemes. It also requires that teachers be aware of classroom culture, of patterns of participation, of levels of trust and acceptance, of authority and status. The teacher's role extends far beyond creating an "orderly environment" to building one in which students' ideas are respected, where all students participate and intellectual risk-taking is the norm.

Teachers also need to learn *when* the interactive, constructivist forms of teaching and learning are called for and when other less demanding, conventional strategies are appropriate. The vision of practice engendered by teaching for understanding does not assume transmission strategies are inappropriate for all tasks. Some learning objectives—learning new vocabulary in a language class or learning the sequence of key events in a history class, for example—might be best achieved through drill-and-practice or lectures. Key to students' learning and accomplishment is teacher judgment about choice of educational method and mix in overall classroom practice. Teachers should use a variety of classroom arrangements flexibly in accord with classroom goals and dynamics.

Teaching for understanding also requires new strategies of assessment and valuing students' work and progress. The new standard for teaching replaces conventional "teach and test" strategies with analytic reflection on classroom life and their connection to students' learning. Ongoing evaluation of classroom life and student thinking processes, rather than episodic paper and pencil tests, informs teachers teaching for understanding.

Challenges for Practice and Policy

Substantial enthusiasm for this new vision of teaching and learning exists in many quarters, but practitioners, researchers, and policymakers have very limited understanding of what it requires of teachers or of education policy. This book is about these practical and pragmatic problems. The chapters that follow portray both the practice of teaching for understanding and the aspects involved in taking that journey. We take up the challenges of changing the practices, beliefs, and assumptions that reinforce and perpetuate notions of teachers as transmitters and students as passive receivers of knowledge.

Many of the practical problems associated with teaching for understanding, problems which exist even for teachers committed to this vision of practice, are inherent in the organization and operation of America's schools. This vision of practice conveys fundamentally different values about authority, responsibility, and knowledge. How do you organize for this kind of instruction? Orchestrate the discourse? For example, the nonstop, five-period teaching schedules that regulate the workplace life of most high school teachers mean that even "superteacher," fortified with passion and multivitamins, would be unable to teach for understanding on a sustained basis, in all classes, all day long. Even teachers accomplished in teaching for understanding would have to make strategic decisions about how to apportion the energy and concentration teaching for understanding consumes. Traditional "five times five," five classes for five periods a day, carves teachers' time and attention in ways that constrain teaching for understanding both pedagogically and in terms of teachers' energy and attention budgets.

Expectations and norms existing in the typical school workplace also constrain teaching for understanding in subtle and explicit ways. As this book illustrates, lack of support from one's colleagues or from administrators places fundamental restrictions on practice, will, and spirit. Teaching for understanding departs from the kinds of teaching and learning activities administrators are accustomed to evaluating and overseeing. Teaching for understanding requires teachers to be learners, constantly reviewing their practice and renewing their content and pedagogical knowledge. Yet under current norms, "needs improvement," an assumption central to this vision of professional growth and responsibility, is a black mark on teacher evaluation forms. How can teachers admit their need to know? Expose pedagogical uncertainties?

This notion of practice also deviates from conventional expectations about what students should know and how they should understand their role. These departures from orthodoxy matter enormously. Teachers wonder: Have the sixth graders entering my classroom been "properly prepared"? What are students' expectations about my role? Will they have behavior problems? Teachers who strive to teach for understanding in traditional school contexts report that the criticism by their colleagues is painful, demoralizing, and difficult to endure.

Parents and members of the community also question the value or legitimacy of the learning produced in classrooms where teachers and students construct understandings of a knowledge domain together. The "products" of these instructional environments do not comport with test makers' frameworks, parents' expectations about "real school" or "real knowledge," or their concerns for their youngsters' success in the track-placement derby or the college admissions race.

These practical constraints exist even when teachers have acquired the knowledge and concepts integral to teaching for understanding. Compounding these issues is the question of how to impart and sustain the knowledge, capacity, and professional beliefs essential to teaching for understanding and what the enabling resources or institutional arrangements may be.

What, for instance, is the role of the school or district administrator if tightly designed lesson plans and predetermined objectives, fact-based assessment systems, and teacher adherence to specified curriculum guides and materials are contrary to the vision of teaching and learning pursued under the rubric of teaching for understanding? What role can district administrators play to enable school environments that support teaching for understanding and teachers' efforts to acquire the necessary knowledge and confidence to implement this vision of practice?

If teaching for understanding assumes ongoing learning and reflection on the part of teachers, what are the implications for schools of education and teacher training programs? What should a teacher credential certify? How do education schools teach teachers to teach and to learn? What notions about the nature of knowledge and learning must be revised? How can schools of education manage and support the sorts of institutional and individual change assumed by these questions?

Questions no less complex and difficult arise for policymakers. What does this vision of practice imply for accountability schemes, for curricula reforms, for standard-setting efforts, for teacher licensure? How can the policy system manage simultaneous expectations of teacher as expert and teacher as learner? How can policymakers manage their impatience, and the impatience of the public, for evidence of success when conventional measures of student outcomes do not match the new standards. And even more fundamentally, how can policy affect the kinds of arrangements, resources, norms, and supports essential to teaching for understanding? Is it any more possible for policymakers to construct productive learning opportunities for teachers if they do not know the territory than it is for teachers to construct effective learning situations for students when they have inadequate knowledge of their students or their subject matter? A serious, fundamental, and unavoidable question is whether policymakers can ever understand the realities associated with this concept sufficiently to develop policies that enable it. Or does this uncertain, situational, constructivist form of teaching by its very nature preclude a direct policy role?

Likewise, what are the roles of the other institutional actors in supporting reforms to implement teaching for understanding? Schools of education and professional education organizations traditionally have had only episodic and superficial connections with the K–12 school system. Does the vision of teaching and learning advocated by reformers call for change in the nature of those relationships, and if so, how?

The vision of teaching for understanding, of students and teachers engaged in constructing new knowledge, promises the kind of learning for both teachers and students that many educators, researchers, and policymakers judge most valuable to individuals and to society. This is the kind of teaching that engages students in the problems of a subject matter, in the process of asking questions and seeking answers, and in pursuing deeper understanding of their world. However, difficult and exceedingly complex questions arise about the kinds of institutional or policy arrangements necessary to enable such teaching, the kinds of resources necessary to build the requisite knowledge and commitment among teachers, and the changes required in existing arrangements. These questions largely are unanswered and not even well understood.

Notes

1. See, for example, the concept of teaching and learning outlined in America 2000 (1991); American Association for the Advancement of Science (1988); Eckert & Knudsen (1991); and Greeno (1991).
2. This view of teaching and learning has been developed by a number of scholars. See, as examples, Ames & Archer (1988); Ball (1990); Greeno (1991); Palinecsar & Brown (1984); and Prawat (1989).
3. See, for example, Good (1989); Mortimore, Sammons, Stoll, Lewis, & Ecob (1988); Newmann (1990); and Shulman (1987).
4. For discussions and illustrations of this co-construction of classroom learning, see Ball (1988); Ball (1990); Brown, Collins, & Duguid (1989); Grant (1988); Lampert (1988a); and McDiarmid, Ball, & Anderson (1989).
5. These demands are elaborated in Ball & McDiarmid (1989); Carpenter, Fennema, Peterson, Chiang, & Loef (1988); Grossman, Wilson, & Shulman (1989); Lampert (1988a, 1988b); Leinhardt & Greeno (1986); and McDiarmid, Ball, & Anderson (1989).
6. Hargreaves, 1988.
7. McDiarmid, Ball, & Anderson, 1989, and Peterson, Fennema, & Carpenter, 1991.

References

America 2000. (1991). *An educational strategy to move the American educational system ahead to meet the needs of the 21st century.* Washington, DC: U.S. Department of Education.

American Association for the Advancement of Science. (1988). *Science teaching: Making the system work.* Washington, DC: AAAS Publications.

Ames, C., & Archer, J. (1988). Achievement goals in the classroom:

Students' learning strategies and motivation processes. *American Psychological Association, 80*(3), 260-267.

Ball, D. L. (1988). *Knowledge and reasoning in mathematical pedagogy: Examining what prospective teachers bring to teacher education.* Unpublished doctoral dissertation, College of Education, Michigan State University, East Lansing.

Ball, D. L. (1990). Research on teaching mathematics: Making subject matter part of the equation. In J. Brophy (Ed.), *Advances in research on teaching: Vol. 2. Teachers' subject matter knowledge* (pp. 1-48). Greenwich, CT: JAI Press.

Ball, D. L., & McDiarmid, G. W. (1989). *The subject matter preparation of teachers* (Paper no. 89-4). East Lansing: National Center for Research on Teacher Education, Michigan State University.

Brown, J. S., Collins, A., & Duguid, P. (1989). Situated cognition and the culture of learning. *Educational Researcher, 18*(1), 32-42.

Carpenter, T. P., Fennema, E., Peterson, P. L., Chiang, C. P., & Loef, M. (1988). *Using knowledge of children's mathematics thinking in classroom teaching: An experimental study.* Washington, DC: National Science Foundation.

Eckert, P., & Knudsen, J. (1991). *Research in support of science and mathematics education.* National Science Foundation. Stanford, CA: Stanford University Publications.

Good, T. (1989). *Classroom and school research: Investments in enhancing schools* (Laboratory policy paper). Columbia: University of Missouri. (ERIC Document Reproduction Service No. ED 308 191)

Grant, G. (1988). *Teaching critical thinking.* New York: Praeger.

Greeno, J. G. (1991). Number sense as situated knowing in a conceptual domain. *Journal for Research in Mathematics Education, 22,* 170-218.

Grossman, P. L., Wilson, S., & Shulman, L. (1989). Teachers of substance: Subject matter knowledge in teaching. In M. Reynolds (Ed.), *Knowledge base of the beginning teacher.* Washington, DC: American Association of Colleges for Teacher Education.

Hargreaves, A. (1988). Teaching quality: A sociological analysis. *Journal of Curriculum Studies, 20*(3), 211-231.

Lampert, M. (1988a). *The teacher's role in reinventing the meaning of mathematical knowing in the classroom* (Research Series No. 186). East Lansing: The Institute for Research on Teaching, Michigan State University.

Lampert, M. (1988b). What can research on teacher education tell us about improving quality in mathematics education? *Teacher and Teacher Education, 4*(2), 157–170.

Leinhardt, G., & Greeno, J. G. (1986). The cognitive skill of teaching. *Journal of Educational Psychology, 78,* 75–95.

Leinhardt, G., & Smith, D. (1985). Expertise in mathematics instruction: Subject matter knowledge. *Journal of Educational Psychology, 77,* 247–271.

McDiarmid, G. W. (1989). *What do prospective teachers learn in their liberal arts courses?* (Paper no. 89–8). East Lansing: The National Center for Research on Teacher Education, Michigan State University.

McDiarmid, G. W., Ball, D. L., & Anderson, C. W. (1989). *Why staying one chapter ahead doesn't really work: Subject-specific pedagogy* (Paper no. 88–6). East Lansing: The National Center for Research on Teacher Education, Michigan State University.

Mortimore, P., Sammons, P., Stoll, L., Lewis, D., & Ecob, R. (1988). *School matters.* Berkeley: University of California Press.

Newmann, F. M. (1990). Higher-order thinking in teaching social studies: A rationale for the assessment of classroom thoughtfulness. *Journal of Curriculum Studies, 89,* 541–554.

Peterson, P. L., Fennema, E., & Carpenter, T. (1991). Using children's mathematical knowledge. In B. Means, C. Chelemer, & M. S. Knapp (Eds.), *Models for teaching advanced skills to disadvantaged students* (pp. 68–101). San Francisco: Jossey-Bass.

Prawat, R. S. (1989). Teaching for understanding: Three key attributes. *Teaching & Teacher Education, 5,* 315–328.

Shulman, L. S. (1987). Knowledge and teaching: Foundations of a new reform. *Harvard Educational Review, 57*(1), 1–22.

Part One

Views from the Classroom

2

Collaboration as a Context for Joining Teacher Learning with Learning About Teaching

Deborah L. Ball
Sylvia S. Rundquist

I hope I'm not too late to request Deborah's math program[1] for next year. To the point, my reasons are purely selfish; I feel weak in CSMP and math in general, and I want to become a better math teacher. I believe this experience would provide an excellent opportunity to do so.

Sylvia S. Rundquist
Letter to her principal

Since the fall of 1988, Deborah Ball, a professor in the College of Education at Michigan State University, has been teaching mathematics on a regular basis in the third grade classroom of Sylvia Rundquist, an elementary school teacher at Spartan Village School in East Lansing. The two have shared students and space, as well as the specific responsibilities for evaluating students' progress and reporting to parents. This chapter explores their learning in the context of that collaboration.

The work for this chapter was supported by the Michigan Partnership for a New Education, by the College of Education, Michigan State University, and by a grant from the National Science Foundation (TPE #8954724). The authors would like to acknowledge Ruth Heaton, Katherine Laatsch, Margery Osborne, Kara Suzuka, and Suzanne Wilson for their helpful comments on earlier drafts of this chapter. We would also like to acknowledge the other contributors to this book for the helpful context that writing it together provided for our own learning.

13

When Deborah began working in Sylvia's classroom, their motivations for the collaboration differed. On one hand, Sylvia saw Deborah's teaching in her class as an opportunity to improve her mathematics teaching, which she considered her weakest suit. For Sylvia, it seemed an unparalleled professional development opportunity. She had concerns about how it would work logistically, for she knew little about how Deborah would fit with the style and standards of classroom management with which she was most comfortable. Sylvia claimed to be "rigid" and not very flexible and wondered about sharing her classroom. She was a little nervous about it, but she nonetheless pursued the opportunity with enthusiasm and conviction. In a letter to her principal, she wrote that Deborah would provide her with a "secure setting in which to improve (her) self." Little did she know at that time the significance of what she had written.

Deborah's starting point, on the other hand, was not to consider her work in Sylvia's class as "professional development" for Sylvia at all. Although she acknowledged that it might offer opportunities for Sylvia's learning, Deborah did not consider her role to be providing "inservice." With thirteen years of elementary school teaching experience, including three of intensive staff development work, Deborah perceived the collaboration as the opportunity for her to resume day-to-day teaching and to develop her own mathematics teaching. If now as a teacher educator she was responsible for helping students learn to teach, it seemed to her that continuing to develop her own understanding of teaching was analogous to the need for an English teacher to continue to extend her own knowledge of literature or language. In her work, teaching was the content, and Deborah sought extended space in which to develop her own knowledge of this content. Additionally, as a researcher interested in studying teacher change, Deborah saw daily classroom teaching as an opportunity to gain an inside view of the challenges entailed in acting on some of the contemporary visions of good teaching: What does it mean to "orchestrate classroom discourse" in which "students make public conjectures and reason together about mathematics"? What is entailed in helping students construct mathematical understandings collaboratively? Or in learning to rely less on the teacher and more on mathematical evidence and argument? How does a teacher create opportunities for students to acquire depth—and what does it really mean for depth to be at least as important as breadth—and at the same time be responsible to students? How can responsiveness to students be balanced with responsibility for equity in opportunity?[2] From inside the teacher's role these issues look different from how they look from a policy or teacher education perspective. Deborah saw this as a chance to use her work as a teacher as one tool for understanding problems of change. And out of this work she has published several articles which focus on practice, on the challenges of trying to teach mathematics for understanding.[3]

Thus, with different starting points and goals, the two set out on what has proven to be a fruitful and satisfying collaboration. Deborah has been able to examine closely, from the inside, some of the specific and difficult dilemmas of teaching. Having Sylvia to talk with about particular tasks, children, and interactions has contributed substantially to this work. We have unpacked in close detail a myriad of considerations embedded in particular pedagogical decisions. We have analyzed specific problems. And we have examined subtle elements of the classroom culture and norms. Through these conversations, Sylvia has found herself on a fascinating personal voyage of change and discovery. However, nowhere have we tried to examine what this relationship has meant for her as a practicing teacher. Instead, all "products" of our collaboration have revolved around what we have been *learning about teaching*, about the challenges inherent in trying to teach mathematics in ways that are intellectually honest and genuinely responsive to children. This chapter is our first attempt to examine the other side of the coin: *teacher learning*. We focus here on the collaboration itself and what we have been learning as teachers. Although the chapter reflects what we have each been learning, we follow Sylvia's learning most closely, for her personal experience and narrative has often been invisible in our focus on "this kind of teaching."

This chapter has three main sections. First, we describe the history and circumstances of our collaboration, exploring the ways in which it is "collaborative" and what we mean by that. The second section explores three areas of teacher learning that have emerged as thematic in this case: mathematics, teaching and learning, and self. The first two areas are predictable; the third, while not surprising, is often unacknowledged in conversations about collaboration. We examine both *what* we have been learning as well as *how* we have been learning these things in the context of our work together. What kind of context for learning has our work been? How has the collaboration made these kinds of learning possible? In the conclusion we explore the notion of collaboration as a context for teacher learning. In what sense is our work together "collaboration"? Examining conversation as a metaphor for the processes and form of our partnership, we highlight the thematic shape of our work together and raise questions that extend beyond our particular story.

Framing Our Collaboration: History and Context

We began our work together in the fall of 1988. We have had an arrangement that does not on the surface seem "collaborative," for we do not, in the strictest sense, teach *together*. Four days a week, Deborah teaches mathematics to Sylvia's students. Amid the widespread clamor for the reform of school mathematics, Deborah has been exploring what is entailed in teaching mathematics "for understanding" by trying to *do* it. One aspect of this work is to find tasks and ways of working that have mathematical integrity and are also engaging to a diverse group of eight-year-olds. Another has been to be responsible to—and simultaneously challenge—the demands of a public school system. For example, the standardized test scores matter in this context, as does speed with basic arithmetic facts. What would it involve to try to be responsive to students while also being responsible to the district curriculum?

The mathematics period is a little over an hour long, usually right after lunch. During this time, the class often works on just one or two problems. The problems Deborah selects are intended to generate mathematical investigation and even controversy. Interested in what makes a problem good, she has been investigating what engages third graders and has been considering what is offered by applications versus "pure" mathematical investigations. Usually the problems are built from the previous day's work, with an eye on where the students need to head. The class often begins with students exploring the problem of the day individually. As part of the class, students keep mathematics notebooks in which they record all their work and in which they also write about that work. Deborah encourages students to confer with others sitting nearby. After ten minutes or so (depending on the problem), students move into small groups and work further together. The second half of the class period is spent in a large group discussion, during which individuals and groups present their solutions and discuss the ideas embedded in the problems.

While Deborah teaches, Sylvia watches, and sometimes attends to small tasks in the room. Happy enough not to have to teach math, she likes watching her students with another teacher. Sylvia, an experienced educator but relative newcomer to elementary school teaching, considered mathematics her weak suit. She had been teaching third grade for two years before she began this work with Deborah. The district was using *CSMP (Comprehensive School Mathematics Program)*,[4] an innovative curriculum centered on problem solving and mathematical reasoning, and Sylvia, like many of her colleagues, found it confusing and hard to teach. She often felt she did not understand the point of the lessons. Because of its spiral curriculum, Sylvia also had difficulty following the development of content. She hoped that watching Deborah, whom she considered an expert with *CSMP*, would give her answers. Not only had Deborah taught this curriculum herself, but Sylvia knew she had also helped other teachers with it.

During the class, Sylvia keeps notes to herself in a spiral notebook. She keeps track of the problems and records interesting approaches or comments that we hear from the students. She also is often busy with visitors who regularly come to the class. Explaining what students are doing, or why Deborah may be responding in particular ways has provided an ongoing context for Sylvia to formulate her ideas about the teaching. Around the edges of this daily classroom time, we exchange observations and worries about particular students. We notice subtle issues about a mathematics task, and we point out things to each other about a particular group of children's work or some aspect of the group discussion. We take note of individual children.

In addition to these conversations we make in borrowed moments, we have also met deliberately every week. Each Tuesday morning at seven o'clock we convene at a local coffee shop to talk about content, curriculum, students, room arrangements, parents, and other topics. Across the first two years of our partnership, the questions and notes in Sylvia's notebooks set up these regular conversations. She would want to retrace a problem the students had been working on. Or she would want to talk about a particular child. Sometimes she had an idea for how she might rearrange the room that she would want to discuss. During the third year, Sylvia bought a computer with a modem for home and virtually overnight entered the world of electronic communication. Soon she was writing messages to Deborah almost every night, as well as most mornings before school. Although we had always talked regularly, the advent of electronic mail significantly increased the amount of communication between us.

Learning in the Context of Our Collaboration

As we look back over our work together, we see that what we have been learning has clustered in three areas: mathematics, teaching and learning, and self. Much of this learning has spun out of the conversations we have learned to have—and to depend on—in our work together.

During the first year of Deborah's work in Sylvia's classroom, mathematics framed the developing relationship. Whereas many teachers and reformers overlook—or ignore—the role of subject matter knowledge in teaching for understanding, it was Sylvia's starting point. It was clear to her that to follow students on a variety of trajectories the teacher would need ample and flexible understanding of mathematics. Thus, from the beginning, many of Sylvia's questions centered on mathematical content and curriculum. For example, she would bring up one of the problems that the students had worked on and want Deborah to explain it to her. She felt quite embarrassed, thinking that she should know the mathematics that underlay the problems. Even as she grew increasingly willing to admit that she did not, she also felt in some ways increasingly ignorant. While Deborah asked her what *she* thought, Sylvia longed for straightforward answers: "Just like the kids . . . I didn't want to have to think on my own." Working together was clearly a risk; it could contribute to making Sylvia feel less competent. Often during the first year, she was amazed and chagrined to see that her knowledge of mathematics was even more tenuous than she had thought. She thought her math skills and understanding were poor and was afraid to let other teachers know how inadequate she felt. She worried that they might think poorly of her, or even wonder how she earned her teaching certificate. Deborah seemed a lifeline out of those feelings of inadequacy.

Sylvia watched and listened during class. Recording the problem of the day in her notebook, she often explored it herself. Quite often she would get stuck. When working on negative numbers that first fall, the students worked at trying to make sense of subtracting negative numbers; Sylvia was not sure about this either. When trying to figure out combinations and permutations, Sylvia remembered that she had never understood this content in her methods class. She struggled with whether zero was even or odd and whether 3×4 meant the same thing as 4×3. Working on a word problem with multiple solutions, Sylvia would randomly find all the solutions, and then be unsure about whether she had them all.

During the fall of the first year, Deborah was teaching multiplication. One day students were working on figuring out how many ways the classroom could be arranged for all the groups of desks to have an equal number of desks. With twenty-eight students in the class, children proposed arrangements such as seven groups of four, four groups of seven, two groups of fourteen, fourteen groups of two. Some children contested Jenny's proposal that you could push all the desks together to form one group of twenty-eight. While this discussion continued, Sylvia and two education students sat at the back table talking about how you might represent differently 4×7 and 7×4. The desk arrangement problem made clear that, although there were twenty-eight desks in either case, the room would look decidedly different with seven groups of four or four groups of seven. This was intriguing to Sylvia, who had learned that 4×7 was "the same as" 7×4. Her math classes in school had never emphasized representation or meaning, and so she remembered that $4 \times 7 = 28$ and $7 \times 4 = 28$, but she had never thought about the differences in what they represented. This was exciting and eye-opening for her. She formulated a way of thinking about the difference in meaning—that what you are concerned with is the number of groups and the number in each group (see Figure 2.1).

Sylvia found herself unexpectedly engrossed in mathematical ideas. At night she would often continue working on problems that the students had been doing in class. She would show the problems from the class to her husband. Sometimes he would suggest answers, or show her how to do the problems. Across the week, she kept track of the mathematics that puzzled her, and during that first year her questions freqently took up most of our weekly conversations. One morning she fretted, "I just can't get this into my head." She showed Deborah her efforts to try to find all possible arrangements for four numerals. She thought it might be 16, from 4 × 4, and had written many combinations in her notebook. Sylvia remembered when her methods instructor had worked on permutations and combinations with her class, and how confusing she had found this content. Another morning she asked what the definition of a multiple was. Was 0 a multiple of 3? Was –9? She would try to subtract –5 – (–3) and see if she could develop a stable way of understanding that the answer was –2, not –8.

Sylvia also had many "aha" moments while watching the class. One of her favorites was when we worked with beansticks[5] to develop the children's understanding of place value and regroup-

Figure 2.1. Differences in the Meaning of Multiplication.

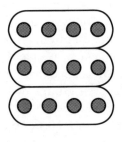

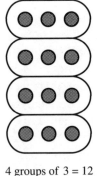

3 groups of 4 = 12   4 groups of 3 = 12
    3 x 4 = 12   4 x 3 = 12

ing. Sylvia was delighted with this because, for the first time, "borrowing" made sense with these materials. She was enthusiastic about departing from the traditional mechanical approach to subtracting 47 – 19 ("cross out the 4 and put a 3 and put a 1 with the 7, which makes 17"). She saw the sense in talking about "trading in" a beanstick for ten loose beans, and then subtracting nine from the seventeen, and one stick from the remaining three beansticks (see Figure 2.2).

During the first year, many of Sylvia's questions were curricular as well. She had asked to work with Deborah because the *CSMP* curriculum had proved so confusing to follow. When Deborah did not teach from these materials, Sylvia repeatedly asked about "where" we were in that curriculum. For many meetings in a row, she came with her teacher's manuals, hoping we could find a one-to-one correspondence between any of the lessons in our class and the lessons in the textbook. "Have we done N17, do you think?" she would ask. Deborah tried to oblige Sylvia by looking with her at the content of the *CSMP* lessons and trying to map what she was doing against that curricular scheme. She kept promising to make a map of the year—about when they would cover which topics—but she never quite managed to do it. And each time the two met, they found themselves overtaken by the actual mathematics that the class was doing.

Sylvia still worried about *CSMP*. When would Deborah teach the minicomputer? Or arrow roads? Both the minicomputer and arrow roads are particular pedagogical tools used in *CSMP*. The minicomputer is not really a computer, but a device used to represent

Figure 2.2. Using Beansticks to Model 47 – 19 with "Regrouping."

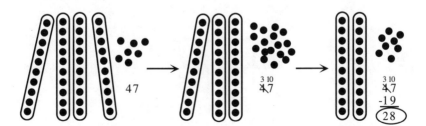

place value and structure of number, as well as to explore operations of addition, subtraction, multiplication, and division (see Figure 2.3). Students use this tool to explore a wide variety of problems, such as how many ways are there to make 20 on the minicomputer? It is also used to model multiplication and addition, as well as subtraction with regrouping, much as the beansticks are. Arrow roads, another *CSMP* device, are drawings used to represent relations (see Figure 2.4). Both the minicomputer and arrow roads are tools chosen by the developers of the curriculum for their mathematical richness and power. They are tools for teaching and learning, just as beansticks, geoboards, or base-ten blocks are tools. In Sylvia's mind, however, they were content. The *CSMP* lesson often appeared to her to be *about* the minicomputer, or *about* arrow roads. The mathematics being explored (for example, the inverse relationship between multiplying by three and multiplying by one-third) was less apparent to her than the mechanics of learning about the tool. Less familiar to her, these tools were what students were supposed to learn. She was worried about what the fourth and fifth grade teachers would think if her students were not well grounded in these. When Deborah chose other paths, Sylvia saw her as doing interesting things but not fully covering the curriculum. And although Deborah talked about how she understood the curriculum in terms of the mathematical goals

Figure 2.3. Representing 47 on the Minicomputer.

Each square has a value:

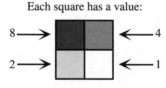

and small checkers are used to denote particular quantities:

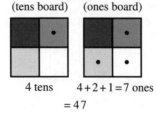

**Figure 2.4. Using an Arrow Road to Model the Inverse Relationship
Between Multiplication by ⅓ and Multiplication by 3.**

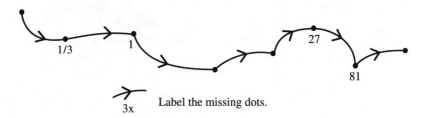

Label the missing dots.

With the "3x" arrow, the number at each dot is three times the previous dot.

to be addressed, Sylvia still worried. When Deborah taught lessons
using the minicomputer, Sylvia was both delighted and a little relieved. She made enthusiastic comments about particular children's
understanding of the minicomputer.

Working flexibly with the minicomputer is not easy. Often
when Sylvia taught *CSMP* in the years before she worked with
Deborah, she had found it hard to keep up in her own mind as she
posed questions for the students. When students presented solutions
to "Find all the ways to make 20," Sylvia sometimes found it hard
to keep up with their explanations. Thinking up fruitful questions
to ask was even harder. She felt anxious as she taught. Teaching
math after lunch, she often could not eat, as her stomach was in
knots. Recently, in an E-mail message to Deborah, she reflected:

> I do know that before DB (BDB) I thought kids
> wouldn't "know it" or be able to figure things out
> mathematically unless I told them how. I usually
> stated the lesson objectives: "Today we're going to
> talk about arrow roads, and we're going to see how
> you can add 10 using an arrow road" or some such
> statement. That is, if I could *figure out* what the les-
> son was trying to teach. More often than not, however,
> I *tried* to figure out what the lesson was teaching.
> After fumbling my way through the lesson in the
> book, I generally closed with asking a question, usu-
> ally a yes or no question—without asking for an ex-

planation—or a how-do-you-know, or a can-you-
show-me sort of question. And was just relieved that
I got through the lesson, and actually didn't pay much
attention to what they had gotten out of it. Guess I
assumed they got something and could build on that
"something" tomorrow, or whenever the next lesson
came along. I wouldn't admit this to many people, but
it was rough, and I had a lot of anxiety attacks.

Despite her discomfort, Sylvia realized that *CSMP* was the district
curriculum, and she worked to try to teach it well. She had the part-
time mathematics resource teacher come and demonstrate lessons
for her. She watched how this woman followed the lesson format
and she picked up some ideas about how to manage the teaching.
Still, Sylvia did not focus on the mathematics.

Working with Deborah, Sylvia's prior worries about *CSMP*
collided with her basic feelings of mathematical inadequacy and
surfaced throughout their first year's conversations. "Why didn't I
learn this when I was in school?" she asked repeatedly. Deborah
reassured her frequently that many people would have the same
questions—that, for instance, few adults really understood subtraction of negative numbers, or probability, or the host of other things
that she asked about. Alone with her anxiety for so long, Sylvia was
surprised. In some ways, it was also something of a relief to know
that maybe these feelings were not unique to her. Deborah suggested that Sylvia's teachers had probably never given her the opportunity to explore mathematics in any meaningful way. Still,
Sylvia wondered whether it had to do with the way she approached
learning, another area in which she was beginning to change.

Sylvia's questions pushed Deborah to articulate distinctions
and shades of meaning and to discover new relationships. For example, Sylvia often asked specific questions about the problems
Deborah designed, such as the one shown in Figure 2.5. Sylvia
asked: "Why did you pick those labels for the circles?" Deborah
explained about hoping the students would notice that all the
numbers that lay in the intersection of multiples of 2 and multiples
of 3 were multiples of 6. She pointed out that no numbers would
go in the intersection of all three circles and that even when she

Figure 2.5. A Challenging Problem.

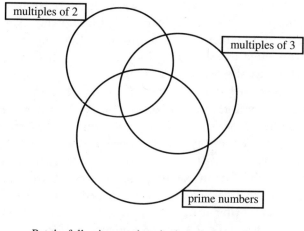

Put the following numbers in the string picture:
0   2   10   12   18   9   -7   21

challenged them to find one that could go in there, they would not be able to find one, since prime numbers, by definition, cannot be multiples of other numbers. Sylvia asked about -7 and Deborah was challenged to explain why -7 is not prime if 7 is.[6] Frequently Sylvia's insatiable curiosity offered Deborah opportunities to clarify and extend her own understandings: Is 1 a prime? Why not? Is 0 a multiple of every number? Deborah would usually respond with, "Let's see if we can figure this out. What do *you* think?" The uncertainties of teaching were underscored as she taught, watched closely by Sylvia, who she knew would ask her pointed questions about her interpretations of students' solutions, the turns the problems took in class, and where the class was headed.

Although Sylvia had hoped for answers, she was game, and gradually she became used to Deborah's returning queries, just as she saw her working with students. And she triumphed in stumping her husband occasionally. Gradually Sylvia began to think of herself as capable of learning and figuring out mathematics. At the end of the first year, she even found herself liking it, but decidedly not eager to resume teaching it. Whereas she had once thought of math as "cut and dried," she now saw it as complicated and fraught with shades of meaning and interpretation. This, while surprisingly interesting intellectually, did not, however, leave her feeling secure about trying to help students learn it. Although her concept of mathematics and mathematics teaching was changing, Sylvia still felt underprepared to teach this kind of mathematics to students. Paradoxically, as she learned more mathematics, she became increasingly convinced that she did not know what she needed to teach. Sylvia grew increasingly focused on issues of teaching and learning, of the teacher's role, of the classroom culture.

Then, in the fourth year, Sylvia began to reach, as a teacher, for the mathematics. While Deborah continued to teach most of the mathematics, Sylvia began teaching a few lessons. When something came up in class, she wholeheartedly pursued it, rather than suggesting that they bring it up "when Dr. Ball comes." And, most significant, she began designing the students' homework, carefully crafting problems that she thought embedded worthwhile mathematics and extended what was happening in class. Although she had worried about dealing with the content, she was ready now. As the fall of the fourth year wore on, she grew increasingly enthralled with this task. Reflecting on her embracing of it, Sylvia felt that it offered her a safe opportunity to begin thinking for herself about the curriculum—about the special blend of mathematical insight and knowledge of students and learning. She could think about good problems, but, because it was a homework assignment, she did not have to—yet—put it all together interactively and orchestrate a discussion of the problems.

A moment of great satisfaction for Sylvia came around the same time when she attended a district mathematics inservice. While the leader presented new ideas for teaching mathematics, Sylvia found that she was familiar with all of what she heard. And she even found some of what was said to be just plain wrong mathematically. She wrote to Deborah that night, "[The leader] simply announced that 3×4 and 4×3 were the SAME! Val and I strongly disagreed with her, and she agreed that they were different, but the end result was the same. Others didn't see them as different. . . . I felt really good. . . . Amen and thank you! (It's working)."

Shortly after that, Sylvia made paper snowflakes with the

students. With construction paper squares, Sylvia enthusiastically helped them measure and figure out how to fold the paper before beginning to cut little designs into the folds. She was pleased with how learning about measurement was interwoven with this art project. But, unfortunately, the snowflakes looked unbalanced and not quite the right shape. Over the weekend, she talked about this with a colleague. In that conversation, she realized that using squares as the starting point was a problem, and that starting with circles would be more promising. Sylvia became completely engrossed in thinking about circles. If she gave the children circles, she thought, they could use protractors to measure degrees and fold the circles into different fractional parts easily. Fascinated, she began asking questions about circles that had never occurred to her. She looked up the word in her mathematics dictionary and found that a circle is defined as "the set of points in a plane at a fixed distance, the radius, from a fixed point, the center." She wondered about what "plane" meant in this case, and how this definition of circle evolved. She became curious about the history of circles and sought materials to read. She imagined ways to have the students explore circles. "I could do it my old way and just say a circle is . . . and tell them, but I'd rather have them do some inquiring!" she wrote. Sylvia found herself intensely excited, and also a little surprised at this excitement. It was thrilling to be thinking about a new thing, and to be able to pursue her excitement about a piece of mathematics with confidence and eagerness.

An important postscript to this section is that writing about Sylvia's learning about mathematics in this chapter has been difficult for us. Although mathematics has been an important part of Sylvia's focus, we have felt it curiously risky to expose her self-doubts to others. We both are deeply aware of the widespread expectation that teachers are supposed to know what they teach, that being a qualified professional implies knowing the content. To admit that she did not feel comfortably grounded in the mathematics she was expected to teach could appear to be an admission of being ill-qualified as a teacher. As we asked others to read drafts of this chapter, however, we received affirming comments from colleagues who felt exactly the same. Our worries receded but never entirely disappeared. In the end, we included this part of the story because we think it crucial for others to understand the depth of the feelings of alienation and inadequacy that can shape a teacher's attitude toward mathematics, and thus toward teaching mathematics. Moreover, the anxiety that accompanied our revealing this is part of the context in which many teachers face off with mathematics—whether in the privacy of their classrooms or in front of others.[7]

Learning About Teaching and Learning

I have learned that children already come with a lot of knowledge, and that they can teach one another. I didn't feel that way before. I felt that I had to be the teacher, whatever that meant. But anyway, I am thinking more about what it means to teach. A lot of the teaching in the classroom goes on between children, and the teacher acts kind of like a facilitator, picking up on the comments that children make that are purposeful for discussion. . . . It takes a great deal of finesse . . . to be able to do that [S. Rundquist, cited in R. Nevins, 1991].

While the first year of our collaboration was dominated by conversation about mathematics content and curriculum, the advent of the second year brought a shift in our focus. Mathematical questions surfaced periodically, but we found ourselves talking more about teaching and learning. Deborah was writing about some of the problems she faced in trying to teach mathematics for understanding,[8] and, more used to each other and to the ways we each worked with students, we shifted our focus. Sylvia found herself changing the way she interacted with students in other subject areas, especially science and language arts. She began questioning her reliance on the basal reading text and turned increasingly to children's literature. She found herself asking students about their thinking more often, and she noticed that she often followed their ideas rather than sticking to what she had planned.

When she was first teaching, Sylvia relied primarily on what she remembered her teachers doing as a guide for her own practice.

She did not concern herself with what students already knew. She assumed that they did not know what she was teaching and saw her job as to give them something to put into their heads. When she returned to the university to gain elementary school certification, she began hearing a lot about the importance of connecting teaching with students' prior knowledge. She never integrated this with her mathematics teaching, however, seeing mathematics as isolated. As she watched Deborah teach, she began to realize that the students had a lot of mathematical insight, that they were learning from one another as well as from Deborah. She saw how they came up with ideas for the problems that Deborah posed, and how she orchestrated a discussion about those ideas. Sylvia saw how new mathematical ideas developed out of these discussions in the class. She saw Deborah doing less telling and explaining, more listening and questioning. She also saw that class periods often ended without closure, without definite answers to the problems with which they had begun.

Sylvia found herself opening up and experimenting with her role in other parts of the day. She heard herself asking more questions like "What do the rest of you think?" and "Why?" She involved the students more in classroom management issues, like how to arrange the desks. She found herself in lengthy discussions of the pros and cons of various room plans, and even sometimes discovered mathematical interest in these contexts. She invited our class of twenty-eight students to figure out how many different ways they could arrange the desks into equal-sized groups. After considering how well groups of two, four, seven, or fourteen might work, some students introduced the idea of making groups of two different sizes (for instance, two groups of five desks and three groups of six). Sylvia also began to stray from text-based presentations in science and began doing more of what she called "facilitating." This made her very nervous at times: students said things that she knew nothing about and she could not decide whether to go with what they had brought up or to change the subject. She felt good when she had the courage to stay with it, because she felt she was not shutting students down.

Although Sylvia found herself drawn in the direction of paying more attention to students' ideas and opening up her classroom to make their ideas more central to the curriculum, Deborah and Sylvia had some different ideas about what Sylvia called "management." Actually, both "manage" the class well: that is, the classroom environment is calm and students work well. But some things that bothered Sylvia were of no concern to Deborah. Indeed, Deborah was oblivious to some things. Sylvia noticed the child who was playing with a small rubber band in her lap and could not ignore the one with his feet up on his desk. She felt the noise level rise during small-group work, and although it was not chaotic, she could not relax. Deborah, intently crouched by a student's desk, appeared not to hear the chattering voices. When Sylvia would cautiously tell Deborah that she wished she could learn not to care when students put their feet nonchalantly on top of their desks, it would turn out that Deborah had not even noticed the child. Deborah paid so little attention to the clock that the students were always late to physical education and recess. And she rarely remembered to take roll at the beginning of the afternoon.

At the same time, the routines that the students learned in mathematics class were appealing to Sylvia. They learned to come in from recess, take out their mathematics notebooks, and begin working on the problem of the day without any direction from Deborah. They learned to listen politely and attentively to other students, and it was rare to hear anyone snicker at anyone else's idea. Only eight years old, they participated effectively in a half-hour (or more) discussion every day. Always in motion, Deborah orchestrated these discussions from all corners of the room and rarely broke in with admonishments. Sylvia and Deborah talked a lot about these routines, what it took to establish them, and how they carried across the day. Sylvia noted Deborah's calm and serious attention to students. She identified qualities of tone and manner that she thought contributed to the ethos of the classroom environment—and management. Waving her hands from the back of the room, she also tried gently to help Deborah learn to keep track of the time and to notice students who were fooling around.

Together we talked about norms we wanted to foster in our classroom. We considered the role of the teacher. Deborah often worried about closure, for many classes ended without firm conclusions. When class discussions grew increasingly muddled, Deborah wondered how to decide when to take a firm hand, when to redirect the students' thinking, when to show or explain a crucial point or idea. While Sylvia tended to feel more comfortable that the content had been "covered" when Deborah was more directive, she also began to notice evidence that students did not necessarily "get it" just because either of them offered an explanation. Deborah and Sylvia analyzed lessons in which Deborah had played different kinds of roles, examining closely what individual students seemed to have learned. Both were particularly intrigued with students who appeared to be tuned out but would suddenly pop up with an important insight, well connected to what the class had been working on. Focused on the teacher's role and its relation to students' learning, these discussions, grounded in our shared experience of the mathematics class, contributed to our growing understanding of some of the subtler elements of teaching.

Sylvia began to realize that she could give more to and get more from her students if she placed more emphasis on their ideas. As she focused increasingly on their thinking, she started to learn a lot more about her students than she ever had before. She also developed new insights into her role and what it meant to teach. But it was scary. She repeatedly felt her heart race during class, her stomach tighten, her face grow warm. It was a lot more uncertain than what she had done before.

We explored what it meant to consider our class a "learning community." Sylvia talked about it explicitly with the students and wove it thematically through their discussions. She involved them in decisions about the class and their areas of study. One day she found herself in the midst of a small assignment which she had designed and which proved to be confusing to the students. Chagrined at her oversight, she nevertheless decided, rather than fix it herself, to see if the students could deal with the problem. They managed just fine without her, talking with one another about it and modifying the task inventively. Sylvia was immensely pleased. Later she wrote:

> They got a big kick out of my comment that I ought to be sitting in the chairs and *they* ought to be up front doing the teaching. Even though I am known as the

"teacher," this is just another example of how we are
a community of teachers and learners and it isn't
always the teacher, as she may be known officially,
who is doing the teaching. It was a thrilling moment
for me and I've thought about it off and on this weekend, as I am proud of the fact that I can take these
risks, and hoped it boosted their feeling of importance
in the classroom and life in general, and perhaps
broke down some of the walls that exist between
adults and children (I won't say teachers and learners
in this context). . . . Anyway, I hope I will remember
this "moment" for a long time to come, as it's really
more of a "milestone moment" than anything else. It's
really provided me with a lot of food for thought in
the past few days, and is very significant to me and my
discourse with kids.

Sylvia's delight in this moment indicated the changes she felt inside
herself. Once a teacher who felt centrally responsible for all aspects
of her students' learning, she was beginning to revel in students'
roles in the class. She was growing to appreciate stepping off of
center stage, to let the work of the class be developed jointly. Whereas earlier she saw herself as the sole source of information, she was
now seeking ways to get students to share their knowledge with one
another. Sylvia is amazed at what they know and can figure out.
Increasingly, Sylvia defines her work as searching for ways to "get
at the content that is *within the kids*" in a way that they will articulate it in the classroom.

      This way of thinking about teaching and learning was, how-
ever, the root of a new problem for Sylvia. Always organized and
devoted to her work, Sylvia had been one to plan her lessons thor-
oughly in advance. Her principal had even at times expected to be
able to review her plans a week beforehand. Sylvia started finding
herself unable to plan as she was accustomed. For a while she
thought she was tired, or less motivated, or under some kind of
stress. She simply could not write lesson plans. She could not entirely understand it. In late summer, she started saying that she was
not "ready," as she had used to be, before the students came. She

did not fill the bulletin boards or make the desk arrangements or decide what to do first. And on several Sunday nights she looked to Deborah for reassurance about the fact that she had not written any plans. Her work patterns were changing. On weekends she spent time in the classroom, alone, thinking. Whereas when she used to go in on weekends it was to clean up and to correct papers, now she looked for materials, read, and organized areas of the room. She tried to imagine various paths the students might want to take in investigating what was going on with their plants, or their bread mold cultures, or their magnets. She looked for books. She gathered magazines and newspapers. In short, she realized that she was *preparing*, rather than *planning*, for teaching. [9]

In the first phase, learning about mathematics, conversation seemed to provide the primary medium for our learning. But in developing ideas about teaching and learning, more of our learning in this phase came from *doing*, from experimenting within our own practice. Our conversations explored things we were each trying, things we were seeing with the children. Sylvia also relied on Deborah at times to reassure her that her ideas made sense and to encourage her to take risks. As we learned and grew as teachers, opening up more to each other and taking more chances, we also grew closer personally. During the third year of our collaboration, we found ourselves often engaged in conversations about ourselves as women. And once again, conversation became a tool for our learning.

Learning About Self

Depending on how one regards Sylvia and Deborah, different perspectives emerge of what kind of collaboration this is. One angle is that Deborah is a university-based researcher and teacher educator and Sylvia is an elementary school teacher. Although she is nineteen years younger, Deborah is the more experienced classroom teacher of the two, for Sylvia only recently received her elementary school teaching credential. Prior to that, Sylvia was a Chapter 1 teacher, and in the 1960s she had taught special education in Detroit. Before that, she had had a stint as a high school physical education teacher. But another aspect of our partnership centers on who we are as women. We share marriage and parenting as common experiences but are women of adjacent generations and different cultures and class. Sylvia has raised her two children to adulthood and is a new grandmother for the first time; her sons are just a little younger than Deborah's younger brother. Deborah is still in the midst of child-rearing and had her second baby at the end of the first year of the collaboration. The struggles to balance marriage, children, work, and selves has been a recurring theme in our conversations. Who is giving guidance and insight to whom in these struggles varies. In socioeconomic background and expectations of ourselves as women, we differ substantially. Still, Sylvia has found herself suddenly amidst changes she could not have anticipated, some of which she attributes directly to our collaboration and the ways in which it has stretched and challenged her assumptions about herself. Not all of these are easy. Writing this paper has provided us with an opportunity to reflect on this dimension of our partnership and what it is contributing to each of us.

By the third year of our work together, we had grown quite comfortable with each other. We offered mutually reciprocal kinds of help as we searched for satisfactory balances of work, play, challenge, responsibility, and family. On one hand, when Deborah felt overwhelmed with the multiple roles and dimensions of her life, Sylvia offered her support. Valuing family, Sylvia reassured—even encouraged—Deborah when she felt compelled to put work on hold and spend a day playing with xylophones and stuffed animals, or caring for an older but sick child. On the other hand, Sylvia, enticed and excited by the challenge of the new ideas and worlds she was encountering, started spending more time working. Her children grown, she had the time. But it nonetheless meant constructing new rhythms.

Buying a computer was one significant event in this process. In the third year of our work together, Sylvia decided that she would like to have a computer at home. Over the summer, we had been working together looking at some videotapes from the class and she had been examining and enhancing transcripts of the lessons. With her finely tuned ear for the children's voices and ways of speaking, Sylvia was able to hear things that the work-study students who had been transcribing tapes could not decipher. In doing this, Sylvia had begun to use a computer. She had also begun to use electronic mail, which she loved. We started to exchange messages daily. In the fall, she missed that work and missed our electronic correspondence. So, with her husband's concurrence, she decided that she would like to own her own computer.

Sylvia's husband thought this was a great idea. Sylvia conferred with Deborah and with others on campus who used computers and seemed to know a lot about them. One of these acquaintances, a man with expertise in technology with whom Deborah worked, offered to help Sylvia find a good deal and to order the computer for her through a cut-rate source. Meanwhile, however, Sylvia's husband was calling around, gathering information about different kinds of computer systems. He called personal acquaintances as well as local stores. Sylvia, feeling very much the novice in this arena, thought he must know much more about what to ask than she did. In the past, he had always taken the lead on major purchases. After many inquiries, he concluded that an IBM computer would serve the same purposes as the one that Sylvia wanted. She tried to convince him that a Macintosh was what she wanted. Eventually, he was persuaded when their two adult sons agreed that a Mac would be the wiser choice. Even though Sylvia and her husband agreed to buy a computer, making the decision about what to buy and from whom was not an easy one for them.

Excited to be buying something for her that he thought she would really like, Sylvia's husband continued to manage the purchase. He arranged an educator discount rather than have her order the machine through the computer expert on campus. Although he did not use a computer himself, Sylvia's husband attended all the computer demonstrations. He decided that she should have a color monitor, even though she said that nothing she was doing required this more expensive peripheral. When the purchase was completed, he set up the system for her in a refurbished upstairs study. Sylvia was both grateful and a little ambivalent about his taking charge of this undertaking. In the past, this was how they had always done this sort of thing. Still, she was beginning to feel that this was an area that she knew something about—maybe even more than he did—and she felt that she could have taken initiative on this purchase. But she was tentative about it. He was smart about so many things, and it made her feel more secure not to have to take the responsibility for it.

Sylvia spent hours working on her new computer. While her husband worked outside in their garden, she remained upstairs in the study. She became a fast and competent—and voracious—E-mail correspondent. She took home videotapes to analyze and interviews to listen to. At times she thought she felt his ambivalence about her deep engagement in this. She wondered whether her becoming so fluent with the computer was a little threatening to him. For the first time, she had taken hold in an area recognized as "advanced," and this was not entirely comfortable.

Deborah and Sylvia spent many Tuesday morning coffee meetings talking about the computer and about Sylvia's feelings about her husband's role and his feelings. Some mornings there were tears. A computer may seem a simple thing. But altering—or just questioning—roles after years of habit is hard and risky. Deborah, a generation younger than Sylvia, had a different though not unappealing set of patterns in being a woman, wife, mother. Our relationship was the context for us to open up some basic assumptions about our lives and to get the help of another woman in thinking about how we were constructing our lives.[10]

We think that this aspect of our learning has been central to our joint work on teaching. The personal resources demanded by this kind of practice are substantial; and our development as women is highly related to our capacity to create, manage, and gain the right to do what we are doing. We have grown in our recognition of the role played by our own sense of authority in making pedagogical decisions about what we teach and how we teach. Realizing that pedagogical judgments are moral matters for which we are responsible, and that we are authorized and qualified to make those judgments, is a giant step, but one that may be necessary in order to break with modal practices of schooling. And responding to those to whom in the past we would have deferred—such as textbook authors, administrators, and parents—has required a more confident sense of self than is typical for many teachers. Introducing a computer into Sylvia's world at home, simple as it may seem, was a crucial step in our journey together, for it was an opportunity for realizing, facing, and articulating some new aspects of ourselves. In beginning to see herself as competent to make purchasing decisions about a computer and to use that computer on her own, Sylvia provided a context for us to talk about being women, being capable, and interacting with people who speak with authority.

Furthermore, we think that the context we have created for ourselves to learn about mathematics, teaching and learning, and ourselves is responsive to our dispositions and preferences as learners. We can cry, we can admit to feeling anxious, and we can open up more about our worlds rather than just our teaching of a particular subject matter. As whole people, we have been able to touch each other's lives with trust and honesty—this despite our obvious and not-so-obvious differences. The relationship has had a quality of intimacy and reciprocity that has nurtured our interactions and opportunities to learn.

Learning About Teaching from Talking About Teaching

Having to explain what we are doing has contributed to our understanding of what we are doing. At the beginning, Sylvia's questions pressed Deborah to articulate ideas she had held much more tacitly. One prime example of this was Sylvia's questions about Deborah's mathematics problems. Watching Deborah stand at the chalkboard in the dimness of the room at lunchtime, watching her write something, deliberate, erase, and revise, Sylvia asked many questions about the tasks. "How do you know what numbers you want in the problem?" she asked after watching Deborah write and rewrite what seemed to be a simple problem involving fractions. Thinking aloud, we explicitly agreed that asking students to compare the relative magnitude of $\frac{3}{4}$ and $\frac{6}{12}$ was more fruitful than asking them to compare $\frac{1}{2}$ and $\frac{2}{3}$ (since one might answer the latter correctly without observing that the sheer size of the numbers does not indicate which one is greater). Sylvia also asked a lot of questions about particular moves during lessons, practice, homework, and assessment. These conversations have blended our concerns for mathematics, students, pedagogy, assessment, and curriculum, offering us ongoing contexts for learning and articulating what we are learning.

Recently, Sylvia was watching a lesson in which a student

asserted that seven erasers at eleven cents each would cost seventy-seven cents "because eleven times seven is seventy-seven." Sylvia sat up straight in her chair, waiting for Deborah to ask something or say something that would push the student somehow to reconsider his representation of seven erasers at eleven cents as 11×7. Deborah did nothing, asking merely for comments from the other students. Everyone agreed that the cost would be seventy-seven cents, and the discussion moved on. Later that day, sure that this case should have been represented as 7×11, Sylvia questioned Deborah. This issue of the meaning of multiplication was one of the things Sylvia had really grappled with at first, and she was truly puzzled about why Deborah had let the "wrong" interpretation stand. At Sylvia's query, Deborah thought hard about why she had not pressed the issue more with the students. Together, through the conversation, and a few E-mail messages, we were able to articulate some new (for both of us) clarity about how we might think about moments in teaching like that one. Our opportunities to learn about teaching are ongoing and connected, for our history together allows us to continue to develop themes and questions over time.

In our conversations we have been building shared understandings of mathematics and its connections, of what kind of learning we were aiming for, and of what it means to teach well. We have developed a common language and shared notions about the referents for such terms as "classroom culture," "explanation," "understanding," and "problem."

These conversations have increasingly included other people. We have had many visitors, diverse in background, experience in elementary school teaching, ideas about mathematics, and interests. As a result of the recurrent need for us to present our work to others—from a troupe of Jordanian educators, to members of the media, to undergraduate preservice teachers—we have developed ideas about ways to help others understand this kind of teaching. We have learned about their assumptions and puzzles—about eight-year-olds, elementary school classrooms, curriculum, the teacher's role, and learning. For example, visitors regularly ask why apparently "wrong" answers are allowed air time in the class. They ask why there is not more closure at the end of a lesson. They wonder about how Deborah ever covers the curriculum if we do just one or two problems a day. We have become more prepared for the kinds of things people are likely to ask, and we have developed a wider repertoire of ways to explain these elements of the mathematics class. Such questions have also provoked us to think more about some issues we had been taking for granted or not noticing. We have learned, too, ways we might explain the more tentative nature of knowledge about teaching—how to explain that what we are doing is "experimental" and evolving, all in a climate that presses toward a "knowledge base" and predictability of curriculum, methods, and outcomes.

Even writing this chapter together—a new experience for us—has provided an important opportunity for our further learning about teaching and teacher learning, as well as ourselves and our work together. In meetings with visitors to the university in the last few months, we have found ways of talking about what we have been doing and what it has been like to work together, as well as what we are learning about teaching. We see the contributions of this project to the collaboration that stretches ahead of us.

Conclusion

"Collaboration" is a slogan often unexamined and assumed to be inherently good. Some collaborations are not collaborative. Although they involve more than one person, they are not necessarily *joint*. Collaboration—*co-laboring*—implies that different minds and hearts join together in related and common pursuits. Collaboration implies respect and caring, connection and purpose. Looking back over the evolution of our collaboration, we see that we have each learned things that contribute in important ways to our work and to ourselves. Heretofore, we have not made this aspect of our work—its very context—a part of the public view of our collaboration. With this chapter, we have begun to learn what it may mean to let others in on that process. We have begun to learn how to make the context of our work a context for others' learning. Writing this chapter together has opened a new episode in our work together.

We will not teach together indefinitely. Sylvia wants to teach mathematics again, seeking ways to integrate it with other subject areas and goals. Deborah wants to develop her work by investigating what it may take to teach mathematics for understanding in another school context, with different students and in a different community. What does the future hold for us? What does the other side of our collaboration look like? We worry at times about the delicate balance we have created and how we can construct things so that the supports that this context provides for Sylvia in particular can extend beyond the current interactive, collaborative relationship. This is an important question for us about what we mean by "context" and whether the context we have constructed for ourselves is—or must be—temporal. Can the context extend beyond the way we currently have arranged our work? Can we extend the context to the "other side" of face-to-face, daily collaboration?

What does our experience offer to others interested in engaging in or supporting fruitful collaborations? Can a context such as ours contribute to learning and change in the wider communities to which we are connected? Different as we are, we think we represent one case of what might be entailed in bringing people with diverse kinds of expertise together to work on important educational problems. Respect and trust have consistently characterized our interactions. We see each other as equals, but not as equivalent. We notice different things about the children, and pick up on different aspects of the students' interactions. We have used and profited from our differences without valuing one person's experiences and inclinations more than the other's. Our work has epitomized the idea of "learning community," in which different people's contributions are all necessary to the quality and progress of the work.[11]

"Conversation" is central to understanding our work.[12] Conversation is a live part of our exchanges, in person, on the phone, and, within the last year, through electronic mail. Conversation is also represented symbolically in the reciprocity of exchange in our work together. Our work is constructive—building new ideas about teaching, students, content, and about the study of teaching—and we contribute different kinds of things to the undertaking. Perhaps our experience can serve to broaden images of what it can mean for two people to work together to learn more about teaching. Deborah did not "teach" Sylvia how to teach; Sylvia did not provide Deborah with the "reality" of students and classrooms. Instead, we joined hands and minds and learned from and with each other.

Notes

1. There was, in fact, no "program." But the term was the only term that Sylvia could think of to describe what she thought Deborah could offer her.
2. See National Council of Teachers of Mathematics (1989; 1991); and Prawat (1991).
3. See Ball (in press b); Ball, D. L. (1991b); Ball, D. L. (1991a); and Ball, D. L. (in press a).
4. CEMREL, 1979; Remillard, 1990.
5. Beansticks are used to model place value numeration. A beanstick is a wooden popsicle stick with ten dried beans glued on it to represent a group of ten. Loose beans are used for ones, and ten sticks glued together on a piece of cardboard represents a hundred.
6. For curious readers: –7 is not a prime number because the factors of –7 are –1, –7, 1, and 7. Prime numbers are defined as those numbers whose only factors are 1 and the number itself. Number theory (of which consideration of primes is a part) focuses on positive integers.
7. In the context of concerns for mathematics education, we are puzzled by others' surprise at teachers' discomfort with mathematical meanings—and the criticisms leveled at teachers. Teachers are, after all, graduates of the very approaches we now seek to change. To rebuild mathematics teaching and learning will require taking teachers more seriously—and sympathetically—as learners.
8. See, for example, Ball (in press a); and Ball (in press b).
9. See Yinger (1990).
10. Bateson, 1989.
11. See Schwab (1976).
12. Others have used conversation as a metaphor for analyzing collaborative work between teachers and researchers. See Heaton, Reineke, & Frese (1991).

References

Ball, D. L. (1991a). Beginning a conversation about the NCTM *Professional Standards for Teaching Mathematics:* Improving teaching, not standardizing it. *Arithmetic Teacher, 39*(1), 18–22.

Ball, D. L. (1991b). What's all this talk about "discourse"? *Arithmetic Teacher, 39*(3), 44–48.

Ball, D. L. (in press a). Halves, pieces, and twoths: Constructing representational contexts in teaching fractions. In T. Carpenter, E. Fennema, & T. Romberg (Eds.), *Rational numbers: An integration of research.* Hillsdale, NJ: Erlbaum.

Ball, D. L. (in press b). With an eye on the mathematical horizon: Dilemmas of teaching elementary school mathematics. *Elementary School Journal.*

Bateson, M. C. (1989). *Composing a life.* New York: Atlantic Monthly Press.

CEMREL. (1979). *Comprehensive school mathematics program.* Saint Louis, MO: Author.

Heaton, R., Reineke, J., & Frese, J. (1991, April). *Collective reflection: An account of collaborative research.* Paper presented at the meeting of the American Educational Research Association, Chicago, IL.

National Council of Teachers of Mathematics. (1989). *Curriculum and evaluation standards for school mathematics.* Reston, VA: Author.

National Council of Teachers of Mathematics. (1991). *Professional standards for teaching mathematics.* Reston, VA: Author.

Nevins, R. (1991, May/June). Reflections on teaching. *Spartan Village Elementary School Professional Development News.*

Schwab, J. J. (1976). Education and the state: Learning community. In *Great ideas today* (pp. 234–271). Chicago: Encyclopaedia Britannica.

Yinger, R. J. (1990). The conversation of practice. In R. T. Clift, W. R. Houston, & M. C. Pugach (Eds.), *Encouraging reflective practice in education* (pp. 73–94). New York: Teachers College Press.

3

Learning to Hear Voices: Inventing a New Pedagogy of Teacher Education

Ruth M. Heaton
Magdalene Lampert

How are teachers going to learn to do the kind of adventurous teaching that is advocated by current reformers?[1] Who is going to teach them about these new practices? The reform policies present a vision of how schools could be quite different, more exciting, more intellectually challenging, more successful in preparing students to lead productive lives. To work out that vision and construct policies to support it is no small task. But it is one thing to get policies in place that give teachers permission to try to do things differently and quite another matter to ensure that educators, from primary school through graduate school, learn to do the things that the policies advocate. We need new practical conceptions of how to teach and learn basic subject matter "for understanding" in K–12 schools. We also need to learn about how to teach teachers to put these practices into effect and how to prepare teacher educators to work in ways that are consonant with the kind of teaching envisioned in the reforms.

The authors would like to acknowledge the contributions of David K. Cohen and Deborah Ball to the ideas presented in this chapter, the collaboration of Jim Reineke in collecting and sharing data with us, and the generosity of the teachers and principal in the school where we worked together, without whom the project reported here would not have been possible.

A shared interest in teacher education and in the teaching and learning of elementary mathematics in a more adventurous manner is what brought Ruth Heaton and Magdalene Lampert together more than three years ago.[2] Heaton had entered a doctoral program in teacher education at Michigan State University as an experienced and successful elementary school teacher, ready to learn to teach teachers. Mathematics was one of the many subjects Heaton was responsible to teach as an elementary school teacher, but it was not central to her interests prior to graduate school. She taught mathematics mainly by following a textbook, and her students spent much of their time learning and practicing rules and procedures by doing repeated computation. As a graduate student, she began reading about the latest reform initiatives in mathematics education and was puzzled by them. Current policies and research described elementary school mathematics teaching in ways that seemed radically different from what she had been doing successfully in the classroom for the last nine years.

Although current ideas about the reform of mathematics teaching and learning were foreign to Heaton, they were familiar to Lampert, a professor in teacher education at Michigan State University. Lampert, a scholar and teacher educator, had been teaching and studying elementary school mathematics since 1982. In an attempt to invent new relationships among teaching, research, and teacher education, Lampert worked as a fifth-grade mathematics teacher in a small but socially diverse public school. As a researcher, she used her classroom as a site for inquiry into the practices of teaching and learning authentic mathematics for understanding in school—practices of the sort that are being advocated by current reformers in mathematics education and other subjects.[3] These practices are unfamiliar not only to many experienced elementary school teachers like Heaton but also to most teacher educators.

Teacher educators are often strong proponents of reform in teaching, but they lack both analytic and practical experience with the kind of teaching they advocate. In the main, the preparation of teacher educators who will work in universities consists of academic studies in the social sciences and curriculum design; it has little to do with examining the problems of actual practice.[4] Even though they are taught about new strategies for teaching and learning that derive from research and theory, teacher educators are not educated to teach in ways that are different from how they were originally taught, nor are they educated to help others make such changes. The courses they take, and the courses they come to teach, follow the familiar scholastic pattern, organizing instruction according to academic disciplines. The way they learn to talk about teaching and the aspects of teaching that they learn to talk about are framed by important questions in those disciplines rather than by analytic frameworks derived from examining practice per se. In contrast to these conventional norms, Lampert's work has been organized around trying to construct ways of talking about teaching that derive from grappling with the problems of practice.

There are serious calls for the reform of teacher education that parallel the hoped for changes in K–12 education. Teacher educators are being called upon to construct a deeper connection between university programs and practical learning in schools and to build educational programs for teachers that offer richer and more integrated engagement with content.[5] Many schools of education are building new programs that link teacher education courses with classrooms and the serious study of content. But like teachers in K–12 schools, teacher educators need to learn how to do the things that the reforms advocate. Reforms at the policy level can structure programs differently, but what happens in these programs will not be determined by administrative fiat. Much would have to change for current practice to begin to move toward the vision proposed in the reforms. As teacher education is currently organized, prospective teachers do practicums and student teaching, but these experiences are rarely supervised by the same people who teach courses. Subject matter content courses are distinct from methods courses and are usually taught outside of professional preparation programs. There is little institutionalized support for making the connections between what it means to understand a subject and how it can be taught and learned. If professors of teacher education are going to play a larger role in helping teachers learn to teach in ways that take both classroom dynamics and subject matter content into consideration, they will need to learn how to do that. It will not follow simply from writing new course descriptions or giving people jobs to do that are different from the ones they were prepared to do. To reform teacher education, teacher educators will need to learn new languages for talking about practice and new ways of interacting with learners.

Lampert has attempted to narrow the distance between teaching and teacher education by using her fifth-grade mathematics classroom as a site in which prospective and practicing teachers and prospective and practicing teacher educators can examine the problems of an unfamilar kind of teaching practice in the context of daily lessons with a class of diverse learners. This means inventing not only a new approach to research but also a new pedagogy of teacher education: one where the actual problems of practice are central, where the question of what it means to know and learn mathematics shapes the discourse, and where analysis and action are integrated in ongoing work with students in a school context. By making her teaching available for study to people who do not ordinarily engage in the careful analysis of actual practice, she is trying to shape a different kind of conversation about reform based on a different conception of research and the relationship between research and practice. Rather than presenting teachers and teacher educators with a vision of desirable practices based on social and psychological theory, Lampert makes available a situation in which the problems entailed in implementing those practices can be directly examined and understood from alternative points of view. This approach to relating research to practice requires the creation of a new kind of discourse, new definitions, and new rules of argument. Unlike the derivation of practical principles from theoretical frameworks, conversations about teaching problems are ill-structured, multifaceted, and even internally contradictory.[6]

Building a model of this new practice-centered discourse—a discourse that could support a new pedagogy of teacher education—was the focus of Lampert's work with Heaton. Their work together provided Heaton with a situation in which she could explore a different and unfamiliar kind of mathematics teaching. Within the context of this teaching, she could begin to make connections between her experiences as a teacher and her intention to become a teacher educator who would support others in their efforts to teach mathematics differently. Working with Heaton prompted Lampert to reflect on the nature of the work she was trying to do and make clear how it was different from more familiar approaches to teaching and teacher education. Lampert and Heaton structured the ways in which they would interact in order to construct and examine a practice-centered process of learning to teach differently. Heaton arranged to teach fourth grade mathematics in the classroom next to Lampert's. She watched Lampert's fifth grade lessons and Lampert watched her lessons. Both wrote notes on their observations, and they had regular conversations about the teaching and learning that was occurring in the two classes. They examined puzzling examples of students' work together, they shared and collaboratively revised the math problems that they were going to use with their classes, and they discussed important events that occurred in their lessons. In the context of this talk about pedagogical matters, they also worked mathematics problems and talked about the relationship between the content of their elementary curricula and the concepts that are central to the discipline of mathematics.

In this chapter, Heaton and Lampert explore a new pedagogy of teacher education. Using their discussions about teaching and learning as data, they analyze the dialogue surrounding a lesson that Heaton taught in early September. The analysis takes the form of distinguishing the many "voices" that came into play in their conversations about a particular instance of teaching in Heaton's lesson. Lampert comes to see her work as identifying the voices that she brings to understanding teaching and learning, and Heaton comes to recognize that learning to be a teacher educator who can move back and forth between the world of practice and the world of research and reform involves learning to listen to the multiple voices with which she can talk about teaching. As the work Lampert and Heaton did together is analyzed, many striking parallels can be drawn between the issues that arise in teaching mathematics by having learners engage in analyzing and solving mathematics problems together with someone who has studied the discipline and the issues that arise in teaching *teaching* by having the learner analyze and solve pedagogical problems together with someone who has studied the teaching and learning of authentic mathematics in school. In both cases, teaching involves watching and listening to the learner, helping the learner to identify and articulate assumptions, and bringing new perspectives to bear on the interpretation and solution of the problem. This is the work of "hearing voices" to which our title refers.

The purpose of this chapter is to describe something of what we learned from our work together. Although the story is a personal one, it suggests elements of the practices of teaching and teacher education that may be important to consider in the current reform context. We do not claim that the work we did together was uniquely innovative; elements of our practice are present in many places where teachers and teacher educators are working to figure out new ways to teach and learn. But such efforts are little examined and rarely written about.

Heaton begins by describing who she was and what she intended to do when she started her study to be a teacher educator. She sets the context for why she, as an experienced teacher, has decided to learn to teach mathematics differently as part of the process of learning to be a teacher educator. Lampert continues by laying out a vision of the kind of mathematics teaching reflected in current reforms. Her description illustrates the complexity of the kind of teaching Heaton wanted to learn and prepares the reader for the difficulties that Heaton encounters while trying to learn to do this kind of teaching. Heaton follows with a description of one of her math lessons in late September and the perspective she brought to bear on this new way of teaching from her previous experience. This is followed by Lampert's reflections on the notes she took while observing this lesson. The multiple perspectives Lampert brings to the work of teacher education are presented through the multiple voices she identifies throughout her reflections. She models a way of thinking about teaching and learning to teach in the notes she writes to Heaton about the teaching she observed. Through this process, Heaton learns to recognize the multiple voices that she brings to her reflections on the lesson and on Lampert's notes.

Heaton: Dismayed by the Past and
Anxious About the Future

When I entered graduate school and began learning of the latest reforms in mathematics education, I was disturbed to find a mismatch between what was being advocated by reformers and the ways I had been teaching mathematics for the past nine years. I was disturbed because I had been considered a good teacher, by myself and others, and I did not feel that way any longer. While it was true that my students had memorized rules and were able to do the procedures in the textbook, as I learned about the reforms I began to question what my students might have actually understood about the rules and procedures that I thought they had learned. When I considered the lack of attention I had given to a conceptual understanding of mathematics, I began to feel dismayed with my own teaching. The way my students had been doing mathematics seemed different and inadequate when I compared it to the goals discussed in the reform documents. The rules and procedures that I had been successfully teaching to my math classes for years were being pushed to the background while problem solving and mathematical reasoning moved to the foreground. What would it be like to make problem solving and conceptual understanding central to my math teaching? What would it mean to reason and argue about mathematical ideas? How would these changes alter my role as a teacher and the expectations I placed on my students?

When I thought about the way I had been teaching for the past nine years and considered my own experiences as a learner of mathematics, I was not sure what there was in mathematics to be reasoned or argued. I had always conceived of mathematics as a collection of rules and procedures to be learned and the answers to problems were either right or wrong. I found these ideas about mathematics challenged by the reforms and my early encounters with Lampert. For six months, prior to the teaching I did that is described in this chapter, I spent time with Lampert watching videotapes of her teaching, observing in her fifth grade classroom, and talking with her about mathematics teaching and learning. Watching Lampert and her students have long discussions over mathematical ideas helped me to see that there was something to be discussed in math class. I began to see that mathematics was laden with meanings, assumptions, and conditions. When these were opened up to discussion and examined by teachers and students, my notion of straightforward right and wrong answers became quite complicated. I had begun to see how mathematics was more than the rules, procedures, and right answers that I had learned and later taught. There were questions to be pondered and meanings to be negotiated. I saw Lampert and her students grapple with mathematical ideas I had never questioned. I remember being intrigued when I watched them spend an entire class period on one problem. In the past, it was common for my students to work at least twenty problems in a single class period. In the context of a single problem, I saw Lampert and her students delve deeply into areas of mathematics I had never considered. For example, I saw them explore the meanings of and relationships among division, remainders, and fractions in the context of writing stories that would give meaning to the computation "3 divided by 16." I was scared. My fifth graders in the past had never done division where the divisor was bigger than the dividend. Teaching the procedures for doing the long division algorithm to fifth graders had always been a challenge. The thought of trying to teach a conceptual understanding of this algorithm was overwhelming. I had never had my students consider the meaning of remainders; and up until now, fractions had always been a separate topic in the math textbook. I would need to learn how it related to division. I wondered whether or not I could teach students mathematics that I was not sure I understood.

Questioning my own knowledge of mathematics was only one source of my anxiety when I thought about the prospect of trying to teach in ways advocated in the reforms. In the past, my math classes had always been one of the quietest parts of my day. Frequently the only voice heard was mine as I read off the answers to homework, worked problems on the board, directed the use of manipulatives, gave out the next assignment, or answered students' questions as they worked silently on problems. The discourse in Lampert's classroom was much different. I watched Lampert listen intently to students as they worked with one another on a problem in small groups or all together on a problem in whole group discussions. After listening, she seemed to decide on the spot what to say and do next. I worried about whether or not I would be able to hear my students' voices in a similar way. I had never given my students much of an opportunity to talk in mathematics, perhaps because I never realized they could have so much to say. The listening, probing, and decision making Lampert had to do on the spot made the whole class period seem much less predictable than the math lessons I had carefully planned and followed in the past.

I thought what I saw in Lampert's math class bore some similarities to what my students and I had been doing in social studies for the past three years. I had been teaching *Man: A Course of Study (MACOS)*,[7] a social studies curriculum developed in the 1960s and designed to give students opportunities to explore questions and issues related to the fundamental question, what makes man human? The emphasis of this curriculum was on inquiry rather than answers. Many of my social studies classes were devoted to small group and whole class discussions of ideas and points of view. I posed questions I found in the *MACOS* teacher's guide that required my students to think about ideas and construct arguments rather than recall facts or search for right answers. In contrast to my math classes, *MACOS* was dominated by my students' voices rather than mine. It seemed to me that what I needed to learn was how to make that happen in mathematics, but mathematics as a subject seemed very different from social studies.

After watching videotapes of Lampert teach, spending time in her classroom, and having extended dialogues with her about her teaching, we decided that I would begin teaching mathematics the following fall, in a fourth grade classroom neighboring Lampert's. On the one hand, this seemed to make a lot of sense when I thought about the sort of teacher educator and scholar I wanted to be— someone that could move between the world of teaching and the world of research and reform. Trying to teach mathematics in an elementary school classroom for a year in ways consistent with current reforms seemed important to understanding this role. On the other hand, the plan to teach was not merely about teaching; it was about *learning* to teach, and this seemed a bit disconcerting to my "experienced teacher" self. After all, I came to graduate school thinking I knew how to teach and that the next step was to learn to teach others to teach. Putting myself back into the position of a learner with regard to teaching, a place the experienced teacher in me thought I had left long ago, felt risky.

I wanted Lampert to value my past experiences as a teacher and give me the space to be a learner. I wanted to be able to talk to Lampert as a colleague who understood the difficulties of what

I was trying to do from a teacher's perspective. I wanted Lampert to remind me of what I did know as a teacher and help me understand what I needed to learn. I wanted to be able to ask her questions without thinking that what I was asking was something I ought to know. I wanted to feel like I could tell her I did not understand the mathematics or ask her to help me understand the reasoning of a student. I wanted to feel like I was not headed into this place of uncertainty alone.

Lampert: What Is Entailed in Learning This Kind of Teaching?

Heaton and I had a relationship with many dimensions. I was her professor, we collaborated on a research project, and we were teachers of mathematics in the same elementary school. I also related to her as a teacher educator. In that role, my purpose was to help Heaton learn to teach math differently so that she could become a teacher educator with firsthand classroom experience of what it takes to do the kinds of things that researchers and reformers advocate. Having read many of the reform documents on mathematics curricula and instruction, Heaton wanted to try to change her practice. Even though I had not seen her teach math before she came to graduate school, she described to me what she had done and contrasted her approach with the way she saw me teach and the kind of teaching that she read about in the *NCTM Standards*[8] and the *California Framework*.[9] I assumed that her teaching had been traditional because of the way she described her use of conventional textbooks and teacher's guides and her comments about how she followed them quite closely. She had worked in a school district whose math curriculum was driven by performance objectives, and her goals primarily focused on the mastery of rules and procedures rather than conceptual understandings of mathematics.

One aspect of the kind of teaching that was advocated in the reforms that seemed especially important to Heaton as she embarked on becoming a teacher educator was the extent to which it was grounded in a way of knowing mathematics that was very different from her experience. When she spoke about her previous teaching, there was an articulated connection between what she had believed mathematics to be and the way she had taught it. When we began to work together, Heaton was not experienced at the practice of mathematics herself, and she saw mathematics as a set of procedures for arriving at correct solutions to problems. She was competent at doing the procedures and had even been successful at a college-level calculus course. As a teacher, her goal was for her students to be similarly proficient. It was only after she came to graduate school that it seemed to matter that, in her own words, she "didn't have a clue why all those formulas worked." She had done some work with "manipulatives" but saw them as an alternative method for teaching procedures in a way that would be more fun and interesting to the children in her classes. During the time that she was trying to learn to teach math differently, she was also struggling to figure out what it may mean to both do and understand mathematics.

What did Heaton need to learn? And how was she going to learn it? My thinking about the first question was based on my own experience as a fifth grade mathematics teacher working to develop and understand the sort of practice that is called for in the reform documents. My thinking about the second question was based on my analysis of the practice of teaching, on an examination of how teachers use knowledge in practice, and on the study of processes whereby the kind of knowledge teachers need might be acquired. The way that Heaton and I approached our work together was based on ideas about both what she needed to learn and how she might learn it.

There was plenty of evidence that before beginning her work with me, Heaton was a competent teacher, and she had done some teaching in social studies that involved her with the kind of pedagogy that she was aiming to apply to the teaching of mathematics. But the kind of mathematics teaching that she wanted to be able to do involved substantial new learning. The elements of the "new" kind of math teaching that Heaton needed to learn included constructing mathematical tasks that would elicit students' intuitive approaches to quantitative situations, managing individual and small group work on open-ended mathematical tasks, managing whole class discussions in which students would assert their mathematical theories and comment on the assertions of others, and constructing mathematical tasks that would be responsive to and at the same time extend students' thinking into new mathematical territory. She needed to learn how to listen to students and to encourage them to be mathematical sense-makers rather than rely on the authority of the teacher or the textbook to decide what was right or wrong. And in order to put these values to work in the classroom, she needed to learn how to manage mathematical ideas in the context of complex social interactions.

Interactive competence and a knowledge of mathematics are required if mathematics is going to be taught in a way that is responsive *both* to the way children think about number and shape *and* to the structure of the mathematical ideas under discussion.[10] This knowledge is different from what one needs to know in order to competently teach a textbook lesson oriented toward having students remember how and when to do procedures.[11] It is also different from knowing mathematics in order to practice in the discipline; in the classroom, the teacher's knowledge of the subject must be used to make connections between what he or she understands and what students bring to the lesson.[12] The teacher's mathematical knowledge must be held in a form that enables it to be reshaped depending on the kinds of ideas students bring up in a discussion or in the activity of trying to solve a problem.[13]

Lampert: Why Did I Observe Heaton and Write Descriptions of What Happened in Her Lessons?

The approach that I took to helping Heaton learn to do this different kind of mathematics teaching was based on ideas about what teachers need to know and how their knowledge is acquired. In particular, our work together was designed to develop her capacity to create mathematics teaching in relation to how students think about quantity. To help her do this, I observed her lessons, wrote notes about the specific teaching problems that occurred in those lessons, and analyzed Heaton's practice with her in the context of these problems. She also observed me teach fifth grade mathematics twice each week. We created a way of talking together about our teaching that recognized the tensions among knowledge about mathematics, knowledge about students' thinking, knowledge about the social dynamics of the classroom, and knowledge about curriculum as we looked at what each of these domains might have to contribute to the design of practice.

We invented an approach to teacher education wherein both of us could bring relevant understandings from different perspectives to the analysis of classroom events. The ideas about how knowledge is acquired that underlay the new pedagogy in mathematics are relevant to teacher education as well.[14] Just as teaching mathematics for understanding requires the teacher to attend to the social and conceptual context in which mathematical problems arise, teaching *teaching* for understanding requires the teacher educator and the learner to interact in the context of actual teaching problems and try to understand those problems in terms of the circumstances in which they arise. In studies of teachers' knowledge use in practice, researchers from several different perspectives have concluded that understanding teacher thinking involves understanding how teachers respond to an ever-changing situation with knowledge that is contextual, interactive, and speculative.[15] Teacher development programs that are structured around peer coaching or mentoring, where the teacher educator and the learner establish their relationship around classroom observations, are designed to take account of this contextual quality of knowing and learning in teaching.[16] As in mathematics education, the focus in teacher education cannot be limited to getting the right answer, because judging whether or not an answer or a practice is "right" depends on understanding the circumstances in which the problem arises and the conditions under which it must be solved. With this view of knowledge in mind, I believed that what I should be doing with Heaton was looking at the teaching problems that arose in her lessons and examining alternative solutions. This kind of teacher education might have the potential to prepare Heaton to make on-line judgments that took account of the multiple considerations appropriate to constructing good teaching practice.[17] It would also help both of us be more articulate about the process of helping others to change their practice.

Including classroom observation and the discussion of situated teaching problems in my work with Heaton followed a well-established path in teacher development, but it also differed from

this tradition in a significant way because of the attention we gave
to mathematics. Although the concept of "pedagogical content
knowledge" has become useful in research on teaching to describe
the notion that teachers integrate subject matter knowledge with
knowledge about how children learn and how knowledge can be
represented for teaching,[18] studies of mentoring or coaching in
teacher education give scant attention to how a teacher acquires and
learns to use subject matter knowledge in the process of learning a
different kind of pedagogy.[19] On line, in face-to-face interactions
with students, teaching that attends seriously to subject matter (as
current reforms suggest it should) requires the mathematics teacher
to simultaneously manage the exchange of mathematical ideas and
the social and ethical situation in which those ideas are exchanged.[20]
Teacher education, as it is now structured, segments learning about
these aspects of teaching into subject matter and methods courses,
and courses in learning theory and classroom dynamics. The learning teacher is left to make the integration for himself or herself with
no practical or conceptual guidance. Even the new case materials
being prepared for teacher education to bring professional preparation closer to the problems of practice neglect the integration of
subject matter problems with social and ethical dilemmas.[21] To become a different kind of teacher educator—one who could help others to think about the use of subject matter knowledge in the social
and ethical context of classroom lessons—Heaton would need to see
what it would be like to try to do this kind of teaching and get some
help in framing some ways to talk about it.

How does mathematics (or any other subject matter) come
into the teaching picture? How does it connect with the social and
ethical issues that are usually considered aspects of "classroom management"? For teachers and students to do authentic mathematics
in the classroom, they need to learn to work collaboratively on
mathematics problems and reflect on their work both privately and
in a public forum; to do that, they need to be able to use words and
symbols that communicate the ideas under consideration. To teach
students to communicate mathematically, to construct reasonable
solutions to complex problems, to look for and articulate the nature
of quantitative patterns, the teacher needs to be able to set tasks that
elicit thinking and doing and talking of a meaningful sort. He or

she then needs to listen, watch, and probe in mathematically informed ways to see how students are thinking and what they are
learning.[22] Setting a task that will engage students in mathematical
ideas that are targeted for learning can occur in a reflective mode
outside the classroom before the lesson starts, although one would
need to know something about the students involved to produce a
problem that would succeed in engaging them; but the interactions
that need to be crafted by the teacher during and after work on the
problem require more on-the-spot improvisation. Teacher-student
interactions in this task environment are more like a conversation
about topics of mutual interest than like a lecture or the kind of
teacher-directed question and answer session typical of school lessons.[23] Like other kinds of conversations, they need to be constructed by the participants in the course of the exchange with all
participants having a part in determining the content and the direction of the interaction.[24] The meaning that terms come to have
in such conversations derives from the way they are used in mathematical work.[25]

So the question that I faced as someone hoping to help a
teacher learn to teach mathematics differently was, How do you
teach someone to participate in mathematical conversations, in the
role of the teacher, for the purpose of instruction? How do you teach
someone the difference between teaching by improvising a conversation about mathematics in each lesson, focused around a task
designed to stimulate students' thinking in areas where they had
something to learn, and teaching that follows a topic-by-topic
agenda with problems that are laid out in advance in a textbook?
Teaching Heaton mathematical principles would have given her a
better background for guiding students' inquiries and leading the
mathematical conversation in fruitful directions. Teaching her pedagogical principles would have given her ideas about how to interact with students in ways that would support the development of
their understanding. Our work together involved this kind of exchange of information. But Heaton's learning how and when to use
these principles in relation to the kinds of questions that came up
in students' work needed to occur in the context of problems that
arose in lessons. What I wanted to teach Heaton by my observing
and reflecting on her lessons with her is what Shulman calls "stra-

tegic knowledge"—the knowledge that "comes into play as the teacher confronts particular situations or problems, whether theoretical, practical, or moral, where principles collide and no simple solution is possible. Strategic knowledge is developed when the lessons of single principles contradict one another, or the precedents of particular cases are incompatible."[26]

A teacher who has seen mathematics as the straightforward acquisition of rules and procedures and who has been teaching mathematics by following step-by-step teacher's guides and textbooks has to learn that strategic knowledge is appropriate to working on pedagogical problems. This means making different assumptions than one would make if one thought good mathematics teaching was teaching that followed the teacher's guide as closely as possible. At the same time, the teacher needs to learn *how* to invent practice in ways that are likely to produce effective teaching and learning. This kind of learning is a matter of not only acquiring new principles or strategies but also holding that knowledge in ways that make it usable in practice. Heaton was learning the principles applicable to the kind of mathematics teaching she wanted to do from reading the research and reform documents. She had learned some new procedures for interacting with learners from watching my teaching. By teaching her own fourth grade class, she would learn how to cope with situations in which principles conflict and pedagogical strategies raise new problems as they solve others. Teaching mathematics for understanding in the school classroom requires having different kinds of knowledge, but in addition it requires the *coordination* of knowledge about math, about students, about social interaction, about curriculum, and so on. Improvisation takes a combination of knowledge and self-confidence; it follows some framework, but loosely. It requires that knowledge be held in flexible ways so that it can be called upon when it is needed, not in the form of a script, but in the form of a web of multiply connected ideas for things to try. It is not a matter of learning the rules and then following them; it is a matter of casing out the situation you are in on a moment-by-moment basis and responding, watching how students react to your response, constructing a new response, in a cyclical improvisation. It means a willingness to go into a situation without knowing what is going to happen next, to accept that there is not one right way to do things, to rely on yourself to be able to come up with the next good action rather than looking in a guidebook or having some expert tell you what to do next. And there is not a lot of time to stop and think in the classroom when a lesson, especially a large group discussion, is happening.

In the example that follows, Heaton and I describe how we tried to focus on these aspects of learning to teach mathematics in our work together. Heaton describes one lesson that she taught in late September, and then each of us analyzes an incident that occurred in this lesson to illustrate how my observations and our reflections contributed to our understanding of the process of learning to teach—and helping others to learn to teach differently. In analyzing both Heaton's thinking about what occurred and my observations of the incident, we hope to illustrate the voices each of us heard as we try to see a teaching situation from multiple perspectives.

Heaton: Beginning to Teach Differently

By late September, I had been teaching fourth grade mathematics for just over two weeks. Maggie taught fifth grade mathematics in the classroom next door, and we arranged our schedules in a way that allowed us to observe each other teach twice a week and meet weekly to talk about teaching. The focus of these conversations varied with whatever was on my mind at the time. At times we talked about my teaching and the notes Maggie took during her observations. Sometimes I was curious about something I had observed in Maggie's class and asked her questions. Other times, we talked about what I was learning at the university. We both asked lots of questions but not because either one of us expected the other to have definitive answers. Rather, the value of the questions came from the ways in which they forced us to think about and try to articulate aspects of our work that we had never been required to put into words. I needed to think hard about what I had learned in my nine years of teaching that would serve me in these reforms and what kinds of things my changing teacher self was asking my experienced teacher self to unlearn. Maggie, as a teacher educator in this setting, contemplated the multiple dimensions in her work as a teacher of mathematics as she listened, watched, and probed to understand what it was that I understood.

My relationship with Maggie was a new way to be thinking about the goals and social organization of teacher education. We organized ourselves to work in an elementary school. Maggie, an experienced teacher and teacher educator, observed, wrote notes, and gave them to me, which in turn fueled a sustained dialogue between us about teaching. We listened to each other and tried to understand how the other made sense of ideas. But our interactions consisted of more than just sharing ideas. Maggie, as the more experienced math teacher and the teacher educator, used her notes about my teaching as a way to push me to think in new ways about my teaching, my students, and what it meant to understand and do mathematics in ways advocated by the current reforms. Maggie also read and responded to a journal I kept on my teaching. In many ways, our inquiry into teaching paralleled the inquiry into mathematics I saw Maggie and her students doing and that I tried to orchestrate myself. As a student of teaching, like students of mathematics, I was expected to take responsibility for making sense of ideas for myself. Maggie, my teacher, acted as a guide and used her notes and my journal as a way to probe and push my thinking in various directions. Her experience combined with my struggles gave both of us new insight into the process of teaching and learning to teach mathematics.

I was faced with struggles everywhere I turned. The difficulties began with planning. In the past, planning for mathematics had been a breeze. It usually just involved writing down the next two pages of the textbook for five days at a time. Planning was no longer so easy. I was not using a typical textbook. The school district had adopted *CSMP, Comprehensive School Mathematics Program*.[27] *CSMP* was a "new" curriculum that, unlike the traditional mathematics textbooks I had used in my past elementary school teaching, took the subject of mathematics seriously. It was filled with experiences that related directly and indirectly to the world of numbers and their interrelationships and with reasoning about these relationships that seemed aligned with the content and pedagogical ideas of the current reforms. There was a teacher's guide, but no student textbooks. The teacher's guide offered scripted lessons with questions for the teacher to follow and possible student responses. Trying to follow the script and teach in ways that opened up the discourse for my students' ideas presented some problems. We often veered away from the script as my students talked about how they made sense of mathematical ideas. When this happened, the teacher's guide was of little use to me, yet I had a hard time trusting myself to let go of it. For nine years the mathematics textbook had been my primary source of what and how to teach. At the time of the following lesson in late September, I was trying to find ways to use the teacher's guide as a source of problems without trying to follow the script. I planned what I could in advance, but I needed to get used to the idea that many of my plans about what to do in class each day needed to wait until I heard the voices of my students and listened to their thoughts about mathematical ideas.

Finding ways to get students to talk about the sense they made of mathematical ideas was a challenge. In my past teaching, any sense-making of mathematical ideas had usually been mine. Learning how to ask questions rather than give answers was difficult. I was forever biting my tongue and stopping myself midsentence in an attempt to turn my statements into questions and find out how my students were thinking. Figuring out what to do with students' ideas once I got them out on the table was also a challenge. I knew from watching Maggie that there was more to this than just students sharing ideas. Deciding which ideas to pursue, which to drop, and which to suspend for the moment was hard. I was also trying to figure out how to listen to my students' voices, make sense of their ideas, and ask questions in ways that would facilitate a discussion around a single math problem. As I tried to come up with problems to give my students, I was thinking about what kind of problem lends itself to a sustained mathematical discussion. What did I want my students to learn? And what, if anything, were they learning?

The public school in which Maggie and I taught served a university community. The twenty-three students of mixed ability in my fourth grade class represented countries from all over the world and all areas of the United States. Five of the students in my class began the year with a limited ability to speak English. The desks were arranged in clusters of four or five. The students did all of their math work in a spiral notebook. This became a record of the mathematical problems I gave and a collection of each student's work for the entire year.

Heaton: A Lesson in Late September

For one of my lessons early in the year, I had decided to modify two problems from *CSMP*. I had been working hard since the beginning of the school year to establish a routine in math class for working in small groups and participating in whole group discussions. I was also trying to find ways for my students to review and for me to understand what they understood about the meanings of addition and subtraction. When I prepared for this lesson, I looked at the problem posed in *CSMP* and considered it from my perspective as an experienced elementary teacher who had dealt for nine years with students' confusion over greater and less than signs. This is the problem as it appeared in the teacher's manual:

What whole numbers could be put in the boxes?

$$26 - \square > 10$$
$$26 - \square < 10$$

These symbols did not seem essential to the review and reasoning I wanted my students to do in the context of addition and subtraction, so I chose to revise the less than sign to an equal sign. When I put in the equal sign, I realized that keeping the 10 in the problem would limit the number of possible solutions to the problem. The changing teacher in me who held a vision of the reforms reminded the experienced teacher that students need a problem that requires them to think and reason. I thought I should not use a problem that would just call for one right answer. I wanted to deliberately set up a problem with multiple solutions or multiple ways to generate solutions, so I replaced the 10 with an empty box. I wrote the revised problem on the board and students copied it into their math notebooks.

What whole numbers could be put in the boxes?

$$26 - \Box = \Box$$

The students had barely begun to copy the problem in their notebooks when a student asked me, "What's a whole number?" I told her to pose her question to the whole class. Other students began offering examples of whole numbers. "Like 1, or 2. Not 1½," explained one student. "Not 1¾," added another. Several examples were given that included large whole numbers or negative numbers, and there were differing opinions as to whether or not zero was a whole number. I asked the students to consider the numbers written below the red dots on the number line displayed on a long strip of paper around the front of the room above the chalkboard: "What about the numbers you see on the number line around the room? What kind of numbers are those?" Students answered in chorus that they were whole numbers. Next I asked, "Can someone give me an example of a whole number you don't see on the number line?" Students gave examples of whole numbers that were greater than or less than the endpoints of the number line. Given all the examples of whole numbers that had been generated, I thought the class was ready to do the problem until I heard the student who initially asked the question say, "I don't understand. What's *not* a whole number?" I said something about a whole number not being a fraction, to which she replied, "What's a fraction?" I repeated my earlier statement that the numbers that she could see on the number line were whole numbers and suggested she use any one of them to try to solve the problem.

Once the lesson was underway, the experienced teacher in me, who had planned the lesson, was surprised that someone would ask me a question like "What's a whole number?" At the time, this question about whole numbers felt to me like an interference in working the problem I wanted the class to do. Spending time on the directions by establishing a meaning for whole numbers seemed like a waste of time. I had planned that we would spend our time working on the problem, not constructing a meaning for the directions. But the changing teacher in me knew from reading the reforms and watching Maggie teach that I was supposed to be listening to the students. So I forced myself to pay attention to the student's question about whole numbers. At the same time, my experienced teacher voice was telling me that we could get on with the lesson more quickly if I would supply the students with a definition. I compromised by giving the students some examples of whole numbers. When one student said she did not understand, the experienced teacher felt even more guilty about the confusion. I tried to think of a way to respond that would answer the question and move everyone in the class from interpreting the directions to working on the problem. I noticed the number line on the board and realized that the numbers I saw boldly printed beneath red dots on the number line chart were whole numbers. Pointing this out to the students seemed like a quick and easy, straightforward way to answer the question and satisfy the experienced teacher in me that wondered how long it was going to be until these students started working on the problem.

Thinking that the students now understood the directions, I was relieved that we could finally move on to the problem. As I walked around and listened to children work on the problem, I heard them continue to talk about whole numbers. As I listened to their ideas, my changing teacher voice began to raise questions about the soundness of my own definition of a whole number and told me to pay attention to the reasonableness of the ways in which students were talking about whole numbers and the number line in their small groups.

As I walked by one of the boys, he said to me, "We did this last year." I looked in his notebook and saw that he had generated many whole number solutions to the problem, more than any of the other students at his table. I gave him the following problem as something extra to do:

$$26 - \square < 10$$

This was one of the original problems in *CSMP* that I had modified and posed to the class. I wrote the problem in the student's notebook and continued roaming around the room, watching and listening to the children. I did not get back to see what he did with the problem I gave him. The students worked independently for about fifteen minutes on the problem. When I saw that everyone had a set of multiple whole number solutions to the problem in their note-books, we moved on to another problem without discussing what they had just done. I had planned for us to work two problems, and when I looked at the clock, the experienced teacher in me knew that we needed to move on if we were going to get the second problem done. This experienced voice conflicted with the changing teacher in me, who was trying to learn to value the time spent on listening to students talk about how they found their solutions and under-stood the problem. However, all that talk about whole numbers had taken up most of the time that I had thought we would spend on the first problem. The need of the experienced teacher in me to cover the curriculum overpowered any desire on the part of the changing teacher to dwell any longer on this problem.

The problem we moved to was the next one in the *CSMP* lesson plan. It was an arrow road. Arrow roads are representations used by *CSMP* to model the process of comparing and analyzing sets and operations on them. I did not see the connection with what we had done in the first problem or even assume that there should be one. I drew arrows on the board, and the task for the students was to figure out what to label the arrow that connects two numbers. We worked on one arrow at a time. I wrote the arrow and the two numbers connected to it on the board. I began with this:

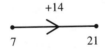

Students copied it into their notebooks and then did either addition or subtraction in their notebooks to figure out what value to give the arrow. When students appeared to have a solution in their note-books, I asked several to explain how they figured out what to label the arrow. After a bit of discussion, I moved on to another arrow. By the end of the class period, we had constructed this arrow road:

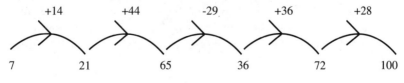

At the time, I saw no connection between what we had done here and the first problem, which had students generating pairs of whole numbers.

When I think back on the exchange now about whole numbers and the number line, more than two years later, with new understandings of mathematical content and pedagogy, I feel slightly embarrassed. Why did I think I had to respond with an answer to the student's question about whole numbers? Why did I think I needed to be the one to define a whole number? I realize that as an experienced teacher, I felt it was my responsibility to clear up the confusion. Working on the problem without some understanding of whole numbers would have been difficult. And the curriculum I was using made me believe that it was working on the problem, not interpreting the definition of whole numbers, that would help my students to learn. But my visionary voice—the voice that comes from studying and valuing new ways to teach and learn—wonders why I thought the understanding of whole numbers that my students used to work the problem had to be *my* definition of whole numbers. The students would have been capable of constructing a working definition of whole numbers themselves. By giving them a definition, I fell right back into the teaching-as-telling mode that I was trying to alter.

Lampert: Talking in Multiple Voices About Heaton's Lesson

I copied the problem that was on the chalkboard into my observation notes so that Ruth and I would have a record of where the lesson had started. While I wrote, I was thinking that this was pretty serious mathematics for fourth graders, beginning to get them into the territory of independent and dependent variables. But before they got into generating the pairs of numbers that would work in this equation, one of the students asked for a clarification of the term "whole number." Ruth answered with some examples and then asked students for more examples. She then looked up at a "number line" displayed above the chalkboard and asked the class, "What about the numbers you see on the number line around the room? What kind of numbers are those?" And she answered her own question: "Whole numbers. These are all examples of whole numbers." Then she asked a further question: "Can someone give me an example of a whole number you don't see on the number line?"[28]

In that moment, several conflicting voices were talking to one another in my head as I tried to think of something appropriate to write in my notes to Ruth. One voice, my mathematical self, would have said, "Oh no! You don't understand the number line at all! The number line is about *continuity*. The number line is one of the great ideas in the history of mathematics; its invention allowed the field to progress in leaps and bounds because it gave mathematics a way to talk about the infinity of numbers *between* zero and one. All of the real numbers are on the number line, not just the "whole numbers." I also worried because Ruth used examples of whole numbers to answer the student who seemed to be requesting a definition. I remembered the sacredness of definitions in my undergraduate courses and how they were used as the foundation for every other assertion you could make in mathematics. Deductive reasoning about quantities is founded on the capacity to define terms unambiguously. And "whole numbers" is not even a good mathematical term because of the questions it raises about zero and the negatives. Mathematicians would prefer teachers to talk about "integers" or "natural numbers."

At the same time that I was having these mathematical concerns, another voice, my constructivist self, asserted the idea that learners cannot appreciate the meaning of a concept unless they grapple with its invention in a situation that requires clarification. This voice would have said to Ruth, "Why don't you just leave it to the students to figure out what the problem means? Let them put their ideas about what a 'whole number' is out on the table and let them argue with each other until they come up with a workable definition." This is my "explorer" voice, the voice of the teacher-researcher, who wants to try out all of the new and interesting ideas about what may happen in classrooms if we actually try to do what the reform documents and the current learning theories suggest. From the point of view of the new pedagogy, mathematical knowledge is not meaningful unless it comes from the child's experience and the meaning of terms needs to be negotiated in classroom dis-

course. Drawing on both studies of how practitioners work in the
field of mathematics and ideas in psychology about the social
construction of knowledge, I and other reformers believe that it is
appropriate to have children make their own situated mathematical
definitions and examine the implications of these definitions rather
than simply accept the definitions arrived at in other times and
places. These constructivist notions collided with what I knew
about the importance and power of mathematical traditions.

As I reflect on my work with Ruth from this distance and
think about what it can contribute to our understanding of a new
pedagogy of teacher education, another set of voices makes its way
into the conversation. In the role of teacher educator, I am also both
a bearer of knowledge and the advocate of negotiated understanding. If I am the "teacher" and Ruth is the "learner," I ought to have
some kind of knowledge about teaching to pass on to her, analogous to my knowledge about the significance of the number line in
mathematics. I have more teaching experience, more familiarity
with the various theoretical frameworks that might be brought to
bear on the problems Ruth is trying to solve, more knowledge about
how fourth graders are likely to think about numbers. I thought I
should have shared what I know with Ruth; but I also thought that
telling her what I know about teaching would have about as much
of a chance of increasing her capacity to understand and solve pedagogical problems as telling ten-year-olds what I know about
mathematics would have of increasing their capacity to understand
and solve mathematics problems. Like the new pedagogy of mathematics that we are trying to construct to support children's capacity
to solve problems, the interaction between teacher educator and
teacher learner has a constructive component. If what Ruth and I
were doing together was research on teacher education, our interaction should have been an occasion to try to create a new way of
talking about practice that would be embedded in classroom problems and not overburdened by all the conventional categories that
I brought to the table. From this point of view, the meaning of the
terms of discourse that Ruth and I would use to talk to each other
would need to be created in the context of our conversation. To have
a truly educational interaction with Ruth, I would need to figure
out why what she did with the number line made sense to her. I

would need to figure out a way to say what I wanted to say about the event I witnessed that would take account of her understanding of teaching and of mathematics.

As if this collection of voices were not confusing enough, there was still another part of my self pulling for attention—my perspective as an experienced and practicing classroom teacher. From this point of view, I understood very well what Ruth was up to when she said that the whole numbers were the ones on the number line up at the front of the room. She wanted to make lots of examples of whole numbers available in the physical environment in order to make it possible for the students to do the assignment. She believed that her students would not learn unless they were engaged in the assigned task, and they could not do this because they were getting hung up on the directions. Ruth cast around, as the student asked for clarification, for some concrete way to make it clear to the whole class what they were supposed to do so they could get down to work. As I looked at the paper strip that was up on the wall, I thought, "She's not wrong. The numerals that are on that paper strip are the numerals that represent whole numbers." And her strategy worked. The student who had been confused, who had asked, "What's a whole number?" and "What's not a whole number?" got down to work and produced appropriate ordered pairs even though her questions had not been answered.

How could I pull all these perspectives together into a written comment that would provoke further conversation, make Ruth think about all these issues, make an occasion for her to learn something important in mathematics, and at the same time convey to her that I recognized that this was a complicated matter, that there was not one right way to handle the situation?

To Ruth at that moment, and to the fourth graders in her class, that chart up on the wall was not the number line I had learned about in my mathematical studies, but I wanted Ruth to see the mathematical perspective on what she was doing while recognizing that her actions made sense from the perspective of a teacher whose aim was to get all her students engaged in the activity of the day. In my notes, I needed to help Ruth realize that the chart on the wall was only a representation of the number line, and as such it emphasized certain features of this mathematical concept (the order of integers) and not others (that there is an infinity of rational numbers between the integers). I also wanted her to question whether getting the students to work on the task she had written on the board was the best thing to do if they had this confusion about the nature of "whole numbers." Perhaps the task could be redefined to include figuring out how to interpret and give meaning to mathematical terms.

The question of how to teach in this situation would be only partially resolved if Ruth had more mathematical knowledge or more knowledge of the process of helping students to construct situated meaning for mathematical terms. I am not sure what I would have done if I were teaching the lesson that Ruth set out to teach. The lesson as presented could get students involved in generating ordered pairs and looking at the patterns that appeared in them, leading them to begin to understand the idea of a function. If I had been teaching this lesson, I would have had to decide whether to diverge from this important mathematical topic and talk about the continuity of the number line; and if I had decided to diverge, I would have had to figure out on the spot how to make the concept of continuity accessible to fourth graders.

My dilemma was similar to the one Ruth faced as a mathematics teacher when her student asked for a definition of a "whole number." The answer to that question is complicated mathematically. The answer to what Ruth should have done in this instance is complicated pedagogically. She needed to say something to the student that would have made her think while not interrupting the flow of the lesson. I needed to say something to Ruth that would signal the issue as one worth thinking about and keep it in mind as a marker for themes we would come back to over and over again.

Here is what I wrote in my notes about the number line incident: "This is interesting → somewhat ambiguous representation; the *numerals* written below the red dots on the number line are being referred to as 'whole numbers'; i.e., 6½ is certainly on the number *line* although the numeral 6½ is not written on the *chart* that *represents* the 'number line.' It is hard to always know how to handle these ambiguities, even when you are aware of them, but the issue of how to use the number line in math teaching is a complicated one. Within *mathematics* the importance of the number *line* is that it represents *continuity* → that is, it represents the idea that there are always more numbers *in between* the other numbers."

As I was writing this, Ruth did something that indicated to me that she too was hearing different voices. When one of the students persisted in expressing confusion about the meaning of the term "whole number," she suggested that the student discuss her question with other students sitting at her table. I acknowledged this attempt to bring the students into the work of defining the terms of discourse by writing in my notes: "There were some interesting discussions among the kids at their tables about the problem, including some talk about what a whole number is and is not."

I wanted to encourage Ruth to take these kinds of risks so that she could have the experience of trying to cope with what happens in the classroom when you open up the discourse. But my reaction to this move was not unconflicted and brought my mathematical self and my explorer self into opposition again. Ruth was attempting to let go of the agenda and bring her students' thinking to the forefront more, but she was also in danger. Turning over the question of what a "whole number" is to a group of fourth graders, even when they are seriously engaged in mathematical thinking, is risky because it is sure to get the classroom discussion into some pretty complicated mathematical territory.

Heaton: What Did It Mean for Lampert to Be Observing Me Teach?

How was I to make sense of what Maggie wrote in her notes? How I understood these notes would depend on who I was and who Maggie was as she wrote them. Was she there to evaluate me, to commiserate, to analyze? I knew we would have a conversation about my teaching, but what sort of conversation would it be? What would be its focus and what sort of language would we use to talk about my teaching? My experienced teacher voice told me to beware of the critical and evaluative language Maggie might use to talk about my teaching. Observations of my teaching had always been done in the context of evaluation. Once a year, my principal was required to visit my classroom and fill out an evaluation form.

One frame of reference I brought to Maggie's observations

came from the vivid memories I had of being observed by my principal. I found his yearly observation and evaluation to be quite nerve-racking. As I taught and he wrote notes, I worried about what he was writing. Did he think I was disorganized? Had I explained something wrong? Did one of my students give a wrong answer? Were there students who were not paying attention? Was someone misbehaving that he noticed and I did not? Did he think I had strayed too far from my plans? As I anticipated the meeting to discuss his evaluation, I worried about whether or not he approved of my teaching. Were there things that I did to which he objected? Were there aspects of my teaching that he thought needed improvement? The answers to these questions were important to me because they determined the status of my job each year, yet, ironically, this annual observation/evaluation process seemed disconnected from both my daily life as a teacher and my professional growth.

My changing teacher voice reminded me that the circumstances and purposes of Maggie's observations and notes were different from what I had previously experienced, but my experienced teacher voice worked hard to convince the changing teacher in me otherwise. My observations as an experienced teacher had always been done in the context of evaluation. The presence of another adult in the classroom had always elicited feelings of being on stage in search of the audience's approval of me. Here I was in my tenth year of teaching, a teacher in the midst of change, feeling the vulnerability and uncertainty of a new teacher. The thought of being on stage was not a comfortable feeling. I felt my teaching to be far from any sort of finished performance, and the experienced teacher in me worried about how Maggie might judge me. The changing teacher in me tried to be open to the possibility of constructing new ways to think about learning to teach and teaching. In this context, learning and teaching were not separate processes for me. In the classroom, with Maggie watching, I was both a teacher and a learner.

In addition to these two voices, I brought several other "voices" to my attempts to make sense of my work with Maggie. One was the voice of a graduate student, learning about both policy and practice in relation to the reform of teaching. From this point of view, Maggie was my professor. She had read all the theories and research that I had read, and more. We had worked together on research projects, and we shared common analytic frames. The scholar in me was trying to learn how to be analytic about what students were thinking in the context of a classroom discussion of mathematics. Understanding what my students thought would immediately inform my own teaching, and if I could write about my teaching experiences, the sense I made of my students' understandings would, I hoped, inform the work of others. The scholar in me was trying to understand what it meant to do research on my own teaching and the ways in which this work was similar to and different from traditional academic research. The limited understanding of mathematics felt by the changing teacher in me influenced the focus of my scholarly work. I tended to focus on the mathematics and worried that scholars who analyzed teaching from other perspectives might criticize the focus of my work. Choosing to analyze my work from a mathematical framework was an opportunity for the changing teacher in me to learn more mathematics.

Maggie was also the math teacher in the next classroom. From another perspective we could talk to each other about school business and empathize about the difficulties of keeping a group of rambunctious kids on task and engaged in authentic mathematical activities. I had watched Maggie teach and talked with her after her lessons, listening to her struggles with the practical implications of trying to teach in a way that paid serious attention to students' understanding. We also shared an understanding of the school context and of the politics of change within the district where we were working.

How would all these voices make their way into the conversations Maggie and I might have about my teaching? The idea that Maggie would be so connected to my teaching, observing me teach twice a week, carried with it mixed feelings. When I thought about Maggie and myself in some ways, it felt less risky; in other ways, more. Thinking about Maggie as a teacher in the neighboring classroom and a person with whom I shared a vision of pedagogy and could talk about teaching appealed to me as an experienced teacher. Conversations about daily practice are rare events for teachers. After teaching for nine years with few occasions to talk about my teaching, I welcomed the opportunity; but to the changing teacher in me, teaching with Maggie in the classroom, a teacher who practiced this new pedagogy and was a scholar, felt risky. I feared that my interactions with students would reveal to Maggie the gaps in my knowledge of mathematics and the limits to my understanding of this new pedagogy. Even though I had taken mathematics through calculus in college, I had not thought about how to make more sophisticated math ideas accessible to students. Yet the graduate student in me knew that, if I could bear the risks, being able to learn from Maggie, my professor, about mathematics teaching and to learn from my own teaching practice in a classroom would be a wonderful complement to the research and theory I was studying at the university; but learning to move between the worlds of scholarship and practice, experiencing and trying to understand teaching from multiple perspectives, was important to learning to be the kind of teacher educator I wanted to become. Because my teaching was being explored from Maggie's and my own multiple perspectives and because my perspectives were often conflicting, the work of teaching and reflecting on it with Maggie was challenging, and at times painful.

An example of the pain I felt during this year of teaching can be seen in the note I wrote in my journal after teaching a lesson and reading Maggie's observation notes: "This teaching is *so* hard. Maybe [a professor of mine] had been right. It would have been better to have some time to mess around on my own before having people observe. . . . It is really hard. One thing that is hard is having things pointed out to me that I already recognize. It's also difficult to have things pointed out that I don't necessarily recognize. I am taking enormous risks." Figuring out ways to learn from the risks I was taking was a constant struggle throughout the year. Fighting the urge to evaluate was a continuous battle.

Heaton: Reflections on the Lesson and Reactions to Lampert's Notes on My Use of the Number Line to Clarify "Whole Numbers"

When I first glanced through Maggie's notes on my response to the question of "What's a whole number?" the changing teacher in me recognized the shallowness of my attempts to get students to understand the idea of a whole number and said to the experienced teacher, "Ruth, how could you be so naive?" As I read more carefully, the experienced teacher in me found some comfort in Maggie's analysis of the number line and her admission that even for her the number line is a "somewhat ambiguous representation." If she has been teaching for a number of years and has knowledge about mathematics and representations that exceeds my own and she *still* finds it ambiguous, maybe I am not doing so bad after all. Maggie's notes highlighted the complexity of the number line and revealed underlying meanings in the representation that I, as an experienced teacher, had never considered in all the years that the number line ran across the front of my classroom.

When I planned the lesson, I never expected that I needed to plan for someone not knowing what a whole number was. I had drawn on my past experiences and attended to the confusion my students might encounter with the greater and less than signs in the problem by revising the problem. Questioning whether or not my students would understand whole numbers never crossed my mind. I thought it was something implicitly understood by everyone, including myself. It was not until I let myself teach in a way that would allow a fourth grader to raise questions about mathematical definitions that I realized it was a concept that neither I nor my students had ever been asked to articulate. At the time, my impatience with the question reflected the distinction I made between directions and working the problem. The issue of whole numbers seemed related to understanding the directions of the problem and unrelated to working the problem. I have come to see that working the problem includes understanding and constructing meanings for the conditions of doing the problem as well as understanding how to arrive at the solutions. I now understand that in mathematics an interpretation of how to do the problem is an essential part of working on the problem. That doing mathematics would involve meaning and interpretation, in addition to finding answers, was something new for me. That I, the teacher, would be responsible for conducting a discussion in which students would construct a situated definition of whole numbers was certainly a new way to think about teaching. After this experience, I became a bit more cautious and thoughtful about the language I used in the problems I wrote on the board. I now see that an interpretation of the directions is a central and important part of working the problem.

Conclusion: Putting the Voices Together

Teacher education in a climate of reform could be seen to be about helping teachers change, helping them to make a simple kind of progress away from bad old practices to desirable new ones. Helping others to make this kind of progress is easier if you are not bogged down in the institutions you are trying to change. The dictionary defines the verb "reform" as "to cause [a person] to give up wrong or evil ways of life." If you are too sympathetic with the perspective of the "enemy," you will be less effective as a reformer. What this means to an experienced teacher who is preparing to be a teacher educator is that it would be best to deny one's past, to leave behind the persons and practices one valued before coming to graduate school and take up the cause of the new pedagogy being described by researchers and reformers. But therein lies a dilemma. The same researchers and reformers who have all these good ideas about how teaching should change have never had the experience of learning about teaching by teaching. They have scant evidence that the practices they envision are possible to implement in actual school settings. Their credibility with practitioners is therefore at risk.

An even more complicated paradox arises from the focus of the reforms on learners as "sense-makers." From this perspective, the ideas that learners hold are to be respected, whether or not they match the teacher's or the expert's ways of thinking about things. Both teachers and teacher educators who hold constructivist beliefs are thus faced with the challenge of respecting both where learners are coming from and where they want them to go. It seems duplicitous to respect children's ways of thinking about mathematics while not doing the same for experienced teachers' ways of thinking about teaching.

Hearing the multiple, oftentimes conflicting voices within Heaton and Lampert is a way to begin to understand the challenges faced by teachers and teacher educators who have an interest in changing traditional ways of teaching mathematics and teaching teachers. It also provides insight into the multiple layers of teaching and learning involved in inventing a new pedagogy of teacher education. Heaton, an experienced teacher, entered a doctoral program in teacher education never expecting that her studies to become a teacher educator would include an examination of her own teaching practice. It became necessary for her to do such an examination when she realized that the pedagogy of mathematics she wanted to teach teachers differed from her own practice of teaching mathematics. She could not live with the dissonance.

For some who enter the world of research and reform, these personal inconsistencies in the worlds of practice and research may not be troubling. Lines are traditionally drawn between theory and practice, research and teaching. For some, these lines are not troubling, and they make conscious decisions to be in one world or the other, to be scholars who contemplate theory and research or teachers who are concerned with the practice of teaching. What we end up with are scholars who tend to devalue the work of teaching and teachers who tend to devalue the work of scholars—both think the other really does not understand teaching. Why would someone want to be a part of both worlds and understand theory and research from the scholar's or reformer's perspective as well as from the teacher's perspective? What is the value in being able to move between these two worlds?

Understanding teaching and learning from multiple perspectives, as a teacher and scholar, allows one to move between the two worlds and understand the relationship between theory and practice in each world. As a teacher, one begins to learn what it might actually mean to try to teach mathematics in ways advocated by research and reform. As a scholar, one learns to articulate what is entailed in teaching and mathematics by analyzing problems of practice.

Constructing a role in which one is attuned to the voices described in this chapter is not without risks. For Heaton, it took courage. As an experienced teacher it required her, in the midst of learning to be a teacher educator, to admit that she needed to learn more about teaching mathematics. It took additional courage to try out this new way of thinking about mathematics teaching with Lampert watching. For Lampert, someone who performs the role

that Heaton wants to learn, the work also is not without risk. Strad-
dling the fence between teaching and research and reform can be
uncomfortable; the conflicts that arise when these worlds clash are
a disquieting reminder of why boundaries between research and
practice make sense.

Notes

1. For a description of "adventurous teaching," see Cohen
    (1988).
2. We are both researchers and teaching colleagues. It is a di-
    lemma for us to know how to handle referring to one another
    throughout this chapter. As an expression of our unusual re-
    lationship, it seems appropriate for us to use, at times, our last
    names and, at other times, our first names. The question of
    what to call ourselves is a central issue related to the role we
    are trying to construct. Thus, the reader should be aware that
    our unorthodox shifting between first and last names—be-
    tween Lampert and Maggie, Heaton and Ruth—has substan-
    tive meaning.
3. For a description of the kinds of practices Lampert has been
    exploring, see Lampert (1986, 1990, 1991, 1992).
4. Judge, 1982; Clifford & Guthrie, 1988; Powell, 1980.
5. See Holmes Group (1986) for more information about these
    reforms.
6. Schwab, 1978; Hammersly, 1979.
7. Educational Services, 1965.
8. National Council of Teachers of Mathematics, 1989, 1991.
9. California State Department of Education, 1985.
10. See National Council of Teachers of Mathematics (1991); also
    Yackel, Cobb, Wood, Wheatley, & Merkel (1990) on social and
    affective supports for co-constructive work in math.
11. See Cohen (1988, in preparation). As to the management of
    mathematical ideas, this is perhaps best described in Greeno
    (1991) where he uses the analogy of getting around in the
    terrain of mathematics. He asserts that competence involves
    being able to get around in the territory as well as having a

sense of where there is to go. The work on curriculum scripts by Putnam (1987) is a contrasting description of the knowledge one uses to do textbook-guided teaching.

12. Ball, 1991; Wilson, Shulman, & Richert, 1987; Cohen (in preparation).

13. Zarrinnia, Lamon, & Romberg, 1987; Lampert, 1987; Cobb, Wood, Yackel, Nicholls, Wheatley, Trigatti, & Perlwitz, 1991.

14. For other versions of this argument, see Ball (1988a, 1988b) and Kennedy (1991).

15. Jackson, 1968; Yinger, 1990; Clark & Peterson, 1986.

16. Little, 1985.

17. This assumption about how good practice is constructed is examined in the work of Spiro, Coulson, Feltovich, & Anderson (1988). Their focus is on medical practice, not teaching practice, but much of what they find about the problems of simplification and reliance on straightforward strategy learning seems relevant to the work of learning to teach.

18. Shulman, 1987; Wilson, Shulman, & Richert, 1987.

19. Exceptions to this are Palincsar, Stevens, & Gavelek (1989) and Gallimore & Goldenberg (1992).

20. This argument is elaborated in Lampert (1992).

21. Barnett (1991) is the exception. See Sykes & Bird (1992) and Merseth, MacDougall, & Lacey (1992) for reviews of these materials.

22. See National Council of Teachers of Mathematics (1991) and Ball (1988a, 1988b, and in press).

23. In terms used by the National Council of Teachers of Mathematics teaching standards, the nature of the "discourse" is different. Doyle (in press) writes about this contrast.

24. See research on literacy learning by O'Conner (1990); Michaels & Cazden (1986); Tharp & Gallimore (1988); and Wells, Chang, & Maher (in press).

25. Kitcher, 1984.

26. Shulman, 1987.

27. CEMREL, 1978.

28. Heaton's comments were recorded on a videotape of this lesson.

References

Ball, D. L. (1988b). *Knowledge and reasoning in mathematical pedagogy: Examining what prospective teachers bring to teacher education.* Unpublished doctoral dissertation, Michigan State University, East Lansing.

Ball, D. L. (1988a). Unlearning to teach mathematics. *For the Learning of Mathematics, 8*(1), 40–48.

Ball, D. L. (1991). Research on teaching mathematics: Making subject matter part of the equation. In J. Brophy (Ed.), *Advances in research on teaching, Vol. 2: Teachers' subject matter knowledge* (pp. 1–48). Greenwich, CT: JAI Press.

Ball, D. L. (in press). With an eye on the mathematical horizon: Dilemmas of teaching elementary school mathematics. *Elementary School Journal.*

Barnett, C. (1991). *Developing cases for use in mathematics teacher education.* Paper presented at the American Educational Research Association annual meeting.

California State Department of Education (1985). *Mathematics framework for California public schools, kindergarten through grade twelve.* Sacramento, CA: Author.

CEMREL, Inc. (1978). *CSMP in action: Comprehensive School Mathematics Program* (Clearing-house no. SE040707). St. Louis, MO. (ERIC Microfiche Collection No. ED226967)

Clark, C., & Peterson, P. (1986). Teachers' thought processes. In Merlin Wittrock (Ed.), *The handbook of research on teaching* (3rd ed., pp. 255–296). New York: Macmillan.

Clifford, G., & Guthrie, J. (1988). *Ed school.* Chicago: University of Chicago Press.

Cobb, P., Wood, T., Yackel, E., Nicholls, J., Wheatley, G., Trigatti, B., & Perlwitz, M., (1991). Assessment of a problem-centered second-grade mathematics project. *Journal for Research in Mathematics Education, 22*(1), 3–29.

Cohen, D. K. (1988). Teaching practice: Plus ça change. . . . In P. W. Jackson (Ed.), *Contributing to educational change: Perspectives on research and practice* (pp. 27–84). Berkeley, CA: McCutchan.

Cohen, D. K. (in preparation). *Teaching: Practice and its predicaments.*

Doyle, W. (in press). Curriculum and pedagogy. In Philip Jackson (Ed.), *Handbook of research on curriculum.*

Educational Services. (1965). *Man: A course of study.* Cambridge, MA: Author.

Gallimore, R., & Goldenberg, C. N. (1992). Tracking the developmental path of teachers and learners: A Vygotskian perspective. In F. K. Oser, A. Dick, & J. L. Patry (eds.), *Effective and responsible teaching: The new synthesis* (pp. 203-222). San Francisco: Jossey-Bass.

Greeno, J. G. (1991). Number sense as situated knowing in a conceptual domain. *Journal for Research in Mathematics Education, 22,* 170-218.

Hammersly, M. (1979). Towards a model of teacher activity. In John Eggleston (Ed.), *Teacher decision-making in the classroom: A collection of papers* (pp. 181-192). London: Routledge & Kegan Paul.

Holmes Group. (1986). *Tomorrow's teachers.* East Lansing, MI: Author.

Jackson, P. (1968). *The practice of teaching.* Troy, MO: Holt, Rinehart & Winston.

Judge, H. (1982). *American graduate schools of education: A view from abroad.* New York: Ford Foundation.

Kennedy, M. (1991). *Teaching subjects to diverse learners.* New York: Teachers College Press.

Kitcher, P. (1984). *The nature of mathematical knowledge.* New York: Oxford University Press.

Lampert, M. (1986). Knowing, doing, and teaching multiplication. *Cognition and Instruction, 3,* 305-342.

Lampert, M. (1987). What is geometry? (Progress Report, Teacher Study, Lab Sites Project). Cambridge, MA: Harvard Graduate School of Education, Educational Technology Center.

Lampert, M. (1990). When the problem is not the question and the solution is not the answer: Mathematical knowing and teaching. *American Educational Research Journal, 27*(1), 29-64.

Lampert, M. (1991). Connecting mathematical teaching and learning. In E. Fennema, T. P. Carpenter, & S. J. Lamon (Eds.),

Integrating research on teaching and learning mathematics (pp. 121–152). Albany, NY: State University of New York Press.

Lampert, M. (1992). Practices and problems in teaching authentic mathematics in school. In F. Oser, A. Dick, & J.-L. Patry (Eds.), *Effective and responsible teaching: The new synthesis.* San Francisco: Jossey-Bass.

Little, J. W. (1985). Teachers as teacher advisors: The delicacy of collegial leadership. *Educational Leadership, 43*(3), 34–36.

Merseth, K., MacDougall, R., & Lacey, C. (1992). Weaving a stronger fabric: The pedagogical promise of hypermedia and case methods in teacher education. Unpublished manuscript, Harvard Graduate School of Education, Cambridge, MA.

Michaels, S., & Cazden, C. (1986). Teacher/child collaboration as oral preparation for literacy. In B. Shefflin (Ed.), *The acquisition of literacy: Ethnographic perspective.* Norwood, NJ: Ablex.

National Council of Teachers of Mathematics. (1989). *Curriculum and evaluation standards for school mathematics.* Reston, VA: Author.

National Council of Teachers of Mathematics. (1991). *Professional standards for teaching mathematics.* Reston, VA: Author.

O'Conner, M. (1990). Negotiated defining: Speech activities and mathematics literacies. Boston: Boston University and the Literacies Institute, Education Development Center.

Palincsar, A., Stevens, D., & Gavelek, J. (1989). Collaborating with teachers in the interest of student collaboration. In N. Webb (Ed.), *Peer interaction, problem-solving and cognition* (pp. 41–53). Elmsford, NY: Pergamon Press.

Powell, A. (1980). *The uncertain profession: Harvard and the search for educational authority.* Cambridge, MA: Harvard University Press.

Putnam, R. (1987). Structuring and adjusting content for students: A study of live and simulated tutoring of addition. *American Educational Research Journal, 24,* 13–48.

Schwab, J. (1978). The arts of the eclectic. In I. Westbury & N. J. Wilkof (Eds.), *Science, curriculum, and liberal education.* Chicago: University of Chicago Press.

Shulman, L. S. (1987). Knowledge and teaching: Foundations of the new reform. *Harvard Educational Review, 57*(1), 1–22.

Spiro, R., Coulson, R., Feltovich, P., & Anderson, D. (1988). Cognitive flexibility theory: Advanced knowledge acquisition in ill-structured domains. In *Proceedings of the tenth annual conference of the cognitive science society.* Hillsdale, NJ: Erlbaum.

Sykes, G., & Bird, T. (1992). Teacher education and the case idea. In G. Grant (Ed.), *Review of research in education, 18.* Washington, DC: American Educational Research Association.

Tharp, R., & Gallimore, R. (1988). *Rousing minds to life: Teaching, learning, and schooling in a social context.* Cambridge, MA: Cambridge University Press.

Wells, G., Chang, G. L., & Maher, A. (in press). Creating classrooms of literate thinkers. In Sharan, S. (Ed.), *Cooperative learning: Theory and research.* New York: Praeger, 1990.

Wilson, S., Shulman, L., & Richert, A. (1987). "150 ways of knowing": Representations of knowledge in teaching. In J. Calderhead (Ed.), *Exploring teacher thinking.* Troy, MO: Holt, Rinehart & Winston.

Yackel, E., Cobb, P., Wood, T., Wheatley, G., & Merkel, G. (1990). The importance of social interaction in children's construction of mathematical knowledge. In T. Cooney (Ed.), *1990 Yearbook of the National Council of Teachers of Mathematics* (pp. 12–21). Reston, VA: National Council of Teachers of Mathematics.

Yinger, R. J. (1990). The conversation of practice. In R. T. Clift, W. R. Houston, & M. C. Pugach (Eds.), *Encouraging reflective practice in education* (pp. 73–94). New York: Teachers College Press.

Zarrinnia, E. A., Lamon, S., & Romberg, T. (1987, March). *Epistemic teaching of school mathematics.* (Program Report 87-3). Madison: University of Wisconsin School of Education, School Mathematics Monitoring Center.

4

Deeply Rooted Change:
A Tale of Learning
to Teach Adventurously

Suzanne M. Wilson
with Carol Miller and Carol Yerkes

Working with a college professor is exhilarating, exasperating, refreshing, frustrating, and rewarding. When we started working with Suzanne, we didn't know what we were getting into! It's always easy to sit back and explore new ideas by yourself because—as an individual teacher within the classroom setting—you are your own judge. But in a collaborative effort, there are strong feelings that you are being judged by others. To successfully build a team, we needed open communication, trust building, and time to be together.
                                    Miller & Yerkes memo, October 1991[1]

Three years ago we began collaborating on a project focused on "teaching for understanding." Naive about what it might mean to blend our minds and worlds, teaching personas and beliefs, experiences and values into an integrated curriculum cotaught by two

The work described in this chapter has been supported by the National Center for Research on Teacher Learning, the Center on Teaching and Learning Elementary School Subjects, and the Michigan Partnership for a New Education. In addition, Wilson's work has been supported by a fellowship from the National Academy of Education. The authors wish to thank Ruth Heaton and Deborah Loewenberg Ball for their counsel while writing the chapter, as well as the other authors of chapters in this book, whose conversation and questions have taught us much about learning to collaborate, write, and teach. We also wish to thank Laura Docter Thornburg and Steve Mattson for their company and conversation while we learn to teach.

elementary school teachers and one university professor, we pursued the idea based on an intuition that we *could* work together and on a commitment to finding better ways to help students learn. We embarked on a collective adventure with our students, one full of uncertainty and doubt, blind alleys, dead ends, a few triumphs.

Cohen describes a Romantic, Deweyan image of teaching that he calls "adventurous teaching."[2] It is a teaching that requires teachers to depend on students, one in which knowledge is viewed as human and constructed. It is a teaching that portrays teachers and students as inquiring together about problems that matter to all, a teaching that asks teachers to become "a species of mental mountaineer, finding paths between innocent curiosity and the great store of human knowledge, and leading children in the great adventures from one to another."[3]

Concerns for this kind of teaching echo throughout current reforms: "teaching for understanding" and "higher-order thinking," "teaching for the twenty-first century," and "new education" are some of the most prominent and popular signals of such commitments.[4] While many assume that schooling must change, however, policymakers, reformers, and scholars alike are beginning to understand the deeply rooted difficulties that have constrained good teaching in the past, consider the recent concern for systemic reform, for restructuring schools, for fundamentally altering assessment, for creating innovative curricula.[5] All these reforms call for radical, sweeping change in teaching practices and in assumptions about schooling and learning. We stand behind these ideals, for we believe, as Cohen states, "that school instruction can be exciting, and must be if children are to learn; that instruction should also be intellectually challenging; that to be either exciting or challenging it must be attuned to children's ways of thinking, to their experience, and to their efforts to make sense of experience; and that some of the greatest intellectual adventures are to be found in the structure and content of academic knowledge."[6]

We recognize how difficult it is to teach large groups of children—who more often than not come from backgrounds varied and little known to us—equally well. We believe that schools and teaching have to change, and we are committed to being part of that change. We see the changes that are necessary as mammoth, and ones that demand creative thinking and action. But no matter the integrity or strength of our commitment, adventurous teaching is little understood. There exist no easy answers, no recipes for action that guarantee results. As scholars and teachers, then, we find ourselves exploring the nature, the texture, the features, the content of adventurous teaching. We want to know what it looks and feels like, what it takes to enact and sustain it, what it means for us as teachers and learners, as parents and administrators.

We have found in the first three years of our explorations that learning to teach adventurously is itself an adventure. We use that word with care, for adventures feel risky but can be exhilarating. They require taking chances, but you can be more or less prepared for them. They often involve teams of people who play different roles. Sometimes there is a predominant leader; at others, leadership is shared. Inevitably, on adventures individuals possess a range of technical expertise and experience and often delegate duties accordingly. Moreover, adventures also often involve vague—or unknown—destinations. They evoke for us mental images of rough trails, peaks and valleys, raging rivers, unfriendly natives, unanticipated wonders. In our work learning to teach in new ways, we have felt ourselves on such an arduous journey, but one full of excitement, intrigue, and reward.

Cohen suggests that the array of reasons typically invoked to explain the failure of school reform—school organization, the conditions of teaching, incentives for changes, flaws in the reforms—go only so far in explaining why classrooms have not changed much in the last 150 years.[7] We agree. We work in a professional development school, an environment in which there are financial and personal incentives, a great deal of intellectual and organizational support, and facilitative and supportive conditions. Yet with all these supports and resources, we have found the process of changing our practice to be difficult and slow. It is our collective experience that changing one's teaching practice, no matter what the conditions, is difficult work.[8] In this chapter, a story of one collaboration aimed at learning to teach adventurously, we focus less on what adventurous teaching looks like and more on the factors that have facilitated our inquiry. We do this in hopes of further exploring what it takes to learn to teach adventurously and what kinds of personal and organizational resources are drawn upon in such work.[9] We begin with a brief explanation of how we came to work together. We then explore the critical factors that have supported our collaboration, as well as some of the unanticipated consequences of our work together.

The Context

Wilson is a teacher educator at Michigan State University and does research on teaching. Miller and Yerkes are elementary school teachers with forty-odd years of experience between them.[10] Several years ago, in an effort to combine her research interests in the subject matter knowledge required to teach elementary school social studies and her practice as a teacher educator, Wilson decided that it would be prudent to teach part-time in a local elementary school.[11] She approached Yerkes, who worked at Kendon Elementary School, a fledgling professional development school supported by the Michigan Partnership for a New Education, and asked if she could teach social studies every afternoon to Yerkes' class. Yerkes did not initially see this project as one that focused on her learning. Although she had a history of participating in research projects in collaboration with Michigan State University, her participation in this project was largely an opportunity to have someone else work with her students. She welcomed this opportunity as much for the relief it would provide from a busy day as anything else. What she might learn from Wilson's teaching, or how it might change her practice, was incidental.

Miller and Yerkes had shared their teaching responsibilities for several years prior to Wilson's arrival on the scene. Miller took responsibility for teaching science and penmanship, while Yerkes taught social studies, language arts, and creative writing. They switched classrooms each afternoon, working with each other's students in those subject areas. In the mornings, they taught reading and mathematics to their own students. This "departmentalization" allowed them each to focus their pedagogical thinking on a smaller set of subjects, with each developing more expertise in selected areas. During the first year that Wilson taught, then, Miller was also present in Yerkes' room. Rolling in with her overhead projector each day, Miller taught science to the students immediately after Wilson. Although they never spoke much, Wilson affectionately referred to Miller as her "mop-up person."

After the first year of Wilson and Yerkes' coexisting in one classroom, Miller joined the team and together we decided to explore what it would mean to integrate social studies, science, and language arts instruction. We created a new curriculum and shared teaching responsibilities, each teaching one-third of the afternoon, forty-five minutes to an hour, four days a week in each of the two third grade classrooms. Miller continued to be primarily responsible for science instruction, while Yerkes and Wilson taught an amalgam of language arts and social studies. We each emphasized writing and oral expression, reading and interpreting texts. And we chose themes around which to focus all the instruction. For example, when we taught a unit on Detroit, Wilson used it as an opportunity to teach geography and map reading skills, Yerkes taught about the history of native Americans in Michigan, and Miller taught about salt and salt mining.

Currently, we plan and reflect together each week during the release time provided by the professional development school's restructuring effort. Miller and Yerkes teach all other subjects to their respective third grades—which they do in the mornings—while Wilson stays at the university and works on her research projects and teaches undergraduate and doctoral classes.[12]

Miller and Yerkes did not enter this project thinking of it as an instance of "teacher learning." Miller's reflections explain the transformation that she experienced:

> This adventure in my teaching helped me to expand as a teacher. Confinement that I experienced within my four walls of teaching never confined my growth as a teacher, because I've never been a traditional teacher. I've always tried to vary my teaching.
>
> When ITIP [Instructional Theory Into Practice] was offered to teachers within the district, I took the class, embracing Madeline Hunter's approach to teaching children. Within that approach, there was "wait time" after asking a question. I had sticks to call

on students randomly. I had closure. I had review planned weeks after a unit ended. I had lots of turning to a neighbor to review or discuss a concept. I filled my teaching with all I learned to help students.

As I look at that paragraph I just wrote, there are lots of "Is." This is where I had confinement. I had no one to communicate with about what was happening in my classroom. Yes, I could tell another teacher about certain aspects of my teaching, but it was never a serious discussion. It was superficial and usually consisted of passing comments.

When I became involved in the professional development school efforts, I went through that process much like I went into ITIP. It was just part of my desire to see what someone else had to offer about student learning. Now 3 years later, I'm beginning to see a bigger idea. This process that I've been involved with over the past three years is not only about student learning—but about teacher learning. Not teachers being informed and told to try a certain idea, but teachers developing many exciting and stimulating avenues for learning. What's exciting about this is that teachers are not alone in the solitude of their classrooms, but teams work together [Miller, memo, February 1992].

Yerkes and Miller were not alone in their naïveté about this project. Although Wilson had originally conceived of her work in Yerkes' room as a project about her own "learning to teach," she never considered what Yerkes and Miller might learn from her, largely because of her own feelings of ignorance and incompetence. After all, she had never taught elementary school before.

Although we all agree this work has been exciting, learning to work together has not been easy. We lead different lives: We read different kinds of books, eat different kinds of food. Wilson travels extensively as a researcher and consultant; Miller and Yerkes have families that demand attention and care. Wilson has been trained as a researcher and writes extensively about her experiences teaching and watching other teachers. Miller and Yerkes have been working in classrooms for years, accumulating experience and knowledge, quietly, unobtrusively. We have different masters to serve, for Miller and Yerkes must think about their colleagues in the school—teachers and administrators alike—as well as their union. Wilson, on the other hand, thinks about her colleagues at the university—teacher educators and researchers—who have expectations of her that differ from those felt by Miller and Yerkes. Our schedules differ: Wilson rushes back to the university for search committee meetings; Miller and Yerkes stay after school to talk with parents. Wilson has some control over how she organizes her work time, while Miller and Yerkes must always be in their classrooms. Our backgrounds differ: Wilson has lived on the East and West coasts and visits friends and family there often. Her dress and manner are decidedly different from those of either Miller or Yerkes, who have spent much of their lives in the Midwest.

Some of these differences may seem trivial or unimportant. But each of them, and more often some combination of them, has colored our adventures in learning to teach, for such learning is at once professional and deeply personal. It requires creating new relationships among school and university faculty, drawing on new resources, trying out new roles and responsibilities. It requires breaking old habits—some of them connected to personal dispositions—examining one's practice critically and honestly, "unlearning" traditional practices and "re-learning" ways to think about teaching and school. Because it is at once personal and professional, it is difficult, probably impossible, to separate the idiosyncratic from the generalizable. On the one hand, our success at collaborating has depended on the people we are: on Miller's serenity, Yerkes' pragmatism, Wilson's zest. On the other hand, there are features of our work together that transcend our personalities. It is those that we discuss here.

Factors That Support Adventures in Learning to Teach

As we think back on our work together, four factors seem critical to us: time and trust, courage and communication. Each seems simple in some ways—and obvious—but our experience has taught us how complex and multidimensional these factors can be. Just as we begin to think that we understand what it takes to communicate, we encounter some new challenge that enriches our understanding of the concept. Just when we begin feeling comfortable in our trust of one another, we encounter something that makes us ever more sensitive to the fragility of our collaboration. Just as our understanding of adventurous teaching continues to evolve, so does our understanding of the ways in which these resources nurture and sustain our adventures in learning. We explain in the next section how our understanding of these four themes has evolved and the impact they have had on our understanding of adventurous learning, and consequently, adventurous teaching.

Discussion of these four themes is structured around a pattern that we have noticed in our learning. If you had asked us before we started working together what factors would make a difference in the success of such a project, we would have more than likely been able to tell you that these four mattered. We knew before we started that time and trust would be crucial. But what we have found over the course of working as a collective is that our understanding of each theme started out as rather simplistic. Over time, that understanding grew deeper, more complex. And somewhere along the line, we began to notice that what we were learning about our own learning had direct implications for the learning of our students. That is, we began to understand the relationship between the resources *we* needed to learn and the resources that our *students* needed. So, we present our discussion of each of our four themes in three parts. We begin by explaining our simplistic notions. We then explain how these notions were altered and enriched over time. We conclude each section by exploring the connections we see between teachers learning in adventurous ways and students learning in adventurous ways.

Time

Interviewer: What does it take to collaborate successfully?

Miller: It takes time, dedication. Things don't happen overnight. Definitely you have to have time. I don't care what anybody says.

If we didn't have this professional development school time, your day is so structured in a regular classroom, by the time you teach something, correct papers, plan your next lesson, if you have any time, you have a family to think about. You just don't have time available to you to think of new ideas, to reflect. So time is number 1 [Yerkes, interview, March 1991].

Of all the resources necessary for such work, time is perhaps the most essential. Time has affected our work in myriad ways. The time we have had to watch one another teach has given us alternative images of teaching and learning. The time we have spent in meetings has facilitated collective reflections on our teaching and learning. The time we have had to write has allowed us to leave a paper trail of our experiences together and has given us the chance to think abstractly about the particulars of our experiences. In short, without such time, there would be no physical and, more important, intellectual space to think about and learn from our experiences.

Time to Breathe. For years, Miller and Yerkes had had no time to breathe during their typical workday. Half serious, half joking, Yerkes told Wilson that the biggest delight of having her teach every afternoon was that there was time to go to the bathroom, to get a glass of water, to make a phone call. These little luxuries had been unknown to her, and were no small reward for the decision to collaborate. Miller expressed a similar view in a letter: "As I look at my teaching, it has never been stagnant. But it was always stifled by time constraints I had as a teacher. So opportunities to share teaching responsibilities were like a blessing" (Miller, letter to Wilson & Yerkes, June 1991).

It is difficult to focus attention on students' thinking and talk when there is little private space in the day. By adding a third teacher to two classrooms, we were each able to have free time, which we used in different ways: writing notes about class, watching someone else teach, grading papers, phoning parents, meeting with other colleagues or visitors to the school. Having these breaks became important, for they provided some emotional and intellectual space in the day, time that enabled us to refocus our attention on the teaching that we *did* do and not feel suffocated by the daily routine.

Time as Part of Adventurous Learning. Our reaction to the quantifiable aspects of time was only a superficial cut on how free time affected our teaching. In addition to providing some rejuvenation during the day, the time began to take on new meanings as we became more and more engaged in watching one another teach— and talking about that teaching. Most notably, time became for us a source of insight into how we might teach in new ways. Unlike typical inservices in which "experts" (often university personnel) visit schools and tell teachers what to do, Wilson's daily practice as a teacher has afforded Miller and Yerkes a different kind of professional development. Yerkes explained in an interview: "I think you need the support of people with new ideas. The only way we change our teaching is to talk to people who are also changing. And you need time to talk to one another. But not on just a one time basis, for it's got to be reoccurring. If Suzanne had come into my room and done a couple of lessons and said, 'Okay, this is the way you teach,' I would not have changed. But because this has been ongoing for several years, I really am seeing changes in myself—in the way I think. It is because of that support of talking with her and with Carol Miller" (Yerkes, interview, March 1991).

She contrasts this with the typical inservice experience: "Workshops can make all the difference in the world, but 99 percent of workshops—at least in my experience—are a waste. It's a one shot deal. Someone comes in, you hear something, you go back, you're excited, but there's no follow through. So then it's easier—it *is*—to go back to what you already know. You feel comfortable with that, you know how it works, and for how long. So that comfort is for *not changing*. With Suzanne here all of the time, now I feel like I can't go back. The things I've learned have changed my thinking about teaching entirely" (Yerkes, interview, March 1991).

By watching other teachers, we have seen teaching and our students from different perspectives. Our conversations and observations have encouraged us to continue experimenting with our own teaching. No one person has determined that "this is the way it should be done." Each of us has extracted from the others' practices something to experiment with, to explore, to model. In a letter to Wilson, Miller explained the effect that such watching had had on her teaching of "systems."

I love watching the interaction that goes on in the classroom while you are there. It lets me have a different perspective of my role in the classroom, the role of the children in the classroom, and I am more thoughtful of *all* the material I teach.

For instance, the science I'm teaching is so different this year. With this unit on Africa, I have decided to introduce the children to just one concept, "system." We brainstormed about what a system was and listed them on the board. They said that a system had things in it, people in it, that the things and people worked together, and that there was a solar system. After this, we looked up the definition in the dictionary to see if our ideas were the same. We found we were right and added other ideas about what a system could be—for instance, that it could be a set of ideas working together, like the rules in our school or the laws in our city. The next day I gave them a booklet with a list of definitions that we compiled the day before on the first page. The rest of the pages were blank. We reviewed the definitions and then broke up into groups of two and listed as many systems as we could. After 10 minutes, we talked about all the different systems there were. . . . We had a good discussion about why these were systems. The next series of lessons was the most exciting I've had this year.

Let me preface this with the fact that in the years past, I would give students a battery, wire, and a bulb and show them how to make the light work. I would then have a discussion about why this is a system and that this is a light system.

This year, I gave them the light bulb, a wire, and a battery and asked "What are these things?" What can we do with them?" I heard comments like, "We're going to make a system." Then they broke into groups of two and discovered how to make the bulb light. In one room, they discovered two different ways. I was so excited! They were teaching me some new ideas! We came back together and shared what they discovered. Then I let them go back to their groups and try these discoveries. Two girls discovered a third way to make the bulb light! . . . The excitement level was very high and they were ALL on task looking for new ways to make the light work. And they did! I was so excited about how smart they were and how much growth can take place in the right atmosphere! [Miller, letter to Wilson & Yerkes, May 1991].

In a postscript to this letter, Yerkes added her observations about what was happening with the students: "The children are looking at answers and not just letting others decide what is right and wrong, but thinking through more for themselves. They challenge answers, are better able to defend their own answers, and seem more willing to listen to several points of view to make up their minds. This holds true not just in social studies and science, but in other areas as well. Students also seem to be making more connections between different subject areas." (Yerkes, letter to Wilson, May 1991).

It was during a conversation that ensued from this exchange of letters that we began to realize how much our own collaboration was a context for us to learn about learning. As we examined ourselves in light of these changes, we wondered at the factors that made it possible for us to experiment, to watch one another and find ways to adapt our own teaching given these new experiences. Watching one another over time, and seeing how children's skills and knowledge developed over a sequence of classes—rather than from a single experience—was exciting and a rich contribution to our own learning. It made us want to find ways to give students the same kind of time to stew in ideas, to consider alternative explanations, to generate and then challenge hypotheses, to explore territories that mattered to them in ways that were genuine.

Time as Part of Adventurous Teaching

You don't teach as much. You really don't. You don't get nearly as much material covered. And that is some-

what frustrating because we have always been told,
"You have to cover this, and this, and this" [Yerkes,
interview, March 1991].

A third way that we have confronted the constraints of time
in our work has been through our willingness to slow down the
curricular clock. Covering the curriculum has been a major theme
in our discussions. It has not been unusual for Yerkes to ask Wilson:
"One question. You're spending forty-five minutes on one topic. I
was thinking, when we're working with the regular classroom, we
can't spend that much time on one topic for that long according to
our minutes and all that—we have a bunch of stuff to cover. You
don't" (Yerkes, conversation with Wilson, May 1991).

As classroom teachers accountable for district standardized
tests and mandated curricula, Yerkes and Miller have both had to
struggle with making decisions about what to teach and how much
time to commit to ideas. Teaching for understanding—no matter
the shape or form it takes—means that students and teachers need
more time together: time to make mistakes, time to go off on tan-
gents, time to let ideas bubble and stew. As committed teachers who
feel responsible to their children, their administrator, other teachers, and parents, Miller and Yerkes have found it difficult to make
decisions about what to take time for and when to move on. Wilson,
because she is responsible only for teaching the piece of the integrated curriculum we planned together, felt less of this pressure. In
some ways, feeling less pressure enabled her to ask questions about
the curricular clock: Why *did* we have to race through ideas? What
happened if we did so? What happened if we didn't? Could we be
sure that students were learning less because we were covering
"less"?

It was hard for Yerkes and Miller to respond to such questions. They had assumed for much of their teaching careers that
coverage was important. Yet, when Wilson asked whether they were
sure that children were "learning" less, they had little evidence to
support the claim. Coverage—and our individual assumptions
about it—became a major question in our conversations: What are
we giving up if we only teach one math problem every day—and
have rich and varied conversations with students around it? What

price do students pay if we spend six weeks studying "scale" instead of the allotted three days? What responsibilities do we have to other teachers in the school, and to the children whom we teach, to make sure that the children are exposed to and explore a host of ideas that matter? How do we select which ideas are the important ones? We are far from answering any of these questions, but we find them guiding our current explorations.

Our experiences with what happens if you do slow down have convinced us that it is worth taking the chance. Consider Miller's experiences teaching about insects. In the past, she had taught students about insects by presenting them with information about their life cycle, habitats, size, and so on. But this past year, she taught the unit in the spirit of an exploration, an adventure that she was taking alongside her students:

> We were coming up with a definition of what an insect looks like. I asked the question, "How many legs does an insect have?" Juan's hand went up: "It has 8 or 10 or 15 legs."
>
> In the past, I would have said, "No, an insect has 6 legs!" And I would have assumed that Juan would correct his understanding in light of my presentation of this "fact."
>
> But instead I wanted to get a feeling for what he was thinking, so I asked, "Can you give me an example?" Juan replied, "A caterpillar has many legs and it's an insect." This opened up a class discussion that showed me that Juan wasn't the only student with this belief. Others agreed with him, yet there were others who didn't. Through much discussion, the class came to the conclusion that we need to say that an *adult* insect usually has 6 legs. [We had a monarch butterfly emerge from a cocoon in the classroom with only 4 legs—so we added the adverb, "usually."]
>
> These conversations are rich and valuable. They build up student self esteem, and a classroom atmosphere of trust and questioning. They allow students to express their ideas, and I have alternate ways

of assessing what they know. It takes time to teach in
this trust-building atmosphere. Many times we scrap
my lesson plans to accommodate a genuine student-
initiated discussion of a piece of subject matter. But if
they truly understand one segment, doesn't this build
on future understandings? [Miller, memo, February
1992].

Taking one whole class period to discuss the number of legs
an insect has meant that Miller could not also discuss other things
about insects she used to in the same time allotment. So time, for
us, becomes a central question and an essential ingredient in developing a real growth in understanding. Children need time to brain-
storm, tinker, try new things, discover new relationships, and even
to take apart understandings that do not work and rebuild them
from their foundations. They need time to be wrong and to learn
from their mistakes. They need time to watch actual consequences
of poor decisions. Too often, we as teachers see them headed for
failure and try to intervene to protect them from the heartbreak of
failure. Yet, as collaborators we have come to realize how important
it is sometimes to fail, and we have begun to question the wisdom
of protecting students.[13]

We give students the chance to do the kinds of things we have
done in our collaboration. This has meant giving them some curricular control so that they can "own" the idea work of the class,
just as we have felt such ownership in the development of our own
curricula. It has meant letting them identify different problems and
try out different solutions, just as we have tried out new ways to
teach. Integral to our experimentation and to the explorations we
want children to engage in is the understanding that there will be
failure—and that there is a lot that can be learned from failure. It
has meant that different solutions, equally sufficient, can exist in
the same classroom, just as it has meant for us developing three
different ways to teach, each true to our developing principles of
adventurous teaching and to our individual personalities, preferences, and idiosyncrasies. Teaching in this way—a teaching that
leaves lots of room for individual and collective exploration, room
for mistakes and dead ends, room for multiple and competing so-

lutions—takes time. We see that in our own learning; we also believe it to be true about learning that matters for our students.

Trust

> It's hard to learn to collaborate. It takes trust [Yerkes, interview, March 1991].

Trust has been another central theme throughout our work. It is scary to invent a new practice, and we have had to find ways to treat our individually felt vulnerability with respect and care. Wilson had to trust that Miller and Yerkes would be open to her experimentation with different forms of teaching and not intentionally do anything to sabotage her efforts. Miller and Yerkes felt an overall responsibility for their students' well-being, and they had to trust that Wilson would take good care of their students' hearts and minds.

What does it take to develop such trust? Time to talk and watch, to develop personal and professional ties with people, to understand their values and motivations and their ways of working and seeing and understanding the world. It takes some sort of compatibility, as Yerkes once remarked: "Suzanne and I have personalities that mesh really well. I think that everybody needs someone like that to bounce ideas off of."

Trust Grounded in Professional Respect. In our case, we began with a trust grounded primarily in professional respect. As Miller explained: "Carol Yerkes and I have two different teaching styles—completely and totally different. I respect other teaching styles and that's what's nice, because Carol respects mine, too. And I think Suzanne respects us as teachers, too" (Miller, interview, March 1991).

With one part intuition, one part professional respect, we began our work by trusting one another's credentials. In addition, Yerkes was impressed with Wilson's decision to be a teacher educator who worked in schools: "I'm sorry, but I've always felt the teachers who taught us to teach hadn't been in the classroom for so long. And especially today, it's even more true that children are extremely different. If she's going to teach teachers, she should know something about schools" (Yerkes, interview, March 1991).

Over time, however, we developed a trust much deeper and much more significant to our ability to learn together. This more complex trust is not a "hands-off, you're-a-professional, I'm-a-professional" trust. Instead, it is a trust grounded in mutual respect and commitment—to learning, to children, to change.

Trust as Part of Adventurous Learning. In a memo they wrote about Wilson, Miller and Yerkes explain: "What we saw in Suzanne was a college professor willing to take risks, willing to leave her comfortable world at Michigan State University and venture into an unknown atmosphere, trying to see if what she was teaching in her world was related to ours. It was easy for her to tell other teachers how to teach, but did this really fly in the classroom? We saw her not as a researcher, but as a gutsy traveler willing to experience the real classrooms" (Miller & Yerkes, memo, October 1991).

Miller elaborated on this in an interview: "Suzanne will do anything and try anything and is not afraid to fall flat on her face. It helps us to know that we can do the same thing. If she can do it, we can do it, too. I think of her as an example. And I think of her dedication to kids, to learning, to finding new ways. Not sticking to the tried-and-true. Always asking, 'Are kids learning? Are they really understanding?' "[14] (Miller, interview, March 1991).

On other occasions, we have talked about the dialectic of our teaching and learning. Yerkes once called us three " 'teacher-learners' . . . with both of us being teacher and both of us being learner at different times. There have been a lot of things that I have learned from Suzanne. I've really changed some things about my teaching and tried some really different things because of her example. And because of her encouragement. . . . So I think that in that case, I am the learner. And then there are other times when she has had an idea and I have gone along and developed it differently. I think that some of the things that *I* have done, *I* have developed, she has incorporated into her teaching, too" (Yerkes, interview, March 1990).

This trust—knowing that the other is asking hard questions, risking failure, taking chances—has made us much more open to

one another's ideas, for we understand them to be fragile and tentative. It has also made us more willing to respond in kind. Such
trust, a trust that grows as you come to know each other as learners,
is not always easy. For us, it has taken patience, for it is not always
easy to tolerate our differences. Yerkes recalled what it felt like to
watch Wilson at first: "It seemed like total chaos. . . . When Suzanne
first came in, it took me a while. It was very difficult to just shut
my mouth and sit there and listen and see what she was trying to
accomplish because to me it seemed really chaotic. It's very difficult
not be be judgmental. I think that's one of the hardest things. I
know there have been many times when I've had to bite my tongue.
To go out of the room, to get away and come back and listen and
watch what happens next" (Yerkes, interview, March 1990).

It was only through watching Wilson's chaos over time—and
talking with her about the work—that Yerkes began to see in Wilson's chaos things that mattered to her as a teacher. For example,
Yerkes began to notice something about her students and their responses to Wilson's questions: "Suzanne has shocked me because I
have been surprised at what kids can know. I go, 'Oh, my God!
They think a lot more than I ever thought!' The poetry, the things
like that that I didn't think could be churned out by third graders
three or four years ago. Now I'm looking at kids and I'm saying,
'Oh, my God! They can think a lot more that I ever dreamed they
could!' Suzanne did that for me." And she reflects about how this
has changed her teaching: "I'm learning to question. I still don't
feel that's a strong area for me, but I see it improving, and not just
in the social studies and science. I'm finding it carrying over into
reading and math and some other things. I'm finding that I'm doing more of letting kids come up with ideas, and questioning them
in hopefully good ways, and making them start to think. A lot less
giving answers, which—of course—is the traditional role for
teachers. We were the information giver and they would just soak
it up" (Yerkes, interview, March 1991).

Wilson, on the other hand, had to learn to trust that Miller
and Yerkes could see something good in her chaos. She initially
called them the "mop-up ladies," because she left them with an
instructional mess of riled and rambunctious students every day.
Gradually, Wilson has had to learn to do less apologizing and more

reflecting on what actually was good in the chaos, and what was not, instead of focusing on the surface confusion. This took time and trust, for it is difficult to feel like you are creating a mess everyday for other people to share, and humor ("mopping up") was much easier to engage in than serious discussion about the substance of the class.

Besides feeling vulnerable and impatient, judgmental and concerned, we have found that part of learning to trust has meant overcoming self-imposed insecurities. Each of us has had to develop her own sense of self-worth, understanding that our very differences can also be our strengths. Looking inward, we have had to make personal peace with these differences, even though the group has always celebrated them: "I don't look at things like Suzanne does. I'm the more practical one. Suzanne does one kind of thinking and I do an entirely different kind. But now I realize that that's what *my* value is. It took me a long time to think of that" (Yerkes, conversation with Miller & Wilson, June 1991).

Although we would all attest to a strong faith and trust in one another, we treat this trust with tenderness and care. Because we constantly find ourselves moving forward, learning new things, taking new chances, we also find ourselves having to trust one another more and more. For example, in writing this chapter we have had to talk about some things that have previously gone unexplored, and we had to trust that our relationship could handle it. When we talked about the reasons teaching for understanding is so difficult, for instance, our conversation turned to the issue of grading. Yerkes complained that "we have to give letter grades." Wilson asked what she would prefer to do. Miller suggested that we should provide assessments that are like the ones Wilson sends home to parents (a combination of a narrative about the child's work and an explanation about the curricular territory being explored). "So why don't you do that?" Wilson asked Yerkes. "What do you think *I* would do if I taught full-time?" Wilson pushed harder. "There must be something in our contracts with the district," Yerkes guessed. "But what would happen if you sent home a description to parents instead and refused to reduce everything to an A, B, C, or S?" "I don't know. I've never thought about it," Yerkes replied. We then brainstormed possible reasons: "It's easier to give an A,"

"Parents expect traditional grades," "It's what we were trained to do."

Conversations like this one are not easy. One person challenges another's assumptions, and an honest exploration of the reasons for behavior inevitably reveal some things we had rather not say out loud. None of us enjoys confrontation, and no one likes looking at one's own flaws. We would all like to be perfect teachers, perfect people. But we are just ordinary people, and sometimes we make a certain decision because it is the easiest thing to do, or the least messy, or the most familiar. And in our talking with one another, we have to learn to acknowledge this and accept it. Learning to face up to the myriad reasons we act as we do really does help us learn to see ourselves and our teaching practice, and we could not manage such discussions without a trust that runs deep and true. It is a trust we strengthen both by treating one another with respect and care *and* exploring what it may mean to push one another even further than we ever thought possible, exploring assumptions we have always taken as "givens."[15]

This trust, a trust that allows individuality and community, is not the kind of trust you develop by saying that you trust someone, or knowing that you *should* respect someone. The trust that really matters in our work is homegrown and rooted in shared trials in which we have dealt with our diversity and repeatedly demonstrated to one another that our respect for that diversity is deep and genuine. In our conversations, we have also come to realize that this is the very trust we are committed to developing among our students. It is a trust that allows us to hold different values, to live different lives, a trust that would enable our students to embrace their own diversity and make the most of it in our collective learning. It is a trust that lets each of us try out half-baked, fragile ideas without fearing the frustration and dead ends, or the rethinking and regrouping, that often accompany creative and exploratory thinking. We want our students to feel such trust because it will enable them to show us—and their peers—their minds' work. Seeing this parallelism between the trust we have come to develop and the trust we want to engender in our classrooms has led us to understand that there is a third way in which trust figures in our collaboration— in our curriculum and instruction.

Trust as Part of Adventurous Learning. Trust has taken two distinct forms in our teaching: developing a trust between teacher and student and developing a similar trust among students. We begin with the former, and move on to the latter.

For us, learning to trust students has translated into learning to depend on them as coadventurers. As Cohen explains, teachers who try to teach in adventurous ways increase their dependence on students:

> For if students are to become inquirers, if their knowledge is constructed rather than merely received, they must take a large responsibility in producing instruction. . . . Teachers must rely less on their own protected performances in lectures or recitation or on materials that they control, such as texts and worksheets. They must accept their charges much more fully as co-instructors. They must find ways to help students expand their intellectual authority—which implies some reduction or transformation in their authority. Teachers must find ways to extend their own dependence on students, which implies relinquishing many central instruments of their authority. Teachers must make themselves more vulnerable, offering students opportunities to fail them, and even inflict painful wounds, in order to help them become more powerful thinkers.[16]

As we explore teaching in more adventurous ways, we find ourselves becoming more dependent on the students and feeling less in control of the teaching and learning. Yerkes recalled the first time she tried something different, crafting a unit in which students did all of the substantive work in small groups: "It was wonderful! It was frustrating! It felt like I didn't teach. I felt like I wasted time because the kids were in groups and doing their own thing. . . . I was feeling frustrated because I felt I wasn't teaching. And yet it was really neat to see what they were coming up with. It's very different because you're no longer "boss." It's probably one of the scariest things that can occur to a teacher" (Yerkes, interview, March 1991).

Becoming more dependent on students is a difficult experience. You have to trust that students will take you to important places. As Yerkes suggests, it is unfamiliar and feels strange. It is scary not to be captain of the ship, not to be able to control where the class travels next. It also requires the teacher to constantly monitor the class's progress: When should the teacher determine the direction a class should go? When should students? How long is long enough to spend on an idea? What happens when a teacher makes an instructional move that threatens the students' ownership of the work? These questions have run throughout our discussions. Consider Wilson's reflections in one afternoon conversation: "I've been feeling really bad about spending so much time on latitude. I really want to be able to explore different kinds of maps with them. So I was trying to push the conversation along a little. I was trying to figure out how to be a little proactive in nudging them toward some closure. But I never feel like I'm doing the right thing—I'm either feeling too pushy or not pushy enough. So I took a chance and said, 'This is how to find the latitude.' Travis really pushed back. He said, 'This is our discussion Dr. Wilson. Can't you just be our reference?'" (Wilson, conversation with Miller & Yerkes, May 1991).

As heartening as it has been to see students engage in dialogue and debate, and to take real interest in identifying and solving problems that matter to them, we are a long way from understanding the role of teacher as guide in such classrooms and how much control teachers need to take over the pace and content of the curriculum.[17]

Learning to create classrooms in which students are willing and able to engage in such discussions is no mean feat. Each year it has taken us nearly six months to develop the norms that are necessary for collective inquiry into ideas. Part of this difficulty is our own lack of knowledge and skill with such teaching; part of it stems from the beliefs and assumptions that our students bring to third grade. Eight- and nine-year-olds are already savvy students of schools and human nature, and it is not always easy to encourage them to collaborate in our adventures into teaching. Students have over and over explained to Wilson that she needs to act more like a teacher—meting out discipline to students who act out. Some students, in an effort to help her in this, have insisted on donning the mantle of behavior police: taking note of who acted well, who acted poorly, and making a report to Yerkes or Miller. It has been difficult for Wilson to return to the classroom day after day and not fall into timeworn and familiar patterns of behavior, scolding children and using traditional means of discipline.

If we want to create classrooms in which everyone has a voice and contributes to our adventures, then we need to trust that students are capable of sharing leadership in our adventures: sometimes as guides, sometimes as leaders of subexpeditions, sometimes as advisers. We have found ourselves giving students power over how well the class goes in order that they may someday acquire the intellectual habits necessary to have power over ideas. And giving them this power means leaving lots of time for them to abuse it as we all learn how to use it. There is no easy process, no set of steps packaged in a tidy curriculum that helps us teach our students to be trustworthy coadventurers. We continue to seek new ways to help them to trust one another and themselves, and we continually make clear our commitment to their minds and our continued respect for their ability to act responsibly and to think well.[18]

Developing trust among students has other dimensions as well. Students can be cruel and harsh, sometimes thoughtless critics of one another. Yet, if we want students to take chances, to guess, to hypothesize, to wonder out loud, they need to know that their wondering will be treated with respect by all. Consider Yerkes' description of the trust and courage that her new ways of teaching math entail:

> In previous years, I would present a new math problem, showing the "proper" way to solve it. Then I would model my thinking as I slowly let the class take over solving similar problems until I felt they "understood" the process. The children would then solve several problems independently while I checked their work to see if they were doing them "correctly." But one thing I *did* notice was any switch in the pattern and I would have to explain each new type.
>
> Today I present a new problem and let the

children individually or in small groups work on solving it. Children discuss their ideas with each other and
try different strategies for solving the problem. Then
children usually volunteer to present their ideas and/
or solutions to the whole class. We may have as many
as ten different ways of solving the same problem.
This process takes a lot of courage and trust. The child
who is explaining must trust the others not to make
fun of his/her solution even if it does not work. When
children do not understand an explanation, it takes
courage to ask for more information. Because more
children take ownership for their own learning, they
keep asking questions of each other until they feel
comfortable with the solution. It also takes courage to
revise your answer when others present convincing
arguments [Yerkes, memo, February 1992].

Again, it has not been easy for us to give students the control
over their own learning, to trust that they will learn to treat our idea
work, their peers, and themselves with the respect necessary to engage in such curricular expeditions. As Miller says, "I have to con-
sciously work at it all the time." She reflects on the change this trust
has provided in her teaching:

When I used to ask a child a question, I did it in a way
I thought would solicit a certain answer. Now I'm still
asking questions but instead of expecting a certain
response, I'm trying to listen to what students have to
say, to try and get at their understanding. This can
take simple shapes in my classroom.

For instance, we had been putting stars on a
map when we received literature from different places
in the United States. The map was attached to a cold
window, and one morning we came in and the stars
were gone. The class was abuzz, and all students were
wondering where the stars had gone. In the past, I may
have said why the stars fell off of the cold window.
Instead, this year I asked, "Why do you think they're

gone?" After many responses about different things
that could have happened, as a class, the students
figured out that the window was too cold for the stars
to adhere to it. Then, instead of me finding a solution
to this problem, the students spontaneously came up
with several ways to solve the problem.

This event ended with me congratulating them
for solving this problem together, that I hadn't even
thought of some of their solutions. The satisfaction
and nodding heads and smiles were outward signs of
their gratification and a continuation of a trust building relationship.

This is not easy for me to learn to do. When I
see students wondering about a problem, I see them
confused or maybe misunderstanding a concept. My
sense of nurturing makes me want to take them and
lead them to understanding. This is still a strong influence within me, but I'm learning to channel it differently. Instead of telling them answers, I *try* to
assume that their reasoning makes sense! By asking
questions I can get a feel for how the child is making
sense of something. It has become one of the biggest
differences in my teaching [Miller, memo, February
1992].

Our understanding of trust and its relationship to adventures
in learning and teaching continues to grow. It is not just a very
human fear of how dangerous it is to trust someone that makes
learning to trust ourselves, one another, and our students difficult.
We feel some pressure about our professional responsibilities. After
all, our students are children. They cannot be held accountable for
making curricular decisions. As adults, we need to make sure that
they have opportunities to learn things that matter. That requires
making hard decisions and becoming comfortable with the uneas-
iness inherent in walking a tightrope between the accumulated wisdom of curriculum developers and our own knowledge of what and
how and when our students may best learn things.

But trusting also requires that we leave room for failure, for frustration, for confusion. As teachers, we were taught to create classrooms that are comfortable and nurturing environments where students feel loved and supported. But as we turn to them as coexplorers, we have to rethink our assumptions about what they can do and how strong they are. We have come to understand the distinction that Hawkins makes between love and respect:

> Long before Bettelheim, Immanuel Kant had given profound support to the proposition that, in human affairs generally, "love is not enough." The more basic gift is not love but respect, respect for others as ends in themselves, as actual and potential artisans of their own learnings and doings, of their own lives; and as thus uniquely contributing, in turn, to the learnings and doings of others.
>
> Respect for the young is not a passive, hands-off attitude. It invites our own offering of resources, it moves us toward the furtherance of their lives and thus even, at times, toward remonstrance or intervention. Respect resembles love in its implicit aim of furtherance, but love without respect can blind and bind. Love is private and unbidden, whereas respect is implicit in all moral relations with others.
>
> To have respect for children is more than recognizing their potentialities in the abstract, it is also to seek out and value their accomplishments—however small these may appear by normal standards of adults. But if we follow that track of thinking one thing stands out. We must provide for children those kinds of environments which elicit their interests and talents and which deepen their engagement in practice and thought.[19]

Our work thus far has taught us a great deal about what children are capable of, and our respect for them as thinkers and collaborators deepens daily. It is out of this respect that we continue to wrestle with what kinds of environments we can develop that will best suit their needs and enable them to continue to develop their individual talents and abilities.

Courage

As we have explored the role that trust has played in our work, we have found it difficult not to also speak of courage. Although we have worked hard to create safe and trustworthy environments for ourselves and for our students, the safety of the context goes only so far in promoting the kind of risk-taking adventurous teaching entails. And so we have learned too the importance of courage.[20] It takes courage and energy to take the chances this work has entailed. This is difficult enough to do alone in a closed-door classroom, but in a collaboration one must do it in front of others—knowing that they are watching you sometimes flounder, wondering how they are thinking about that, trusting that they will treat you gently in the aftermath.

Courage plays a role in such work in several ways. First, it takes courage to take chances: to try new things, to veer from the familiar, to examine one's practice. Examining one's own teaching can be difficult, for it calls into question choices one makes daily, as well as choices made in the past. In one conversation that we had about experimenting with alternative versions of mathematics teaching, Yerkes talked about how long ago she had made the decision to teach children the "basics" in mathematics—how to balance a checkbook, add, subtract. She had thought about using manipulatives but decided that she did not have the time or the inclination to teach children about the deeper understandings of mathematics. Teachers make such decisions all the time: what to focus on, what to give less attention to. In the course of our collaboration, though, Yerkes was beginning to rethink what she had taught—or not taught—her students for the past twenty years. And she found this thinking very painful, for it made her wonder about what students *had not* learned in her classes before this.[21] Before working with other teachers so closely, she had always considered herself an innovative teacher—but watching someone else has really made her rethink those assumptions. She explains:

I hadn't ever defined myself as a more traditional teacher before I started working with Suzanne. I always thought I was a good teacher because my students always seemed to get the knowledge that I expected them to get. And I still feel that I was never a totally traditional teacher because there were always things that I think I did a little differently. But I was still basically more traditional than she is, and I'm still not at where she is. But I see myself shifting and I see that every area that I shift that way, for some reason, the children get more excited about learning. And they seem happier with their own products. I think they have more confidence [Yerkes, interview, March 1991].

Exploring how to teach in new ways has taken other forms of courage. For both Miller and Yerkes, having critical observers enter their room and watch them teach has been difficult to grow accustomed to. Miller explained: "It's scary because you don't know what the other person is thinking when they are watching. But having someone in the room is one thing that I have become used to. It's threatening, yes. But it's not. You have to deal with those feelings within yourself and say what you want to say. But you're learning right in there with the kids and so you put that all aside" (Miller, memo, November 1991).

Writing this chapter, we have drawn on yet other forms of courage, for it has required that we confront each other (recall our conversation about student evaluations). It is also very scary for Miller and Yerkes to state for the record that the way they used to teach seems less than adequate to them now. And working in a still very traditional setting, they run a risk by exposing themselves to administrators, teachers, and parents as "teachers as learners" rather than "teachers as experts."[22] Many people expect teachers to know what to do, and they would find it troubling to read our account, for here we three aver that we are less than clear about how best to teach. We take a chance that some parent will read this chapter and complain about our incompetence; we risk the possibility that another teacher in the school will read this and complain that we are not covering the necessary material for children to be prepared for the next grade level.

These may seem small acts of bravery to the outsider, but any one who has worked in a school knows the pressure to conform, to not make waves, to follow tradition. Moreover, as women we have been raised to try and please; to provide stability; to follow, not lead. Miller offers the following reflection:[23]

> I've changed. I've changed a great deal, especially in my self-confidence. I'm beginning to feel more sure of myself as a person. I am beginning to make decisions that I know are right, even though these decisions may not always be agreed upon by those around me. I'm beginning to tread unfamiliar water and—although it's scary—it's exciting as well! I'm beginning to try to accomplish goals I never thought were within my reach.
>
> I never viewed myself as a leader, yet through this collaboration, I have gained a courage that I never discovered I had before. I have the courage to express my ideas. (This courage seems to be easier for me at my computer than by oral expression, but at least I have discovered this wonderful computer.) I never thought before that I would have the nerve to speak publicly to my peers about teaching, but I have. Though I have a long way to go to be good at this, I now have the courage to try. This courage is there because of a trust built up through this collabora- tion—that it's okay to try, because if you fail, there is support to help you get back up and try again. But on the other hand, too, this support is there to cheer you in your successes. I am a different person because of this [Miller, letter to Wilson & Yerkes, February 1992].

Courage as Part of Adventurous Teaching. We treasure this courage born from our trust, and we are committed to finding ways to help students find a similar courage in themselves. Children need to be able to accept themselves, and one another, in all their diversity and difference. The learning we are asking of students requires that we build trustworthy environments, but we also recognize that it requires a deep-down-inside courage. This is not something that we can guarantee will happen if we only create the right atmosphere. Miller describes how her explorations with adventurous teaching requires courage of students:

> This is not a "comfort zone" that I am building in my classroom, for me or for the students. It's challenging for them to be questioned—a questioning I have come to value because I want to know what they know and how they are thinking—about why they think a certain way. This has been especially true in mathematics. My students were used to "explaining" why a character acted a certain way in a reading lesson, but explaining why you crossed off the 5 in
>
> $$\begin{array}{r} 54 \\ -19 \\ \hline 35 \end{array}$$
>
> was difficult for even the brightest student. It even made one of my brightest students cry and get sick before math was to begin.
>
> And my anxiety level was up there, too. I was used to giving students formulas and if they could follow the plan and get the right answer, they were an excellent student. End of my teaching [Miller, memo, February 1992].

Almost every day now, we witness a courage in some student that stuns us. And it comes in many packages. Aliesha, who has been quiet for months, might raise her hand and ask a question of Juan. Deborah, who has always been a very successful student and finds it very difficult to be wrong, does not cry when Demetrius challenges her solution to a geography problem. Sarah, a quiet thinker who prefers her notebook to class discussions, writes us a message about whether or not her alternative solution to the one proposed in class might also work. Because we each have different ways of being brave, our collective view of our students allows us to recognize the myriad ways their courage emerges in the tasks they engage in. And in our work we continue to wrestle with ways to at once create a trusting environment that provides the outside support for risk-taking while we also struggle to find ways to help students look inward and begin to draw on courage that they have had all along, and may—as Miller discovered about herself—never have known was there.

Communication

A fourth theme in our collaboration has involved learning to communicate. Coming from different worlds, we have different experiences with communication. Wilson, as a researcher, is used to talking to large groups of people at professional meetings, as well as writing regularly for journals and university work. Miller and Yerkes, as classroom teachers, have done little public speaking or writing. On the other hand, they are in constant contact with parents, administrators, and other teachers. Wilson was used to university discourse full of argument and debate, disagreement and challenge. In many ways, her world was dominated with what are sometimes considered male patterns of interaction. Miller and Yerkes were used to their elementary school discourse—polite and respectful, and very female—nurturing, supportive. Challenge and disagreement in their world has, more often than not, been considered something to avoid, bury. For us, learning to work together has meant learning to take the best features from both of these worlds and combine them in a way of talking and communicating that does not replicate either, but allows us to communicate openly and honestly with care and commitment.[24]

Initially, we thought it would be important to communicate on a regular basis: Yerkes and Wilson had been frustrated by the lack of time to talk during their first year of coexistence, and so in the second year we decided to meet regularly. We thought it might also be important to have a system by which we could send each other messages. We established a dialogue journal for this purpose.

But as we worked together, it became clear that communication in our collaboration was about much more than the physical arrangements: having a meeting time and place, having a journal. Instead, communication was about sharing a vocabulary, developing a manner of talking, and developing new habits. We explore each of these in turn as we examine the ways in which communication has played a role in our learning to teach.

Communication as Part of Adventurous Learning. The folklore of school-university experiences contains many stories of teachers complaining about university people's "twenty-five-cent words," jabs at the jargon of research and its unhelpfulness to the down-and-dirty world of real classrooms. It is true that university faculty and school faculty enter conversations with different vocabularies: Wilson is an educational psychologist, and much of her language has developed through her associations with researchers and scholars in that field. But talk of schemata and cognitive maps, mental models and situated learning seem like Greek to Miller and Yerkes, who work and live in a real school where talk is of effective schools and basals, crack babies, and the Michigan Educational Assessment Program (MEAP). Part of learning to communicate has entailed developing a shared vocabulary. Our respect for one another and the different roles we play in our collaboration has made it possible for us to bring our diverse vocabularies together.

Developing a set of words to share, however, was only the beginning of learning to talk to one another. Wilson came from a world of scholarship in which everything she wrote and did was to be supported with a well-developed and highly articulated rationale. She had also learned habits of discourse that enabled her to argue with opponents who readily challenged the claims she made about research or teaching. The academic world she lived in was much like one long oral defense in which people enthusiastically inquired, argued, debated, discussed, and challenged one another's ideas. The air at Michigan State was full of such arguments, and Wilson was accustomed to actively participating in them.

Miller and Yerkes, on the other hand, had been working in the isolated world of their individual classrooms. Conversations among teachers stayed at the level of schedules and assignments, not the substance of their work. As Miller explained:

Working together has been a really good thing for me.
I've been more thoughtful and vocal with other people. I've always been an introvert with my teaching.
I've always had a good feeling about my teaching,
about my class, no matter what. But it'd have been
nice to *talk* with others. It's changed me, the risks I've
taken have made me grow. What risks have I taken?
I've become more vocal. I've never been vocal about
the things I've done. I've never been vocal about my
failures. I've never talked to other teachers about how
we were teaching. . . . Sometimes we've talked about
what we were going to teach, about schedules. Very
little was said about methods of teaching students except the tried-and-true. The teacher standing in the
front of the class giving knowledge and students sitting at their desks receiving knowledge and accessing
that knowledge with paper and pencil tests [Miller,
letter to Wilson & Yerkes, June 1991].

Asked how it felt to become more vocal and to explain more about
her thinking, Miller replied, "Scary! Awful! It's the hardest thing
in the world for me to do. It's not easy to learn to explain yourself,
and to argue for what you believe" (Miller, interview, March 1991).

Learning to talk about teaching has been at once exciting
and scary, for it has meant articulating things long left tacit. It has
meant learning to challenge, to question, to debate—discourse characteristics that were not part of the school in which Miller and
Yerkes work. It began to dawn on us how important it was to be
willing to argue one summer when the whole school had a professional development school meeting. During that meeting, another
university person was arguing about her plans for the following
year, and leaving little conversational space for teachers to raise
questions or to challenge her. Moreover, the teachers had no practice with challenging someone's proposal and remained silent. Wilson, coming from the university, was familiar with such debate and
engaged the faculty member in what became a rather heated argument about collaboration while Miller and Yerkes looked on.

After the discussion, we had lunch together and Miller and

Yerkes shared with Wilson their discomfort during the discussion. "I thought you were all getting mad at each other," Miller explained. "I was very uncomfortable with the conflict," Yerkes added. After a few moments, Miller observed, "Yet, if we want children to argue with one another about their ideas and challenge each other—in polite and respectful ways—we have to be willing to learn to do that among ourselves."

It took us a long time to learn to voice concerns and disagreements. Nearly two years into our collaboration, Miller wrote Wilson a letter questioning her curricular choices:

> Dear Suzanne:
>   I don't believe I'm sitting at my computer at 3:30 A.M., but I had a thought about—of all things— teaching latitude and longitude. I'm thinking about Liz, a girl who is very thoughtful about this whole idea of up and down, back and forth lines to find places in the world. She seems to really want to understand this notion, but too many ideas are cropping up at once and it confuses her. Can the class be trying to ask too many questions to begin with about latitude and longitude? Can we just introduce only one degree and talk about just that line—be it a line of latitude or longitude—and ask the class to tell all they can about that one degree, and stick to that one degree, understanding it totally? I'm thinking that it would help the class to focus on just one concept.

The letter stimulated a long series of letters and conversations among the three of us in which we discussed the role of confusion in learning. For example, Wilson wrote a letter (May 1991) to both Miller and Yerkes in which she explained:

> First, I'm not sure what the best way to learn things is. Schools have always assumed that there is either something linear (first we learn this, then we learn this) or that there are building blocks (you have to learn these basics before you can learn this more com-

plex stuff), and curriculum has presented information
to kids in linear and block-like ways. But when I think
about my own learning, I think of it as much more
messy, circular, back-and-forth. For example, when I
think and learn now, I go back and forth between
practical things and abstract things, between basic
ideas and the bigger pictures that they fit in. It is actually helpful for me sometimes to look at an idea as
it is embedded in a complex web of relationships—
even when I'm not completely clear on the individual
idea—because looking at it inside those relationships
helps me sharpen my definition and understanding of
it. [I'm not sure that any of this makes any sense.] So,
one of the reasons I haven't chosen to present one idea
at a time has something to do with my sense that
maybe learning—real learning—is not clean and simple, that it does involve messing around with a couple
of ideas at once, that it does mean bouncing one concept off of another in an attempt to look at both their
relationships and their individuality.

In response to this, Miller reflected in a conversation among
the three of us: "After I read what you wrote yesterday about confusion—and the more you talked about it in that letter, during the
class—the more it hit home to me that really, one person's confusion leads to another person's discovery and that leads to another
confusion. And eventually they came up with the idea of the up and
down and I saw where you were trying to get them and where it
eventually led them. And it was their discovery. So I'm feeling better
about confusion."

This exchange was only the beginning of a longer conversation we continue to have about our assumptions about learning—
how kids learn, when they learn, why they learn. We differ about
many things—what we know, what we believe—and learning to
communicate has been in large part learning to respect those differences without avoiding them, learning to discuss them openly
and honestly without one person domineering or another remaining silent. In searching for the best way to talk to one another, we

have worked hard to combine what we consider good about our different worlds—the willingness to challenge from the academic world with the concern for care and tenderness from the elementary school world—in a way of interacting that allows us to grow, but grow because we feel we can talk honestly and openly in comfortable ways.

Learning to communicate, however, has meant more than just developing a way to communicate among ourselves. As we develop our collaborative relationship, our roles and responsibilities have merged somewhat. Wilson has become a member of the faculty of the elementary school, learning to work with other teachers and the administrator, as well as parents and the community. Meanwhile, Miller and Yerkes have been drawn into her world—invited to speak about their work as teachers in a professional development school, as collaborators with university faculty. And because our lives continue apace, there is not enough time in the week for talking about everything that we want to say about our teaching and learning.

As our roles change, and the amount of material we want to talk about ever increases, we have had to develop new habits and skills of communication. Initially, Wilson had proposed the idea of a joint journal, something in which we could talk to one another and a means for documenting our learning and work. But the journal failed to become a consistent part of our work: "When we started the journal with Suzanne, it was just one more thing to be done that I probably haven't done for about three months. It wasn't convenient for me. There are so many different things you need to do as a teacher, but no room. They pull you in a lot of different directions, and the journal writing is just another pull. Is it as important as talking to parents or putting together a letter? You have to decide" (Miller, interview, March 1991).

Our use of the journal has been sporadic, and we have found the most benefit from our weekly conversations. As Miller describes them, "Our Wednesday afternoon meetings are a kind of writing." But as Wilson's travel and university schedule sometimes press on her ability to make all those meetings, we have also experienced some frustration in being able to communicate. This frustration drove Miller to write one letter at 3:30 one morning in May 1991, which she ended by saying, "Suzanne, I probably wouldn't be here at my computer sharing this with you if you could be with us on Wednesday afternoons. I miss our discussions. And I get very frustrated that I can't talk to you after class. We must set up a time to talk!"

As a consequence of this frustration, we decided to try letter writing as a form of communication, a form that felt comfortable to both Miller and Wilson. Yerkes agreed with this decision, only later sharing with us her own reservations: "I have to say that when you guys said we were going to write these letters, I freaked out. I just don't like to put things down in black and white. I have trouble saying what I'm saying. I felt it was going to take too much thinking to put down what I was thinking" (Yerkes, June 1991). Yet eventually, Yerkes too adapted to writing letters, albeit they were less frequent and shorter than Wilson's and Miller's. One of these she ended with the following: "Now, Suzanne, I hope you're excited that you got me to think tonight and even to risk putting down my thoughts on paper. See, you can teach an old dog new tricks. A fellow traveler—Carol Y."

Recently, we have also begun to experiment with technology, using electronic mail and other communication systems as ways to reduce the distance between our separate places of work. But every time we add another task to our work, the work expands in size, and we are ever sensitive to balancing our needs to attend to our teaching, to our students, to our own learning, to each other, to our community, and to our families.

Communication as Part of Adventurous Teaching. It is not surprising that we have recently found ourselves exploring ways in which the lessons we have learned about communication have implications for our students. We believe that they too need ways to keep track of their thinking and growth, and we have experimented sporadically with the idea of portfolios. Wilson has had students keep journals of their daily work; Miller and Yerkes have encouraged students to write more often. In all of our teaching, helping students learn to communicate, in written and oral forms, has become central, for we now understand how important this has been to our own individual and collective development. Learning to document and give voice to your mind's work is an essential piece of becoming an adventurous learner (and teacher). We are only begin-ning to think about how to integrate concerns for communication into the experiences that students have in our classrooms, but we are excited about the possibilities of using alternative assessments as well as technology (electronic mail, for example) as means for facilitating communication among students and teachers in our rooms and in our schools.

Conclusion

This has been a difficult chapter to craft, for several reasons. For one, the collaboration we describe here is a living, breathing, ever-changing phenomenon, and it feels awkward to try and describe something that changes even as we try to hold it still long enough to describe it. Writing this chapter has reminded us that in the very act of writing about this relationship, we have once again changed it.

But there is another reason the chapter has been difficult, for the story here feels more rosy than the one we lived. It is true that we have experienced great success in our collaboration, and an ef-fort born out of professional interest and responsibility has led to a deep, enduring friendship. But there has been nothing easy or simple about the process, and we have not felt particularly wise about the ways in which we went about it. It has been messy, con-fused, much like an inordinate amount of our teaching these days.

Cohen was right to suggest that change in teaching is "gla-cial." In our collaboration, and in our teaching, we feel only that we have taken the "fumbling first steps down an unfamiliar path." And we are nowhere near understanding what it takes to teach adventurously, for as Miller and Yerkes are quick to say, "We're still traditional teachers."

Wilson disagrees, for there seems nothing traditional about their enthusiasm and devotion to learning and change—a devotion that has continued even in the face of hard times: confrontations with other teachers in the school, questions from parents, disagree-ments among ourselves, battles with other university personnel. But it is also true that if an impartial outsider strode into one of our classrooms one day, there might be very little that appeared innovative, adventurous, radical. Our experiences have taught us much about what we now call the "order of magnitude" question in learning. The changes Miller and Yerkes have experienced in their teaching and thinking seem enormous to them, yet those changes are as much in their minds and hearts as they are in their practice. Miller and Yerkes can see how their interactions and talk with students has changed in subtle and less subtle ways. But an outsider might see little that seemed new.

Yet perhaps this is the way that permanent, important change starts. Our learning is in our roots, in the very ways that we see and understand and think about our responsibilities as teachers and our relationships with students. We do not, however, feel like seedlings or fragile flowers easily uprooted with a single sweep of the hand. We feel more like those weeds one battles on spring days whose roots run deep and long, weeds that keep returning no matter how many times they are uprooted. Likewise, the changes we have made will not go away; as Miller and Yerkes have both said, "The problem is, you can't go back."

There are many things we still do not know about teaching, but one lesson seems clear: as teachers trying to invent a practice, we have gained a great deal of insight into what it might mean to ask the same of students. The greatest source of our insight into the nature of adventurous teaching has been our own experiences trying to enact such a vision in our classrooms. It is scary and unnerving to try to change your teaching, your curriculum, your assessment, your role and responsibilities, your students' assumptions and habits of mind (as well as their parents'). It must be equally frightening for students to define and identify their own problems in mathematics, or history, or biology. It is frightening to try to do that in front of other people—as teachers working collaboratively or as students talking openly.

Contextual factors can make a difference, but in ways none of us fathomed before we started this work. Time is critical, but not so much for the bathroom break it provides; it is the time to watch someone else work on ideas that has been the greatest resource for us. And trust has been critical, but not the trust that comes from professional respect; rather it is a trust that opens you up as a learner to see, to experience, to experiment. Learning to communicate has reinforced something that we already knew to be true: that in communicating your ideas to others, you develop them as well. Courage seems the strangest thing to discuss, for no one of us feels especially brave, although we recognize courage in our students. But the changes that are required in teaching are enormous, and the problems so critical that radical change is necessary. So maybe our change has come from fear of what may happen to students if school and university faculty *do not* join forces and facilitate necessary changes, not from some courage. We prefer to believe, however, that we are—like many teachers and most students—hopeless Romantics, who believe anything is possible, even classrooms full of adventure.

Notes

1. Throughout this chapter, we draw on written documents that we have collected during our work together. These include transcripts of interviews with observers, transcripts of weekly conferences, letters written to one another, a dialogue journal used sporadically, and memos written for other purposes about professional development schoolwork. In some ways, it feels strange to quote ourselves, for as authors of this chapter we could simply choose to rephrase or rewrite the words we have said or written earlier in our collaboration. But we have two reasons for drawing on such documents. First, what we describe in this chapter is learning and change, and we believe that showing readers the differences in our talk (and thought) over time (as reflected in notes we have written to one another) is one method of documenting some of that learning. Our second reason is related to the issue of voice. This chapter was primarily—in an official sense—written by Wilson. She took the lead in writing it, and its final tone and texture very much bear the stamp of her authorship. But the chapter is a story told by all three of us, and we struggled with ways to allow both our shared and individual voices to emerge. By using the notes and memos and words of individuals, we hope to provide the reader some sense of how our minds and voices differ, as well as agree. All the interviews cited in this chapter were

conducted by Laura Thornburg, a graduate student at the Michigan State University College of Education.

2. Cohen, 1989.
3. Cohen, 1989, p. 29.
4. See, for example, reports by the Carnegie Forum on Education and the Economy (1986); the Holmes Group (1990); and the National Council of Teachers of Mathematics (1989).
5. See, for example, discussions of systemic reform by Smith & O'Day (1991) and discussions of school restructuring by Elmore & Associates (1990).
6. Cohen, 1989, p. 28.
7. For a review of trends in educational policy, see Chapter Seven; Cohen (1989); Cuban (1984); and Cuban (1990).
8. In this chapter, we talk a lot about the language we use to describe our learning. Here we talk about "changing our practice," and at other points we talk about "learning to teach." We do not believe that change and learning are interchangeable, for there have been times when we have learned something and it has not resulted in any change in our practice. And there have been times when we have changed our practice, but little learning has resulted. However, in the mess that is the work of teaching, we find ourselves sometimes changing, sometimes learning, and seldom sure which came first, and how they are related. For that reason, we use "change" and "learn" interchangeably in this chapter, more because we have experienced them as a dialectic, not because we view them as isomorphic.
9. For descriptions of adventurous teaching, see Chapters Two and Three.
10. As we noted previously, we have struggled in this chapter with the question of voice and how to present ourselves as a collective and as individuals. There are many things that we can state in chorus, for we have an identity, a history, a language, and some understanding that we have acquired together. But we also remain three distinctly different learners, teachers, thinkers. For the purposes of this chapter, we use "we" for the collective, but when we need to make points about individuals, we refer to one another by our last name. We chose to use

last names for two reasons. First, Yerkes and Miller have the same first name, and we felt that readers unfamiliar with us would find it difficult to keep track of Carol Y and Carol M. Second, Wilson is a researcher whose work is cited by others, and it is always her last name that is used in such references. Because we see ourselves as peers, and because we wanted to represent the voices of teachers with equal stature, we chose to use everyone's surnames. This seems awkward and distancing to us, for we are now close friends and like to present ourselves informally and personably, but it seems the most reasonable solution. In our work, the distance between the individual and the group is neither as formal nor as distinct as it might appear in this chapter.

11. Wilson's decision was influenced by a commitment of Michigan State University to support faculty who want to explore such roles, and she is among a small clan of such teacher educators, which includes her colleagues Deborah Loewenberg Ball, Daniel Chazan, Ruth Heaton, Magdalene Lampert, and Janine Remillard. See Ball (in press); Lampert (1991); and Wilson (in press) for examples of such work.

12. Miller and Yerkes are also involved in other professional development school projects that involve university personnel, and those individuals often join the ranks of teachers in our two rooms. Most notably, they work with Janine Remillard, a mathematics teacher and teacher educator, on a project focused on learning to teach mathematics for understanding. We cannot begin to disentangle where we have learned the lessons we talk about in this paper, and we know that many of them have benefited from and depended on our work with Remillard.

13. We use words like "mistakes," "wrong," and "failure" with great care. We wonder a great deal about what constitutes failure in our classrooms—in the case of teacher or student— as well as what it means to be "wrong." Often, for example, what at first blush appears to be a mistake to us turns into a great idea. Moreover, when something feels "wrong" to us, it does not necessarily feel wrong to our students. But sometimes it does. And in our work watching students struggle with

ideas, we notice two faces of failure or error: the cognitive and the emotional. Although we can rationally and openly aver, "It is okay to do something that doesn't work out," that rationalization does not make us any less human. We feel bad when we do not do something well, sometimes out of frustration, sometimes out of anguish. Likewise, our students feel anger, frustration, embarrassment. To say that "anything goes" does not save us from deeply felt emotional reactions to not "getting it right." We chose to use the words "failure" and "wrong" in this chapter not because we think constantly of failure and error in our work and the work of our students, but because we want to remind readers of the emotional aspects of learning.

14. Actually, Wilson *is* afraid of falling flat on her face, and does not like it when she does, for several reasons: one part frustration, one part embarrassment. She would prefer to "get it right." But primarily such travails worry her as she thinks about what students are learning during these adventures.

15. The trust is both in one another and in one's self. We explore the issue of trusting oneself in the section on "courage."

16. Cohen, 1989.

17. This problem is exacerbated in our case, for we are at once dependent on our students and dependent on one another. In developing an integrated curriculum, we have tried to find a way of exploring aspects of science, social studies, and language arts that complement one another. But if our students make a choice to focus on one idea in their discussions with Yerkes, and an entirely different idea in their work with Miller, that integration can begin to disintegrate.

18. The question of how to help students learn to share such responsibility continues to plague us, and we differ in the ways we explore the possibilities. We do believe that there is no linear process, no step-by-step procedure that takes students from no responsibility to new levels of responsibility. If we begin our work with students by treating them with lack of respect (by not allowing them voice, by making all of the decisions, by controlling what they do and when), then there

is no reason for them to trust us when we later give them such respect.

19. Hawkins, 1978.

20. As we mentioned previously, another way to think about courage is as a resource that becomes available when one learns to trust oneself. This overlap in trust and courage points to the ways in which our themes are interrelated. For the purposes of this chapter, it seemed right to examine each separately.

21. In collaboration, we have found that a by-product of calling into question one's own assumptions is sometimes an implicit calling into question of one's colleague's assumptions. Miller's willingness, for instance, to question the ways in which she teaches writing may give Wilson pause to wonder the same things about her teaching of writing. Alternatively, Yerkes' decision to ask questions about her management system might make Miller wonder whether she should do the same. What we learn from one another's example can sometimes be exciting, and at other times annoying: There are just so many changes one can try to make at once, and just so many questions one can juggle in one's head. Three people calling into question different aspects of their teaching has led us into what feels like a swamp of change, where nothing seems certain, and everything seems worthy of scrutiny.

22. Miller and Yerkes have over and over again noted the significance of the support that they receive from their principal, Dr. Wheeler-Thomas. As Yerkes has written: "In order to effectively change teaching practices, you need an administrator who encourages new ideas and is willing to withhold her judgment. For instance, many principals expect each day to be divided into neat compartments where they can see each subject is given the proper amount of time. New ideas about teaching do not have each content area in neat packages; rather, ideas flow across all areas and each contributes concepts to the whole. Administrators must allow flexibility and trust each teacher. Teachers must also trust that administration will back them up even when they fail, for any attempt to genuinely learn something new requires some floundering along the way" (Yerkes, memo, February 1992). Although we

do not take up the issue of administrators as support in this chapter, we note here that there is much about the school context that also supports or inhibits the kind of learning and teaching we are exploring.

23. The following quote comes from a personal communication between Miller and Wilson, one that begins with a caveat: "Suzanne, this is not an easy subject for me to write about. I've started to write about it many times, but I keep starting over. None of the stories seemed right. Somehow, what I've experienced in the classroom with the students is less sensitive for me to talk about. What I've experienced personally is not so easy."

24. It has been difficult for us to craft a way of interacting that melds these worlds, for we want to be able to challenge one another, but not confront; nurture, but not shelter. We think we are a long way from creating a way of talking that allows us to work within these two worlds in a manner that has integrity and grace.

References

Ball, D. L. (in press). With an eye on the mathematical horizon: Dilemmas of teaching elementary school mathematics. *Elementary School Journal.*

Carnegie Forum on Education and the Economy. (1986). *A nation prepared: Teachers for the twenty-first century.* New York: Carnegie Corporation.

Cohen, D. K. (1989). Teaching practice: Plus que ça change. . . . In P. W. Jackson (Ed.), *Contributing to educational change: Perspectives on research and practice* (pp. 27–84). Berkeley, CA: McCutchan.

Cuban, L. (1984). *How teachers taught: Constancy and change in the American classroom.* New York: Longman.

Cuban, L. (1990). Reforming again, and again, and again. *Educational Researcher, 19,* 3–13.

Elmore, R. F., & Associates (Eds.). (1990). *Restructuring schools: The generation of education reform.* San Francisco: Jossey-Bass.

Hawkins, D. (1974). I, thou, and it. In *The informed vision: Essays on learning and human nature* (p. 48). New York: Agathon Press.

Holmes Group. (1990). *Tomorrow's schools: Principles for the design of professional development schools.* East Lansing, MI: Author.

Lampert, M. (1991). Looking at restructuring from within a restructured role. *Phi Delta Kappan, 72,* 670–674.

National Council of Teachers of Mathematics. (1989). *Curriculum and evaluation standards for school mathematics.* Reston, VA: Author.

Smith, M., & O'Day, J. (1991). Systemic school reform. In S. H. Fuhrman & B. Malen (Eds.), *The politics of curriculum and testing* (pp. 233–268). New York: Falmer.

Wilson, S. M. (in press). Mastodons, maps, and Michigan: Exploring the uncharted territory of elementary school social studies. *Elementary School Journal.*

5

Creating Classroom Practice Within the Context of a Restructured Professional Development School

Sarah J. McCarthey
Penelope L. Peterson

A wave of reform is producing new images of schools and new patterns of organization within them.[1] Professional development schools envisioned by the Holmes Group are designed to foster teaching and learning for understanding, create a learning community for diverse learners, and promote thoughtful inquiry for adults as well as children.[2] Consistent with these goals, restructuring efforts by both individual schools and school districts have focused on transforming the nature of teachers' work and reorganizing governance systems to develop new roles and relationships among school personnel, build new coalitions of support, and define new concepts of accountability.[3] Integral to these reforms is the creation of supportive contexts in which teachers can reflect on their

The research reported in this chapter was supported by a grant to the Consortium for Policy Research in Education (CPRE) at Rutgers University and Michigan State University from the Department of Education (DOE) Office of Educational Research and Improvement (OERI) (Grant No. OERI-G008690011-89). The opinions expressed here do not necessarily reflect the position, policy, or endorsement of the OERI or the DOE. We thank the teachers and principal at the school for their willingness to participate in our study. We also thank Richard Elmore for his contributions to our research and Michelle Parker for her assistance with data collection.

teaching and improve their practice with the help of colleagues.[4] The literature suggests that individual teacher change must be viewed within the context of the collective of teachers, administrators, and students in a particular school.[5]

In this chapter we consider the nature of teaching contexts and their effects on classroom practice through case analyses of two teachers on a primary team, Julie Brandt and Melissa Benton, who teach in Webster Elementary School,[6] a "professional development school" that has been involved in major restructuring efforts since 1988–89 within the context of district restructuring efforts that began in 1985. Within their own primary team and within the whole school, both teachers have come to be regarded by the staff as experts in teaching their chosen subjects—reading and writing for Brandt and mathematics for Benton. In these cases, we explore the practices that each teacher created that were consistent with teaching for understanding. (For more examples of teaching for understanding, see Chapters Two, Three, and Four.) We explore why each teacher created these practices, how the practices came about, and the teaching contexts that did or did not support the practices. In particular, we examine how other individuals in the school and district contributed to the growth of Brandt's and Benton's knowledge and expertise and discuss the connections between this new knowledge and major reform ideas being advocated by researchers and practitioners at the district, state, and national levels. We also consider the extent to which differences in subject matter and disciplinary knowledge may contribute to the variations in classroom practices of these two teachers.

The Contexts in Which Brandt and Benton Teach

Located in a major metropolitan area in the south-central United States, Webster is a large elementary school with approximately five hundred students in kindergarten through fifth grade. Children are bused to the school from other areas within the county as part of the school district's desegregation plan. As a result, children in the school represent the ethnic and socioeconomic diversity of the urban metropolitan area, with 26 percent coming from African-American families and 25 percent receiving free or reduced cost lunches.

The county in which Webster is located began major restructuring efforts in 1985 when a group of district administrators and principals came together to develop a shared vision for education reform. Leaders of the district's restructuring team conceptualized their efforts as aimed at changing rules, roles, and responsibilities in the schools.

Webster began its restructuring efforts in the fall of 1988–89 following a summer retreat in which the teachers and the principal developed the motto for the school, "Expect the best, achieve success!" and piloted two major organizational changes—teaming and multiage grouping—with two teams of teachers in the school. By the 1990–91 school year, staff at the school had chosen to expand teaming and multiage grouping to include all teachers and students in the school.

Teaming meant that four teachers shared responsibility for all the students on their team, and within each team teachers had a common time to meet and plan together. Three to four teachers and approximately 120 students constituted each team. Multiage grouping meant that students on each team spanned several grades. A purpose of multiage grouping was to allow for adaptation to students' learning needs and abilities and to promote success by eliminating grade-level retention of students. Although each teacher still taught in her own classroom, students within a team moved from classroom to classroom during the day, and each team's classrooms were grouped next to each other. Within each team, teachers chose to specialize so that each teacher taught the subjects she regarded as her area of expertise. In their primary (grades 1 and 2) team, Brandt chose to specialize in reading, and Benton chose to specialize in mathematics.

Restructuring also involved the provision of new opportunities for teacher learning and professional development. Beginning in 1987, teachers had access to the Professional Development Center, which was funded by the school district and a private foundation. The center included a professional development library, a curriculum resource center, a materials center for special education students, a computer education unit, and a grants assistance office. Webster teachers also participated in workshops given at the Professional Development Center and were particularly interested in using literature-based instruction in their reading programs.

During the 1989–90 school year, the school district provided Webster with a staff member, Jay Ross, from the Professional Development Center and a large local university. He acted as a liaison among the university, the school district, and the school. His role with the university involved placing and supervising student teachers; he tried to select teachers who would allow innovations by the student teachers. Because Ross's area of expertise was writing and he had participated in the National Writing Project, he served as a resource for teachers in the school who wanted to learn new ways of teaching a process approach to writing. His own philosophy of learning included engaging students in authentic tasks and having students use their own experiences. Researchers and practitioners who had influenced his thinking included James Moffett, Donald Graves, and Grant Wiggins. Ross's work at Webster fit with the school's decision to focus on literature-based instruction in beginning their reform efforts.

The Case of Julie Brandt: Building a Literate Community

Brandt is a primary grade teacher who assumed the role of team leader for the first pilot team when Webster began restructuring. She described herself as having been a traditional teacher who used workbooks and basals prior to restructuring, although she acknowledged that when she was a middle school science teacher, she had used many of the discovery-oriented materials. When we looked inside Brandt's classroom, we saw innovative reading and writing practices.

Beginning readers read "predictable" books and identified labels from cereal boxes and Pizza Hut boxes, while older students were arranged in small groups according to the books they chose to read. Students often read aloud to one another and wrote responses in their logs to the books they were reading. Brandt also read aloud to the students and discussed the stories with students for main ideas and enjoyment, without using specific comprehension questions. While students wrote on topics of their own choice, or related to a topic such as "feelings" that she chose and discussed with them,

Brandt had individual conferences with students about their writing. She encouraged them and asked questions about their work. Children collaborated by writing together; they also proofread one another's work.

The classroom was organized for students to meet in both small groups and the large group. Brandt had designated one corner near the back of the classroom as a "literacy corner." It was set off by two adjoining bookshelves. Small carpet pieces for students to sit on while writing or reading were spread out in the space. Student-written stories hung from a clothesline near the corner, while students' drawings labeled "I never saw a . . . " decorated a nearby bulletin board.

In the corner opposite the literacy corner a round table provided another place for students to write. Student-drawn titles of picture books were stapled to the side bulletin board under the sign "Have You Read?" Other evidence of an emphasis on writing included a bulletin board decorated with photographs that said, "Write About It." In the front of the room a table had books displayed that students could choose to read. A large floor space for students to gather to listen to the teacher or other students read occupied the front center. A rocking chair labeled "author's chair" was centered in the front of this space. Student desks clustered in two large groups that faced each other.

The Writing Lesson

We observed a session that Brandt held in the spring of 1990 with one of her primary grade classes. Students had been coming to this class each morning throughout the year for writing. During the one-hour session students wrote pieces on topics of their own choosing.

Brandt began the session by asking students to share with the group the topics they were writing about. One pair of students offered that they were writing an ABC book. When Brandt asked them which students in the school might especially appreciate their book, the girls responded "the kindergartners and preschool kids." Brandt called on several children to share with the rest of the class the topics they were writing about. One student was doing a "pop-up book" with pictures and words, another pair of students were writing about baseball's greatest players, while another student was writing about aliens who come from Mars. Two students were creating a map for other students to find the treasure; another student was writing about a time capsule that went back to when knights lived.

Discussing Collaboration. After the boys who were writing about baseball volunteered their topic, Brandt asked how students who were writing together had decided to divide up the work.

Brandt: How many of you are working in pairs? How many of you have two working on a book? I will be anxious to see and I'd like just a couple of you to share how you've decided to split up the work. If you have an author and an illustrator. If you're both being author and illustrator. Tell us a little bit about that. Courtney.

Courtney: Um, we take turns, like I will write one chapter and she draws a chapter and she draws the picture on that chapter and then I take, then I draw the picture on chapter 2 and she writes it.

Brandt: I see. That's an interesting way to do it. Sheri.

Sheri: Uh, first I'm drawing the pictures for a cover and Wanda is making . . . pictures and then when we finished . . . I'm going to write them and she's supposed to color and then she writes some.

Brandt: Good, it sounds good. You've got that well worked out. Nate, how are you and Adam doing yours?

Nate: He knows how to draw the Simpsons and everything, and we'll let him be the illustrator, and I'll be the author.

Brandt: All right, three different ways we have. That's good. You worked that out yourselves. Chris?

Chris: Me and Matt will take turns.

This discussion led to Brandt's pointing out to the class that she had noticed that a student, Courtney, had figured out how to indicate dialogue by using quotation marks. She commended

Courtney's efforts and explained how the child had reached this conclusion.

Writing Conferences. After this brief discussion, Brandt asked students to begin writing either alone or with their partners. Students gravitated to different parts of the room. Some students went back to write in the literacy corner, others sat on the floor or at tables; still other children sat together at their desks.

As students wrote, Brandt went around the classroom having brief conferences with individuals or pairs of students. Her comments were supportive in nature. Occasionally, she asked a question about what a student was writing or gave a suggestion. The following interaction with Curtis was more extensive than most of her conferences, but it provides an example of what she discussed with students as she circulated. Curtis was writing a book about guns by himself.

Brandt: Do you know what you could do? You've told me a lot of different ways that they could use them [guns]. Now you could go off into that with the army now. If you run out of ideas for just that because you told me some about the army, you could show them in use. You could show some of your army. You could get off into some action in your story if you'd like to. If you get stumped, think about that; keep that in mind. See, you've got good starters there, and you may want to go off now and add more to it if you get stumped. How else could you do that?

Curtis: Make like mens like you see them shooting . . . or you can have like a man right here and a man running and a man shooting.

Brandt: You could.

Curtis: Something like that . . .

Brandt: You could. If you could tell people something about guns, what would you like to tell them? What are some things you want people to know that you hope your children would know about them or what might you want to tell them?

Curtis: They're dangerous.

Brandt: And what else would you want them to know?

Curtis: That they can kill you if you shoot yourself.

Brandt: Okay.

Curtis: And, umm, that never shoot them at people.

Brandt: Okay, that could be another way you could go, Curtis. You could make it a safety book. You could be teaching a lesson in your book. I mean, if we're having this, having children read this you might want them to learn the lesson from that. All of those things that you know we're not sure that they know. So that's another way you could go with your book—to make it a gun safety book to tell them the rules, teach them that. Okay?

Curtis: This is what I . . .

Brandt: It looks good. It looks good. Think about it, and if you want to give them some rules you go with it the way you would like to. But you've just given me two or three different ideas. If you're stumped for a way, you could go and make more about your story. The safety idea or the army idea either one, but it would be nice for you either way. They'd enjoy an army story, or they'd enjoy your ideas about safety, about what to do and why they're dangerous and how they're dangerous. It's very good.

Offering Help to Others. Brandt continued to circulate among students until about five minutes before the session was over. As she talked to individual students, she noticed that several students had offered help, such as doing illustrations or proofreading for other children. She formalized this by getting students' attention and asking for volunteers to tell the others what strengths they had to share.

Several students offered their services to others. For instance, Jackie indicated that she could help other students with their covers; Curtis offered help in drawing; Kim offered help with spelling; and Courtney suggested she could help with coloring. Brad offered help with making backgrounds; Sheri suggested she could help students who had trouble beginning their stories; and Jessica suggested she was good at proofreading. Brandt encouraged each of these offers and told students they should take advantage of the help offered by other children.

Looking at Brandt's Practice

Brandt seemed to be building a community of students within her classroom in a number of ways. First, by having students share their topics with one another and read to each other through the author's chair, she was establishing real audiences. She encouraged this community to extend to the rest of the school by suggesting that the two girls who were constructing the "ABC" book could read their book to the kindergartners and preschool children.

Second, a sense of communal learning took place as students not only worked together on their stories if they chose but also shared with the rest of the group how they made decisions about dividing up the work. Later in an interview, Brandt noted that she had students tell how they divided the work because it provided students with more options about how to work together.

Brandt built on the ideas of the children and gave credit to the students for the development of these ideas, such as discovering how to indicate dialogue through quotation marks. Even if students were not working directly together, she suggested that they talk to one another during writing to share their ideas and to practice telling their stories before writing. Encouraging students to both develop their own strengths and take advantage of other students' talents, Brandt set up a situation in which students could provide one another with help on particular aspects of their stories.

How Brandt Thought About Her Practice

Brandt described her practice as changing, and she characterized these changes as developmental. First she was a traditional teacher who used the basal materials. She found that she was discontented with what she had been doing and began to do some reading on her own, including Lucy Calkins.[7] She gradually tried new ways of teaching for understanding through incorporating a reading-writing-phonics program entitled "Success" into her teaching. In writing, she said that she initially gave students "creative topics" about which to write but found them constraining after a while. Although she had not been through the National Writing Project herself, she had read articles, visited other teachers, and invited Ross into her room. She found that the most important feature of her changes was trying ideas out with children, watching how they responded, and then revising her teaching according to what students enjoyed and learned. She believed that she used a literature-based approach to teaching, but then moved into a total whole language program in which students drew from their own experiences as well as the books they read.

Brandt's comments about her changing practice suggest that she had moved beyond a model of knowledge transmission toward one of knowledge transformation. Three key features of her knowledge and beliefs included (1) her ideas about students drawing from their own experiences, (2) integrating skills into students' own writing, and (3) building a community. After experimenting with providing students with topics and beginnings of stories, Brandt discovered that "the best kind of writing came from their own experience, things they were interested in, things they wanted to write about. . . . Story starters were not within their experience."

The most difficult thing to let go of was students getting "the skills" through their reading and writing. To reassure herself that students were learning the skills appropriate for their grade level, she went through the teacher's manuals and compared their objectives to what she was teaching and found that students learned skills such as capitalization and punctuation within the context of their own writing. Over time, she came to look to the students rather than the textbook to make her plans.

Having students write from their own experiences was also an important aspect of Brandt's practice and one that helped her want to build a feeling of community among her students: "[Students] come to school having had so many experiences—both good and not so good—and I think it's [writing] a good catharsis for them. . . . Even your innermost thoughts you can't share with someone, you can share through your writing."

Brandt described several incidents of violence and abuse that were expressed in students' writing; other students in the class asked questions, but became protective and helpful toward the abused

students who read their pieces. Given other studies that have doc-
umented the inherent risks to children of opening up these
discussions,[8] Brandt's successful negotiation of these topics is particularly noteworthy. Brandt attributed this type of closeness that
she built within her classroom to the teaming and the sessions in
which teachers and students discussed problems: "I think that's one
of the advantages of the teaming and the teacher-based guidance.
These children feel close together and they're such a team and they
really sympathize, empathize. They really care about each other."

Brandt hoped to build on that feeling of closeness and care
among students in her classroom. She and her colleagues built this
feeling of being part of a team by having the same 120 students for
four years, by using the metaphor of a baseball team when talking
directly with students about team membership, and by participating
as a team in a three-day camping trip.

These features suggest the ways in which Brandt was creating
her practice and her underlying thinking about her practice. What
could account for these practices and beliefs that were consistent
with teaching for understanding? How do her practices reflect
school, district, and national goals for elementary students in the
area of literacy and new ideas and knowledge about teaching?

Although Brandt was quite motivated to seek and use new
knowledge herself, as evidenced by her reading on her own, she was
connected to school, district, and national efforts to create new literacy practices. Brandt attributed the changes in her classroom practice
to the restructuring efforts, her work with Ross, who was the liaison
from the professional development center, and her other connections
at the center. Brandt went to the center for materials, for inservices,
and to talk to teachers from other schools. Her thinking and practice
were also influenced by new ideas brought into her classroom by
student teachers from the university who were placed in the school
and supervised by Ross. In addition, Brandt reported that her principal and colleagues were supportive of her innovations.

Coherence and Connections Across Contexts

Brandt invited Jay Ross into her classroom on an ongoing basis—
two or three times weekly. He did demonstration writing lessons

and worked alongside Brandt in responding to children's writing. Brandt identified his visits as a major influence on her changing practice; she described him as credible because he was actually in the classroom teaching children. Through Ross's teaching writing in her classroom, Brandt had the opportunity to see new knowledge in use. Ross's demonstrations share some similarities with Ball's mathematics teaching in Rundquist's room (see Chapter Two). Both demonstrators provided opportunities for the teachers to see new ways of teaching in actual classroom settings. The teachers saw Ross and Ball, the demonstrators, as credible because they worked with students.

Ross introduced the Success program—a "transitional program" from traditional skills to literature-based instruction integrating reading, writing, and phonics. However, Brandt became dissatisfied with the program because it advocated reading any books, not necessarily quality literature. It provided a set of topics for students to write about that she found rigid, uninteresting, and distant from the children's experiences. Ross helped her to move beyond Success. One particular example she noted was the day that Ross demonstrated students' writing from their own experiences without any assigned topics or story-starters. She was shocked and delighted when students expressed pride with the pieces they had shared with one another.

Besides providing demonstration teaching, Ross also stimulated reflection through the articles he left for the teachers. Brandt said, "There was not a day that I walked to my mailbox that he didn't have some kind of literature in there." She found that Ross was so encouraging of her new practices that she could anticipate what he wanted her to think about next.

Gradually, Ross worked with her to take ideas from Success, to take aspects of a literature-based program, and to try out ideas from the Writing Project to develop her own curriculum. Ross was available to Brandt outside the classroom as well; teachers felt free to call him at home, and he joined the team for a camping trip. He acted as a resource and often as part of the team.

Similar to Miller and Yerkes' team (see Chapter Four), Brandt's team acted as a support system and sounding board and provided motivation for each other. Initially, the team discussed ways of grouping students and assigning teachers to subject matter. Over time, teachers on the team began to discuss individual students, curricular units, and themes.

Brandt regarded the school as a supportive place where the principal and the teachers were working together. Participatory management in which teachers were involved in making decisions helped her feel free to try out new ideas. She found that she did not have to be bound by the curriculum guide and that she could "personalize her program," putting herself into it.

The district provided resources in the form of sustaining on-site staff development, materials, and personnel to support Brandt's efforts. When restructuring efforts began, Brandt took advantage of many of the workshops at the Professional Development Center, particularly those on "literature-based instruction." Literature-based instruction involves using material such as "Big Books, trade books, and chapter books" instead of basal readers. The emphasis is on reading authentic materials for meaning; skills are taught within the context of the students' own writing or as issues emerge from the literature students read. Students are encouraged to discuss their ideas with the teacher and other students in the form of individual or small group conferences. Students often have many choices about materials they read and activities in which they participate.

District efforts were important in providing workshops at the Professional Development Center and securing an on-site coach (Jay Ross) who had access to larger reading and writing resources and had connections with a larger community of practitioners and scholars (for example, the citywide Writing Project and the National Writing Project, the district language arts expert, and faculty at the local university). The district had also provided initial support for a district person to work with Brandt and her team members in positing the goals of their restructuring efforts. The district provided support for Brandt to visit teachers in other schools who were implementing literature-based approaches in their classrooms. In addition, Brandt had her own informal, personal connections with people involved in the district's restructuring efforts through her husband, who as head of the district's restructuring team was spearheading reform efforts at the district level and at local school sites.

Although the philosophical ties were not explicit, Brandt shared with the district language arts coordinator, Carol Hall, and the liaison person, Ross, a view of literacy learning. This view was focused on reading for meaning and connecting to students' own experiences, and provided opportunities for students to read and write authentic texts and discuss those with the teacher and other students. Carol Hall's vision of a literacy program was that it should involve students in talking about books in discussion groups, the students should have choices about what they read, they should read and write "real" texts, and they should have opportunities to communicate in a very literate environment. The focus should be on reading for meaning and for relevance to students' own experiences. Ross's philosophy of learning was that it is a natural process. He wanted students to use their own experiences and to make connections between learning in school and out of school. Brandt's philosophy included making skills meaningful and having students learn them within the context of their own writing.

Brandt worked with people at the local university to write a grant proposal for thematic teaching and purchasing trade books. They were successful in getting $4,200 for books, resource people, and field trips related to language arts studies. The professors who taught the children's literature classes helped Brandt choose appropriate books for the classroom.

The connection that Brandt made between research, new knowledge, and practice from the larger community of practitioners and scholars at the national level was often mediated through the person of Jay Ross, who provided materials. When asked what authors she had read that influenced her ideas about reading and writing, Brandt mentioned John Goodlad, David Elkind, and the book *The Art of Teaching Writing* by Lucy Calkins. She also attended presentations in which national speakers motivated her.

The Case of Melissa Benton and Her Mathematics Practice

Although Benton was a relatively new (third year) teacher, she felt that she taught mathematics much differently from the way she originally did when she had students work from a book four days a week. She described her former practice as boring, both for her students and for her. Now she saw mathematics as exciting, both for her students and for her. Benton saw this as quite a change for someone who had hated math in high school because she was never any good at it. How did this change come about in Benton's feelings and thinking about her mathematics teaching practice?

Benton taught at another school before Webster Elementary. She chose Webster because it was part of a major "restructuring" effort in the district. When asked what restructuring meant to her, Benton described it as using "more innovative ways of teaching and better ways of teaching" and as "more hands-on." She credited her principal for the important role that she played in encouraging her and providing opportunities to adopt a new math program. Benton described her principal as "real open" and supportive of trying out "anything new." The previous year her principal had provided the opportunity for Benton to visit another school that was using a new activity-based mathematics program called Box It or Bag It Mathematics (B or B). Right away she knew it was for her and decided to take the workshop offered by the school district that summer. She chose to be one of the two teachers on her primary multiage team who taught mathematics. The team consisted of four teachers and approximately a hundred first and second grade children. Benton was now nearing the end of her first year of using the program. As she saw it, the basis for the major changes she had made in her mathematics teaching practice was B or B Mathematics.

Engaging Students in "Active" Mathematics Learning

Benton roused her first and second grade students to begin thinking about mathematics class by announcing that they were going to have a "a regular calendar and games day." The "calendar" segment consisted of a rapidly paced series of lecture-recitation activities led by Benton from a position at the side of the room standing in front of a bulletin board with an eye-catching array of mathematics activities. The activities, many with a "teddy bear" theme, occupied most of the side wall. From her position in front of the calendar, Benton conducted the whole class calendar activities in an upbeat, fast-paced tempo. She seemed ready to burst with excitement and energy as she led off the recitation in a clear, strong voice:

Benton: Let's start with the calendar. Chris, what's the date of today?

Chris: The fifteenth.

Benton: The fifteenth, May the fifteenth. According to our pattern what's it gonna be?

[Note: The calendar, labeled "May," consisted of a series of squares arranged in columns under the names of the days of the week. Each square of the calendar had a different-colored flower with the number of the day on it. At this point in the lecture-recitation, the calendar consisted of flowers with these colors and numbers: (1) orange, (2) yellow, (3) purple, (4) purple, (5) yellow, (6) blue, (7) blue, (8) blue, (9) yellow, (10) orange, (11) yellow, (12) purple, (13) purple, and (14) yellow.]

Chris: Um, blue.

Benton: Blue, raise your hand if you can tell me the pattern this month. OK, let's all say the pattern for this month.

All: Orange, yellow, purple, purple, yellow, blue, blue, blue, yellow, orange, yellow, purple, purple, yellow, blue . . .

Benton: What's tomorrow gonna be?

All: Blue, blue.

Benton: How do we know that it was a pattern? Lauren?

Lauren: It repeats itself.

Here Benton might have probed further her students' understanding of the pattern by asking how they knew that the next flower should be blue, why they thought it should be so to form a pattern, and what they thought the pattern was. For example, in answering "It repeats itself," Lauren might have been referring to the fact that the blue flower repeated itself or she might have been referring to the larger sequence of nine colors that was partially repeated—orange, yellow, purple, purple, yellow, blue, blue, blue, yellow. Rather than probing her students' understanding, however, Benton assumed that by her answer, "It repeats itself," Lauren had the same understanding as she did. Benton reaffirmed her assumed understanding by repeating Lauren's words, "It repeats itself." Then she added obliquely, "After we get an orange, then it started over again, and that's how come we know it's a pattern."

Turning to a slate that hung next to the calendar, Benton queried the class for the abbreviation of the day of the week (Tues.), the name of the month (May), and the date and year (15, 1990). Her students replied by chanting each of these in unison. Benton called on Michelle to give her another way to write the date, and Benton responded with "Five dash fifteen dash ninety." Benton affirmed Michelle's answer by writing "5-15-90" on the slate.

What followed then was a brisk march through a multitude of additional "calendar" activities with Benton at the lead. Each of the activities involved some materials that Benton had made and posted on the board. To the observer, who was new to this class-room, these activities passed by with a speed that left her gasping and a blur that left her dazed. But to Benton's students, well versed in this routine, these activities seemed to be all part of the game, and her students entered into it actively and enthusiastically by respond-ing singly or in unison to her familiar questions for each activity. Some of these additional calendar activities included counting the number of tally marks that had been made so far that month (fif-teen); deciding whether this number of tallies was an odd or even number by placing the number in the odd or the even column on a chart; adding another penny to the "money purse" to make fifteen cents; adding 162 to the number line because it was the one hundred sixty-second day of the year; representing the number 162 in terms of the ones, tens, and hundreds places; and dressing the "today" bear, the "yesterday" bear, and the "tomorrow bear" with the ap-propriate clothes—jerseys emblazoned with "Tuesday, the 15th," "Monday, the 14th," and "Wednesday, the 16th."

Benton led into the final calendar activity by announcing, "Now it's time for . . . " with a rising inflection followed by a dra-matic pause. Benton followed her dramatic pause by announcing the next activity, "INCREDIBLE EQUATIONS!" Because this was Benton's favorite activity, and she wanted this to be her students' favorite activity, too, she made her voice sound exciting so her students would think, "Oh, this is pretty exciting!" It was as though Benton were "willing" her students to be involved through catching her own excitement. The major task for this lecture-recitation activity involved the students' coming up with as many different equations as they could that equaled 15—the day of the month. One at a time, Benton called on individual students, who each gave an equation. If the equation was correct, Benton then affirmed it by writing it on a slate next to the calendar. Benton did not ask students to explain how or why their equation was correct. If the equation was incorrect, she directly prompted the student by giving clues on how the student might make the equation correct. In a few minutes, the children had listed twelve different equations that equaled 15:

3×5	$1{,}000{,}000 - 999{,}985$
$5 + 5 + 5$	$20 - 5$
$100 - 85$	$\$1.00 - .15 - .75 + .05$
$22 - 11 + 4$	$10 + 5$
$10 \times 10 - 85$	$2{,}000 - 1{,}000 - 1{,}000 + 15$
$20 + 5 - 10$	$2{,}000{,}000 - 1{,}999{,}985$

Satisfied with the results of the students' endeavors, Benton moved into the "game" portion of the mathematics lesson. She passed out to each child the materials needed for the game—a "general materials" box containing a slate, chalk, erasing cloth, small plastic cups, and beans and a game sheet consisting of a "honeycomb" of hexagons. Within each hexagon was a two-digit or three-digit number or an equation. Each child's sheet was different. Then Benton stood at the front of the room and read a word problem from an index card. Students got to color in a square when the answer or the equation on their sheet solved the word problem read by Benton. For the word problems that could be solved by using addition or subtraction, Benton expected her students to write the appropriate addition or subtraction computation on their slates.

The object of this Honeycomb game was to "win" by being the first to color in a row or diagonal of hexagons on the sheet.

When they got to a "tough one," Benton directed her students to use the beans and the cups from their boxes to find the answer to the "division" word problem that she posed: "Shelly had 20 pennies. She wanted to divide them evenly between 5 kids." Benton had each student take out 5 cups, count out 20 beans in his or her hands, and then put the beans into the 5 cups so that each cup had the same amount—four beans per cup. After the students had 4 beans in each of their cups, Benton announced that the answer was "4," and she showed them two ways to write the division calculation on their slates, using the two different symbols for division. After several more problems, the game and the class ended when one student "won" the game by having correctly colored in a row of hexagons on his sheet.

Ways That Benton Was Creating Her Practice

One change in Benton's practice was that she came to see herself in the role of a leader in the classroom. Indeed, the principal, who viewed Benton as the math expert in the school, also described her proudly as our "cheerleader"—an apt metaphor considering Benton's youthful demeanor, spritely figure, and voice, which conveyed constant excitement and enthusiasm.

Perhaps the most important way that Benton thought her practice was different was her new approach to math as "fun and exciting." Why was math more exciting for her? As she saw it, it was because she was *doing* different things each day and because she was *playing games* with the students. She attributed her new love of teaching math to the new program that she chose, Box It or Bag It Mathematics,[9] which provided directions for how to make and use the different activities that she was now doing in math and the games that she was using. Benton thought math was the subject she was best at teaching, because she had been "newly trained and the kids love it, and they understand it, and it's satisfying" for her. She believed her children understood math better because they were "actively involved."

With the activity-based mathematics program, Benton felt

that her children were more actively involved in mathematics because "they can touch it, feel it, see it, and do it." Benton believed
that children learned math better with the new program, rather than
by using a mathematics book that she said was boring for them
because they were not actively involved. She compared learning
mathematics to learning to cook: "If you had to learn how to cook,
if you read a book about it, it's not going to be as effective as if
you're in the kitchen taking one tablespoon and putting it in, and
mixing it up with what a spoon or a blender. You know, actively
doing it is going to be a lot better. I wish I could remember the
saying, "Show me and I'll learn; tell me and I'll. . . . Especially for
children, especially for kids, if they're actively doing it, it makes
more sense to them." Thus, a third significant way that Benton was
creating her practice involved teaching mathematics to her primary
children entirely within the context of activities, for example, activities related to the calendar, seasonal activities, and game-like
activities.

A fourth way that Benton was creating her practice was by
introducing new mathematical content into her primary mathematics teaching with the Box It or Bag It program. The program authors themselves assert, "mathematics is more than arithmetic."
Further, they argue that "with the advent of computers, geometry,
patterning, sorting, graphing, estimating, measuring, and problem
solving might be considered the 'new' basic skills."[10] Indeed, there
is evidence that Benton included mathematical content not found
in traditional textbooks, for example, her lead-off discussion using
the calendar to identify a pattern. Further, the last two-thirds of the
lesson focused on solving word problems, reflecting a much greater
emphasis on word problems than seen in most primary mathematics classes.[11]

How Does Benton's Practice Reflect New Ideas and New Knowledge?

One way of examining Benton's practice is through the lens of the
authors of the Box It or Bag It program. Another lens for examining
her practice is through the vision explicated by the authors of the
NCTM Standards. In both cases a central issue is, "How do children

learn mathematics?'' In response to this question, the authors of
Box It or Bag It Mathematics assert the following in their
introduction:

> Young children learn best when they are actively in-
> volved in hands-on experiences with a variety of mate-
> rials. Understanding takes lots of time. Children need
> multiple opportunities and experiences in a wide var-
> iety of contexts to construct knowledge. . . . Language
> is a tool for learning and thinking. Children who can
> tell, draw, or act out story problems to illustrate an
> operation or explain to others how they solved a prob-
> lem are closer to understanding a concept than chil-
> dren who labor alone silently over worksheets as the
> daily routine. . . . Mathematics is synonymous with
> problem solving *if* we take every opportunity to ask
> rather than tell, guide rather than direct. [12]

For Benton too, a key element in learning mathematics is the idea
that students need to be "actively involved." Like another primary
teacher, Carol Turner, who saw herself as teaching mathematics for
understanding, Benton believed that students must be "actively engaged," and she would agree completely with Carol's assertions that
"students learn through doing; they don't learn through sitting and
doing workbook pages." [13] But what does Benton mean by "actively
involved," and how is Benton's view similar or different from that
of the Box It or Bag It authors and from NCTM's vision of mathematics education reform?

    What Does It Mean to Be "Actively Involved"? When they
refer to "actively involved," both Benton and the Box It or Bag It
authors seem to focus on the hands-on aspect or physical involvement of the children with the materials. But the B or B authors may
have had more in mind than what is reflected in Benton's perspectives and her practice. For example, they seem to have in mind a
more open-ended pattern of discourse and classroom talk in which
the teacher and students are engaged in reasoning, discussion, and
sharing of possible understandings. However, like Benton, the au-

thors of B or B also seem to assume that *students will learn mathematics by doing activities that involve mathematics.*

A contrasting view is that *students learn mathematics by doing mathematics.* For example, one of the major assumptions underlying the vision of the authors of the *NCTM Standards* is that "The K-4 curriculum should actively involve children in doing mathematics. . . . To convey this active physical and mental involvement of children in learning the content of the curriculum," the NCTM authors state that they intentionally use such verbs as "explore, justify, represent, solve, construct, discuss, use, investigate, describe, develop, and predict."[14]

In keeping with her view that students learn mathematics better by participating in games and interesting activities, Benton drew an analogy with cooking to describe how students learn math:

> The more that they do it this year or any year, the more they're going to retain it. The more I learn to cook brown rice, the more I don't even have to look at the recipe. I've got it in my mind. I may still have to look at the recipe the first 3 or 4 times, but then I've done it enough that I don't need the recipe anymore. It's kind of the same with these [word problems]. They've done these enough now so they don't need the beans anymore. And that's the whole thing—you start with the beans, and you move up to the chalkboard, and you move up to the paper, and then they have it.

For Benton cooking is an apt metaphor for learning mathematics because mathematics is procedural for her. Learning to use and follow a recipe in cooking is like learning to use and follow a mathematical procedure to solve a problem. The procedure may be a computational procedure like addition or subtraction. Alternatively, the procedure may involve manipulating concrete objects (for example, the beans) to count, then moving up to the more abstract procedure of writing and completing a number sentence. The key is that there are mathematical procedures or steps to follow, the steps progress linearly, and a person learns mathematics through practice and repetition involved in doing the procedures over and over.

In an interview following the math lesson, Benton described the purpose of the Honeycomb game activity as "just a review of skills." She expected her students to have learned the way to do a story problem, and she seems to see the Honeycomb game as a way of assessing whether students have learned this skill. This seems to be a very different perspective on the Honeycomb word problem game than if Benton had said that the purpose was to explore students' mathematical thinking, understanding, or reasoning about word problems. Further, Benton claimed that if she had been observed doing this earlier in the year she would have been "teaching the skill of doing word problems."

What Does It Mean to Give Children Multiple Opportunities to "Construct Knowledge"? Benton's view of how students learn to solve word problems can be seen as consistent with the B or B authors' view if we return to their assertion that "children need multiple opportunities and experiences in a wide variety of contexts to construct knowledge." Benton provided her students with multiple opportunities and experiences (using beans, drawing pictures, and so forth) when they were in the process of "constructing knowledge," but once they had "constructed" the knowledge (for instance, the appropriate computation to solve the word problem), she expected them to be able to demonstrate it later. Because in this lesson Benton assumed that students should have already "constructed" the appropriate knowledge, she had trouble with Chris when he suggested a different way of solving the following word problem that she had posed to the class:

> Gina wants to buy a "New Kids on the Block" key chain that costs seventy-nine cents. But guess what? Gina has only fifty-three cents. How much more money does she need to buy the key chain?

Because one of the hexagons on the Honeycomb game sheet contained the equation "$79 - 53 = $," Benton expected the students to write that equation on their slates to solve the problem. As students held up their slates with that equation, Benton nodded approvingly. But one student, Chris, suggested that he solved the problem by adding on. Benton understood his response to mean that he did not understand, and in a dialogue with Chris she pursued the issue until she got him to admit that you need to subtract to solve the problem. Then he obediently wrote "79 - 53 = 26" on his slate. In this case then, Benton missed the opportunity to learn and expand her own knowledge by exploring the depths of her students' mathematical knowledge and understanding.

As discussed earlier in this chapter, learning from her own students and exploring the amazing knowledge and understanding of children was an important way Julie Brandt learned and increased her own knowledge and understanding. Similarly, listening and attempting to understand her own students' mathematical knowledge and thinking could have served as an important impetus for Benton to teach in ways that were more consistent with teaching for understanding. Paying attention to students' thinking has had a significant influence on other elementary mathematics teachers who have been involved in constructivist approaches designed to facilitate teacher change aimed toward teaching mathematics for understanding.[15]

Contexts for Learning and Teaching

In her interview with us, Benton said, "I actually hate math." What she said she meant by math was "higher-level math" such as algebra and geometry. She said that she only loved to teach math now because of the program she had chosen to use—Box It or Bag It Mathematics. She admitted that in getting her degree in elementary education in 1987 she had been required to take no courses in mathematics and to take only one course in elementary mathematics methods as part of her program. Given that Benton was building on her own admittedly limited substantive knowledge of mathematics and of mathematics pedagogy, it is not surprising that she, the perceived mathematics expert in the school, did not appear to have reconsidered her fundamental knowledge and beliefs about mathematics or about mathematics learning and understanding. Lacking substantive knowledge about mathematics, mathematics learning, and mathematics pedagogy, Benton drew most of her new knowledge and information from the B or B program, a program that by itself seems to constitute a somewhat impoverished context for teachers' learning. As the title of the program implies, much of what Benton has learned to do in implementing the program is to *make* and *do* new activities, such as the myriad "calendar activities" displayed on the board and the "general materials box" used by each student. Learning to do B or B Mathematics has provided Benton with scant opportunity to learn new mathematical content, to increase the depth of her own mathematical knowledge and understanding, or to explore the depths of her students' mathematical knowledge and understanding. In embracing the program, Benton embraced the assumption that "appropriate materials and activities alone will do the trick" and "simply working with the proper activities and materials assures that math will be understood."[16] Benton did not reconsider the nature of mathematical knowledge and understanding, and the curriculum did not encourage her to do so. She continued to assume that mathematics is a fixed body of knowledge and facts and continued to treat it as such.

Yet Benton made what she considered to be substantive changes in her classroom practice in the area of mathematics. How do Benton's changes reflect school, district, and national goals for elementary students in the area of mathematics and address new ideas and knowledge about the teaching of mathematics? What may account for Benton's changes?

Like Brandt, Benton worked within contexts that were embedded and complex, and the relevant contexts for Benton were the same as those for Brandt—the classroom, the team, the school, the district, the state, and the nation. Indeed, on the face of it, all these contexts except the classroom appear to be the "same" for Benton as for Brandt. Yet, as we shall see, these contexts differed significantly for the two teachers.

Within her classroom, Benton lacked an on-site "coach" or mentor in mathematics of the sort that Brandt had for literacy and writing in the person of Jay Ross. Although Ross sat in on Benton's class occasionally, he saw his main role as providing her with support and occasionally giving her information (for example, on multiage grouping). Because of this, Benton missed out on opportunities that Brandt had to connect with a larger knowledge base in the subject area, to connect with a larger community of practitioners and scholars, and to engage in the kinds of ongoing conversations with herself and others that may be critical to knowledge growth in teaching.[17]

The team context also differed substantially for Brandt and Benton. While Brandt was the acknowledged team leader in general as well as in literacy specifically, Benton was the "rookie" on her team, in her third year of teaching. In his interview with us, Ross ventured the idea that one reason that Benton got involved with the B or B program was so that she could become an "expert" and "carve out her own niche." But as the "expert" and the only one on her team who taught mathematics, Benton had no one on her team with whom she could have conversations about mathematics, about Box It or Bag It Mathematics, or about the changes she was trying to make in her own mathematics teaching. Although Benton mentioned that another Webster teacher had taken the two-week summer B or B workshop with her, she did not seem to be engaged in ongoing conversations with this teacher about their mathematics teaching.

As was the case for Brandt, the school and the district provided supportive contexts for Benton to innovate and to take risks. The school and district provided resources in the form of sustained on-site staff development, materials, and personnel. As teachers in one of the district's professional development schools, Webster teachers were encouraged to seek out new ideas, develop new knowledge, and work with their teams within the school in "constructing new approaches suited to the needs of their students." Benton described Webster's principal, Cheryl Billings, as "real open" and supportive of trying out "anything new." When asked what restructuring meant to her, Benton described it as "using more innovative ways of teaching and better ways of teaching." During the previous year the principal had provided the opportunity for Benton to visit another school that was using the Box It or Bag It Math program. Then during the summer, Benton took a two-week Box It or Bag It workshop that was offered by her district's professional development center. The workshop was taught by a group of elementary teachers from a neighboring district who were using the program and who had gone to Oregon to be trained by developers of the program itself. As a result, Benton and her team adopted the program, and in mathematics Benton had come to be viewed as the expert and as a resource for other teachers in the school.

While Benton continued to visit the materials library at the district's professional development center to look for mathematics materials and activities during the subsequent school year, she seemed to be very much on her own and disconnected from others in her attempts to innovate, grow, and change in her mathematics teaching. Further, Benton seems disconnected from mathematics education reforms occurring within the state and national contexts. For example, her vision of mathematics and mathematics teaching seems to have been influenced little by views from the larger community of mathematics educators at the state and national level, although the potential for such connections existed. Benton's vision involved implementing what she viewed as an effective, innovative, activity-based mathematics program in which the kids are learning more because she and the kids are having fun and they are all "actively involved." Yet Benton had not changed fundamentally either her view of what mathematics is or how children come to know and understand mathematics. She was still bootstrapping from the mathematical knowledge and beliefs that she herself developed as a student.

As mentioned earlier, Benton had not connected with others who might have had more knowledge and expertise in mathematics teaching and from whom she might have learned and gained access to new ideas about mathematics. For example, the district's mathematics curriculum expert, Marsha Green, was one person from whom Benton might have learned and through whom she might have connected to other professional communities of discourse around mathematics. Intimately familiar with the *National Council of Teachers of Mathematics Standards* herself, Green was currently serving as state president of the National Council of Teachers of Mathematics, and she conducted professional development activities at many schools in the district. Yet she reported that she had never been to Webster, she had never been called on by the teachers there, and she did not know how Webster teachers were teaching elementary mathematics. In a conversation with us, the head of the district's restructuring team indicated that the team had intentionally decided to exclude from their conversations the members of the district's curriculum department, including Green. He felt that they had "old" knowledge and ideas; they did not have the kind of leading-edge radical reform ideas that characterized members of the restructuring team.

By distancing themselves from the district curriculum personnel in mathematics and other areas, the restructuring team missed the opportunity to engage in the kind of learning among policymakers, administrators, and practitioners suggested by Cohen and Barnes (Chapter Seven). By not getting to know Green, Benton missed the opportunity to connect with a person knowledgeable about mathematics and mathematics pedagogy, the *NCTM Standards,* and the current mathematics education reform effort locally and nationally, and she missed out on connecting with professional communities of discourse around mathematics and mathematics teaching.

Relations Between Research, New Knowledge, and Practice

In comparing the practices of Brandt and Benton, we are faced with several questions. Why did Brandt create practices that seem more consonant with "teaching for understanding?" What may account for differences that we see in the ways these two teachers created their practices? Are these differences related to individual variations between the teachers or to variations within the contexts in which they taught?

Both Brandt and Benton possessed personal characteristics that enabled them to take risks and innovate in their teaching, and both teachers were part of a supportive team with a restructured professional development school. However, individual differences between the two teachers and differences within the contexts in which each worked highlight important issues that may account for why Brandt's practice reflected teaching for understanding to a larger extent than Benton's practice.

First, the educational backgrounds and previous experiences with innovation differed for the two teachers. Brandt had been engaged in literature-based instruction for at least two years and had read works by Calkins and others previous to the restructuring efforts, whereas Benton was a relatively new teacher who was just beginning her work in mathematics. Brandt had more background in pedagogies that had similar orientations toward student roles. For instance, she involved her students in doing discovery learning in science long before she began setting up a writing process classroom. Both discovery learning in science and a writing process approach involve cognitively active roles for students in which the students are continually suggesting their own hypotheses or writing from their own experiences. Benton, however, came from a traditional teacher education program and had little opportunity to engage in innovative practices prior to her involvement in the restructuring efforts.

Second, Brandt articulated beliefs that were consistent with her changing practices. Her changing beliefs and practices worked together. Brandt was quite reflective about her practice, often challenging some of her old beliefs. By trying out ideas and seeing students' positive experiences with reading and writing, Brandt came to believe that students' life experiences were important. She moved away from using a specific program, Success, for ideas about teaching and began to look instead toward her students to construct her curriculum. In contrast, Benton depended heavily on the Box It or Bag It program for her curricular ideas. B or B mathematics could have been a step along the way toward teaching for understanding, just as Success was for Brandt and CSMP was for Sylvia (see Chapter Two). However, for Benton, the B or B program was an end in itself. By depending on B or B mathematics activities to carry the day, Benton neither reconsidered the nature of mathematical knowledge as dynamic and changing rather than a fixed body of facts nor attempted to explore and learn from her students' own mathematical knowledge, thinking, and ideas.

Third, although both Brandt and Benton took initiative in beginning new programs, Brandt had a particular vision and increasingly well-developed knowledge in the area of literacy and writing. Ross viewed Brandt as the "spiritual and cognitive leader" of the team, who had a clear direction about what she wanted to accomplish. Brandt's well-developed vision allowed her to pursue her goals, to learn, and to create her practice commensurate with those goals. In contrast, Benton was a "rookie" looking to create her own niche. She was in the process of developing a vision of mathematics pedagogy that depended heavily on the Box It or Bag It program activities and materials, but her vision did not seem to involve either an expanded view of mathematics or an expanded view of the student as a mathematics knower, doer, or thinker. Benton was attempting to "bootstrap" from her own admittedly impoverished mathematical background and knowledge and her own dislike of mathematics itself.

Although differences between the two teachers' backgrounds, knowledge, beliefs, and visions mattered, differences between the teachers' work contexts also mattered. These embedded contexts, while appearing to be similar, actually differed significantly; and these context differences contributed to create dramatically different practices in Brandt's and Benton's classrooms.

Brandt was linked to several supportive communities and had opportunities to engage in conversations at a variety of levels. She had conversations about teaching with Ross, her team, members of the restructuring team, including her husband, and university professors. Through these conversations, Brandt was connected with policymakers in her district, thereby setting up situations for the kinds of mutual learning to occur among practitioners and policymakers as described by Cohen and Barnes (Chapter Seven). Through these conversations Brandt was also linked to larger professional and academic discourse communities. Ross's intensive work in Brandt's classroom played a large role in linking her to these communities. As a liaison among the school, the district, and the university, Ross drew upon his own knowledge and expertise in writing to demonstrate in Brandt's classroom and support her efforts, while reporting back weekly to the district restructuring team. His manner of working with Brandt was particularly effective because he built trust with her and did not impose programs upon her or other teachers. Instead he described his approach to staff development as providing "invitations to learn."

In contrast, Benton was learning on her own how to teach mathematics in new ways. She had no one on her team with whom she could work on Box It or Bag It Mathematics. Benton appeared unconnected to other communities within her school, district, or state from whom she might have benefited and learned through conversations and knowledge sharing. Thus, she missed out on the kinds of opportunities for learning available to Brandt, who had access to professional communities around issues related to the teaching of literacy. Further, the Webster school as a whole was more involved in reforms involving literature-based instruction and writing than they were in reforms involving mathematics instruction. Compared to Brandt, Benton had significantly fewer opportunities to interact directly with members of the district's restructuring team, district curriculum experts, or university professors. Benton also chose to implement an activity-based mathematics program that provided little in the way of new mathematical knowledge or ideas of the kind that might have facilitated Benton's learning and growth of new knowledge in mathematics and in mathematics learniı.g. Thus, the embedded contexts in which Benton worked provided less opportunity for learning and less access to new knowledge and information than did the embedded contexts in which her teammate, Brandt, worked.

What Is Significant About These Cases?

By analyzing cases of teachers working within a "new organization" conceptualized as both a restructured school and a professional development school, we have had the opportunity to examine closely individual teachers interacting within specific contexts and to attempt to unpack how and why diverse aspects of contexts influence elementary teaching. We have attempted to define and describe the contexts in which two teachers work in order to understand what features make a difference in teachers' knowledge, thinking, and beliefs, and in the ways that teachers attempt to create their practice.

Our study demonstrates the complex interactions of individuals within contexts, suggesting that both individual differences within teachers as well as the layers of context within which teachers work affect their thinking and the ways that they create their practice.[18] Through examining the cases of two teachers— Melissa Benton and Julie Brandt—and the contexts in which they work we have attempted to understand "the co-occurrence of, and complex interactions among context conditions that support or undermine particular educational outcomes such as teaching for understanding" (see Chapter Six). We suggest that risk-taking, developing trust with colleagues, and developing coherent knowledge-based visions are important conditions for teacher learning. Further, we suggest that supportive contexts for teacher learning include not only administrative support and a climate for risk-taking but also participation in and linkage among professional communities of discourse. In the case of Brandt, we see both the power of participation in a wide variety of discourse communities as well as the power of connections and coherence among these communities. In this case, linkage occurred mainly in the form of a person, Jay Ross, who served as a liaison, ambassador, and knowledge-carrier among communities.[19]

The key role that Ross played is similar to the role that Heaton is developing for herself as a teacher educator who travels between the university setting and local school districts (see Chapter Three). One question raised by this role is how do teacher educators like Ross learn to enact this role? Other chapters in this book explore this and related questions in more depth (see Chapters Two, Three, and Four).

Ross's role also raises the question of whether using an individual to link communities of professional discourse around teaching is the best way or whether there may be other ways that are equally effective. Further research may expand on our work by studying other contexts in which linkages among discourse communities occur in ways other than through an individual person or liaison, for example, through a formal network.

Notes

1. Elmore, R. F., & Associates, 1990.
2. Holmes Group, 1990.
3. David, 1990.
4. Little, 1988.
5. Richardson, 1990.
6. The names of the school, principal, staff, teachers, and students are pseudonyms.
7. Calkins, 1986.
8. Lensmire, 1991; and McCarthey, 1991.

9. Burk, Snider, & Symonds, 1988.
10. Burk, Snider, & Symonds, 1988, p. 2.
11. Romberg & Carpenter, 1986.
12. Burk, Snider, & Symonds, 1988, pp. 1-2.
13. Ball, 1990.
14. National Council of Teachers of Mathematics, 1989, p. 17.
15. Peterson, Fennema, & Carpenter, 1990; and Wood, Cobb, & Yackel, 1991.
16. Cohen, 1990, p. 317.
17. Prawat, 1991; and Shulman, 1987.
18. See also case studies by Feiman-Nemser & Parker (in press); and Peterson (1990).
19. See also Lampert (1991).

References

Ball, D. L. (1990). Reflections and deflections of policy: The case of Carol Turner. *Educational Evaluation and Policy Analysis, 12*(3), 247-259.

Burk, D., Snider, A., & Symonds, P. (1988). *Box it or bag it mathematics.* Salem, OR: The Mathematics Learning Center.

Calkins, L. M. (1986). *The art of teaching writing.* Portsmouth, NH: Heinemann.

Cohen, D. K. (1991). A revolution in one classroom: The case of Mrs. Oublier. *Educational Evaluation and Policy Analysis, 12,* 311-330.

David, J. (1990). Restructuring in progress: Lessons from pioneering districts. In R. Elmore and Associates (Eds.), *Restructuring schools* (pp. 209-250). San Francisco: Jossey-Bass.

Elmore, R. F., & Associates (Eds.). (1990). *Restructuring schools: The next generation of educational reform.* San Francisco: Jossey-Bass.

Feiman-Nemser, S., & Parker, M. (in press). Mentoring in context: A comparison of two U.S. programs for beginning teachers. *International Journal of Educational Research.*

Holmes Group. (1990). *Tomorrow's schools: Principles for the design of professional development schools.* East Lansing, MI: Author.

Lampert, M. (1991, May). Looking at restructuring from within a restructured role. *Phi Delta Kappan, 72,* 670–674.

Lensmire, T. (1991). *Intention, risk, and writing in a third-grade writing workshop.* Unpublished dissertation. East Lansing: Michigan State University.

Little, J. W. (1988). Assessing the prospects for teacher leadership. In A. Lieberman (Ed.), *Building a professional culture in schools.* New York: Teachers College Press.

McCarthey, S. J. (1991). *Authors, text, and talk: The internalization of dialogue from social interaction during writing.* Unpublished dissertation. East Lansing: Michigan State University.

National Council of Teachers of Mathematics. (1989). *Curriculum and evaluation standards for school mathematics.* Reston, VA: Author.

Peterson, P. L. (1990). Cathy Swift: Doing more in the same amount of time. *Educational Evaluation and Policy Analysis, 12*(3), 261–280.

Peterson, P. L., Fennema, E., & Carpenter, T. (1990). Using children's mathematical knowledge. In B. Means, C. Chelemer, & M. S. Knapp (Eds.), *Models for teaching advanced skills to disadvantaged students* (pp. 68–101). San Francisco: Jossey-Bass.

Prawat, R. (1991). Conversations with self and settings: A framework for thinking about teacher empowerment. *American Educational Research Journal, 28,* 737–758.

Richardson, V. K. (1990). Significant and worthwhile change in teaching practice. *Educational Researcher, 19*(7), 10–18.

Romberg, T. A., & Carpenter, T. P. (1986). Research on teaching and learning mathematics: Two disciplines of scientific inquiry. In M. C. Wittrock (Ed.), *Handbook of research on teaching* (3rd ed., pp. 850–873). New York: Macmillan.

Shulman, L. S. (1987). Knowledge and teaching: Foundations of the new reform. *Harvard Educational Review, 57*(1), 1–22.

Wood, T., Cobb, P., & Yackel, E. (1991). Change in teaching mathematics: A case study. *American Educational Research Journal, 28,* 587–616.

Part Two

Enabling Teaching for Understanding

6

Understanding Teaching
in Context

Joan E. Talbert
Milbrey W. McLaughlin

What factors in the environment of classroom teaching influence
how a teacher defines the goals and means of teaching and learning
and how well she or he realizes the new vision of education practice?
And, more specifically: what conditions in the multiple contexts of
teaching—the students in a class, colleagues in a department or
school, school administrators, local and state educational policies,
and so on—make it more or less likely that a teacher will embrace
a vision of "teaching for understanding," will venture the long and
risky process of relearning to teach in this vision, and will persist
in the endeavor? Answers to these questions are crucial if we are

Research for this paper was supported by funds from the U.S. Department
of Education Office of Educational Research and Improvement (Grant No.
G0087C0235) to the Center for Research on the Context of Secondary
School Teaching (CRC), Stanford University. Any opinions, findings, and
conclusions expressed here are those of the authors and do not necessarily
reflect the views of the sponsoring agency. We are grateful to Julie Cummer
for help preparing the chapter for publication, to CRC research colleagues
for help collecting and analyzing the interview and survey data summarized
in the chapter, to Brian Rowan and Richard Elmore for collaborating on
the literature review for this chapter, and especially to the hundreds of
teachers in California and Michigan high schools who contributed to our
research.

to foster and design teaching contexts that enable, rather than constrain, the new vision of teaching and learning.

In 1987 the Center for Research on the Context of Secondary School Teaching (CRC)[1] embarked on the mission to integrate various lines of work on teaching contexts and conduct new, multimethod research on context conditions that affect teaching and learning.

The center's work, like other policy research, aims to inform educators, administrators, and policymakers about levers for improving the conditions and quality of education. We began our research program by reviewing the major lines of context-effects research in an effort to identify context conditions that affect the nature and success of teaching.[2] We considered, for example, the findings of research in sociology and in psychology on the effects of student grouping and tracking practices on learning and educational attainment, of interdisciplinary survey research estimating "school effects" on educational outcomes, and of related research isolating features of effective schools.

At the same time the center launched a three-year field research project in sixteen secondary schools with diverse student and community contexts, diverse school missions and district cultures, and contrasting state and sector policy contexts. A distinctive feature of our research is its bottom-up, teacher's-eye perspective on teaching within these diverse embedded contexts. This view of teaching and the contexts within which teachers work differs from that of researchers and policymakers who look at practice from the outside-in, considering teachers and their work from established frameworks of policy or social science paradigms. The teachers' perspective frames teaching in terms of the daily communion of students, subject matter, and dynamics of the school setting. It makes problematic the relevance of particular policies and theoretical variables popular with social science for understanding the day-to-day realities of teaching.

This chapter retraces our journey through the research literature concerned with context effects on educational outcomes and evaluates the contributions and methods of these lines of research from the vantage point of our bottom-up perspective on teaching in diverse secondary school settings. We aim to "hold up a mirror" for school context researchers to see how their work contributes to the knowledge base needed to promote teaching reform.

Since the research literature emphasizes organizational contexts of teaching—school systems and school cultures—we began, and now summarize, our review of the literature at these outer layers of teaching contexts and then moved inward to the subject and student/classroom contexts. Each section peels away and examines another layer of teaching context, including, in order, educational sector and system, school organization, and classroom. Following the course of our inquiry, our discussion then moves outward from the classroom nexus of teacher, subject, and student to the broader social and institutional environments that permeate primary and secondary school teaching.

While our critique of the context-effects literature is concerned generally with how well research informs understandings of context effects on teaching practice, we are also interested specifically in what it can say about conditions that enable or promote "teaching for understanding" (hereafter TFU).[3] In other words, what can the context-effects research traditions tell us about the likelihood that a teacher will embrace and act on TFU principles for instruction? The core principles of this new vision of instruction include (1) a conception of knowledge as *constructed* by the learner and therefore *situated* in the context of prior knowledge, skills, values, and beliefs; (2) a conception of teacher as *guide,* as *co-constructor* of students' knowledge; and (3) a conception of the classroom as a *community of learners,* in which shared goals and standards, an atmosphere of mutual trust, and norms for behavior support students in taking the risks and making the sustained efforts entailed in serious learning. (See Chapters Two, Three, and Four.)

School Context Effects on Teaching

Concerns with the design of educational systems, school climates, and curricular structures that improve student outcomes define the contours of extant context-effects research. While teachers and teaching have rarely been a focus in these lines of research, they implicitly comprise key mediating variables in context effects on student learning outcomes. For example, if private schools have better cognitive outcomes than public schools, this must be because teaching in the private sector is superior, on average. Similarly, lower learning gains in low-track classrooms implies generally inferior teaching in these settings.

In our review of the literature, we attempt to bring teachers and teaching out of the shadows of research findings into the fore. We ask what extant traditions of research can and cannot tell us about context effects on teaching goals and practices and, specifically, on the likelihood that a teacher would teach in ways that promote deeper student understanding of subject matter.

School Sector and System Conditions

Differences in the educational success between public and private schools have been a primary focus of school-effects research conducted over the past decade. Researchers have explored differences between sectors on such dimensions as governance, curriculum and instructional practice, accountability, funding arrangements, faculty autonomy, and material resources.[4]

In a few highly publicized studies that used national survey data on school conditions and student test performance, researchers reached the conclusion that private schools do better than public schools, after other variables relevant to educational success are controlled.[5] Each study generated considerable debate on the adequacy of controls for confounded variables, adequacy of the tests for measuring student learning, and problems of comparing sectors as a basis for public education policy.[6] As with most context-effects research we have reviewed, these studies do not analyze or seriously discuss the nature of teaching and learning in sampled schools; indeed, teachers and teaching are absent from the studies, except as informants on school conditions. The research has been used to support policy initiatives to extend public funding to private schools.

The studies of sector effects have yielded various theories about which organizational conditions affect educational quality and in what way. Chubb and Moe,[7] for example, extrapolate from their study's findings to conclude that institutions of democratic control generate bureaucratic controls in the public education sector that are inefficient and ineffective. In contrast, according to their argument, the market context of private schools establishes both quality control and responsiveness to parent and student clients because, the authors imply, parents and students know how to choose, evaluate, and regulate the quality of teaching in classrooms and schools. The realities of school contexts make this a questionable simplifying assumption in all but the most superficial terms.

The proposition that bureaucracy undermines educational success is prominent in a broader research literature concerned with organizational effects on educational quality, as well as in debates surrounding centralization initiatives such as national tests and curriculum. Of most interest is the work specifically concerned with effects of bureaucracy, or increased centralized controls in American education, on teaching and learning.

Several researchers document ways in which bureaucratic controls brought about by recent educational reforms have negatively affected teaching and learning.[8] They argue that the work of teachers is becoming more routinized as state education agencies and local school systems increasingly implement standardized curricula and use standardized achievement tests to assess the performance of students, teachers, and schools. Since available texts and tests stress basic skills outcomes, teachers are pressured to use methods of "direct instruction" to teach to the objectives of minimum competency and basic skills achievement tests.[9] Consistent with the argument are test data over the past several years that show rising scores in basic skills areas but declining scores in writing, science, mathematical problem solving, and analytic reasoning.[10]

In interviews with elementary school teachers in Tennessee during the first year statewide minimum-competency testing was implemented, Susan Rosenholtz[11] found evidence that teachers do in fact alter their instructional practices in response to these policies. She found that virtually all the teachers interviewed altered the content of instruction to conform to the content of the tests. Similar findings were reported by Darling-Hammond and Wise[12] in their study of teachers' responses to districtwide testing systems. They found that standardized testing altered the curriculum content and pacing of instruction and led teachers to teach directly to the content of the tests. Studies of "competency based" education provide additional evidence of the power of bureaucratic regulation to control teaching and learning. This form of instruction, with pre- and posttests tightly linked to specific curricular objectives, prompts teachers to regard student learning as test results and to adopt fast-paced teaching directly to the test.[13]

Clearly, the state and district levels of school organization are increasingly important contexts of teaching in U.S. public schools.[14] And many states have formulated policies and accountability systems that emphasize basic skills and routine, fact-oriented instruction—controls compatible with traditional teaching practices.[15] However, a blanket condemnation of bureaucracy or centralization in education seems unwarranted on a number of grounds.

First, the content of centralized educational policies and the kinds of controls exercised are important variables unexamined by the studies we reviewed. California, for instance, has been developing state curriculum frameworks and assessments that embrace the new educational standards. Further, these new instructional standards and directives are being initiated through a "soft" control strategy—incentives as opposed to mandates, accompanied by substantial resources and local programs to support teachers' professional development. Whether or not successful, centralization of this sort is designed to challenge the kinds of routine teaching that researchers have called the product of bureaucracies and to enable teachers' capacity for professional judgment, which the researchers argue is squelched by bureaucracy.

Second, the concept of bureaucracy is richer theoretically than the researchers acknowledge, and dimensions or features of bureaucracy that can or do support teachers' professionalism and TFU are systematically ignored.[16] In this regard, the trend toward increased controls over teachers' subject and pedagogical content knowledge embraces a core principle of bureaucratic organization and a strategy, again, to enable teacher professionalism. While this strand of the current reform movement was initiated largely outside educational bureaucracies—through, most notably, the Holmes Group;[17] the Carnegie Forum on Education and the Economy;[18] and the recently established National Board for Professional Teaching Standards—the strategy assumes that school systems will implement the professional controls in hiring practices and perhaps in their own evaluation systems.[19] By establishing standards for deeper knowledge of specific subjects, this kind of bureaucratization should make it more likely that teachers will be prepared for TFU.

Further, the argument explaining educational bureaucracy as an outgrowth of democratic control misrepresents the different, multidimensional structures in which schools operate. Missing from these analyses is the important point that the more centralized systems in other countries—France, Japan, Australia, as examples— are both less governed by democracy and less bureaucraticized than ours on dimensions other than hierarchy, or centralization. The various dimensions of bureaucratic organization—hierarchy, work rules, specialization, and impersonal standards and control—can and do vary independently of one another, and of democratic principles of educational control, across educational systems.

Similarly, local school systems are not the homogeneous institution such analysts as Chubb and Moe[20] imply. The public sector embraces substantial diversity in form and function of schooling. Within America's school districts exist specialized schools, magnet schools, schools with innovative "house" structures, small schools and large schools. Democratic controls have not produced an undifferentiated public school bureaucracy. And the democratic controls to which Chubb and Moe refer differ themselves in their nature and influence within the public school system. For example, states with strong traditions of local control generate little state presence in local school policies and procedures. In contrast, states like California and New York, with their elaborated state-level frameworks, examination schedules, and curricular standards, comprise significantly different contexts for local educational decision making. Differences in collective bargaining among states and districts is another feature that engenders fundamentally different forms of democratic control. Chubb and Moe ignore, as do other analysts of this persuasion, this complexity for purposes of analytic simplification. But in doing so, they model a reality that departs in important ways from the enterprise they aim to change.

Our review of this literature has been rather discouraging, in sum. Most discouraging is how quickly researchers have moved to simplify complex problems—to isolate *the* offending variable, like bureaucracy—and to reach simple solutions that go far beyond empirical evidence, like endorsing public support for parental choice of private education. The simplicity, we believe, is in large part a product of routines and standards for research. Not unlike standards for education that enforce transmission teaching, standards for research assume simple, straightforward answers to enormously complex questions. Called upon to reach such conclusions, policy researchers generally follow the norms of social science: they conduct studies in order to "isolate" effects of particular variables. This routine often mistakes statistical significance for substantive significance. Does the statistically significant one-item difference in the reading scores of two groups really have substantive import? This research approach also inevitably leads to simple conclusions: *x* variable causes *y* outcome, after all other relevant variables are controlled, enforcing this tendency to simplify complexity and move quickly to identify *the* problems and solutions in the "bullet" market for educational research—decision makers' demand for crisp "bulleted" implications for policy from a study or line of work. In reality, the *ceteris paribus,* or "all other things being equal," assumptions of this line of research are at best problematic.

A related problem is that research traditions that place premiums on quantification and on advancing theory prompt researchers to ignore the time- and space-bound nature of their measures and findings. Abstractions of routine social science can mislead, especially when used within the highly diverse and changing context of U.S. education. For example, in our view, the effect of bureaucratization on teaching is highly conditional: it depends fundamentally on the *nature* of centralized policies and on the *interaction* of the policies with other context variables, such as local standards and norms for teaching, relevant resources, and a school's professional community.[21] Conclusions from this line of research are much too decontextualized to be of value in identifying levers to influence teaching generally or in designing contexts that promote TFU. The salience of a particular context, or a particular variable, depends on the context in which it is embedded.

Internal Organization of Schools

Another line of research concerned with context effects on teaching and learning focuses on the internal organization of schools. This work, often called "effective schools" research, has sought to isolate organization conditions that promote school success.[22] As with other research reviewed thus far, the effective schools studies rely on traditional, standardized achievement tests to measure school success, and thus their findings are not useful in understanding what school conditions can shape different *kinds* of teaching and learning and how they can shape them. Further, this line of work venerates the school as *the* focus and unit of analysis for studying how workplace structures and cultures affect teachers and teaching— thus ignoring internal contours of organization and teachers' professional communities. This tendency is consistent with the top-down bias of context-effects research, in which the administrative structure of the system defines the important layers of organization for research and policy; the school is the smallest organization unit that has an administrator.

Nevertheless, the effective schools research is useful in drawing attention to the culture of the school workplace as a critical feature of the context of teaching and learning. Regardless of what is being learned, students and teachers are much more engaged in school work when staff members share educational goals, when the principal provides teachers with resources and encouragement to improve their teaching, when teachers collaborate and share in developing practice, and when teachers and students relate to one another as persons outside the classroom context.[23]

This line of argument suggests that a strong, schoolwide community is needed to engage teachers and students in the enterprise of education. It posits school community as an important condition of educational success and has supported a substantial effective schools reform movement over the past few years.[24] However, as we note, connections between this organization variable and particular forms of teaching and learning in classrooms are highly problematic. Widespread district and school participation in effective schools programs to generate more communal forms of organization, or increased specialization among school missions in large urban districts to generate greater client commitment, are reform strategies likely to yield uneven effects on TFU in U.S. classrooms.

We also end up disappointed with this line of research as a guide to constructing environments to enable TFU or even to understanding better the important contexts of teaching. Again, the research and conclusions are too simplistic and therefore can mislead as well as lead. First, the contingencies involved in both constructing a schoolwide community and establishing this norm of educational practice are not analyzed. For example, our research suggests that strong schoolwide communities are rare indeed among public high schools. The capacity for such a community to develop seems to depend importantly on small school size or a very special, encompassing school mission; the research conclusions thus may apply more to elementary than secondary school teaching contexts.

Even under such rare conditions where distinctive school communities are found—in special mission secondary schools, such as the performing arts magnet in the CRC sample; in private schools, such as our academically selective girls' school and our school for students unsuccessful in traditional school settings; and in elementary schools with strong principals—value consensus may have nothing to do with the new standards for TFU or may even enforce traditional teaching standards. This line of research and argument fails to consider the various *kinds of school communities* that can develop under different circumstances. For example, the immediate environment of public schools—populations served, curriculum policies, teacher assignment practices—may make the construction of a school community very different from one public school to another. [25]

In the typical high school of about twelve hundred students, the *high school department* is a primary organizational context of teaching. As indicated by measures of teacher collegiality, the extent of collaboration and support among teachers in the typical high school varies substantially across high school departments in the same school. [26] Thus, departments can more or less approximate a community of colleagues and more or less support members' capacity for effective practice, sense of professional efficacy, and commitment. Whether or not a strong department community supports teacher learning and practice of TFU is yet another question and a needed complication for this line of research. Most surely, teachers need to be linked themselves or through colleagues to the wider discourse community in which TFU standards are understood and promoted.

Moreover, we are finding that teachers' collegial relations, standards for teaching, and opportunities to learn are not tightly bound by the school workplace. We see, in particular, the pivotal role that *professional networks* can play in teachers' interest and capacity to learn new forms of teaching. For example, large and growing subject area networks such as the Urban Math Collaborative and the Bay Area Writing Project have promoted the professional growth of large numbers of high school mathematics and English teachers, respectively. Teachers participating in these networks see them as critical contexts of their work and professional development.[27] Also, as evidenced by the chapters in this book, university–school collaboratives—as well as district subject specialists who participate in TFU discourse communities—play a similar role in promoting improved teaching practice among elementary school teachers. While the existence of such extraschool contexts of teachers' professional communities does not challenge the importance of the school context in supporting teachers' success, it may be that professional networks and discourse communities outside the school are more important than, or at least an influential complement to, school-based community for diffusing and enabling TFU in American classrooms. As our data show, the subject area department is also likely to be a key context for high school teachers, in that colleagues who teach the same subject can be important in sustaining and engendering enthusiasm for the subject and commitment to courses and classes on a day-to-day basis. By exalting the school community as *the* normative context of teaching, this line of research misses both more proximate and distant boundaries of teachers' professional communities that can fundamentally frame teaching practice.

Class/Student Context of Teaching

The class-level organization of elementary and secondary school teaching differs radically, with implications for the meaning of class assignment and composition for practice. School organizing norms usually keep elementary school students and teachers together for most subjects and hours of the day and divide secondary school students' and teachers' days into time periods, usually about an hour in length, devoted to particular subjects/courses and classes of students. Lines of research on the class context of primary and secondary school teaching are quite disparate and offer very different perspectives on how the class context, and particularly student composition, affects teaching practice.

A major line of research concerned with class-level effects in secondary schooling analyzes the educational consequences of student tracking, a common though not highly institutionalized practice in U.S. secondary schools.[28] Research on tracking is a long-standing tradition in the sociology of education and stratification[29] and only recently has examined teaching and learning processes across tracked high school classes.[30]

In contrast, most research on classroom instruction has been conducted by psychologists aiming to improve the design of instruction in primary and secondary school classrooms. Since findings of such research could be important for understanding teachers' judgments about classroom practice, we need to consider their messages to teachers. The key issue for us in reviewing these disparate literatures has been: what class variables influence teachers' judgments about best practice and, specifically, the likelihood of TFU? Here we consider observations from educational psychology on different learners' needs and move to the sociological analyses of classroom teaching.

What differences in students' learning needs might prompt teachers to adapt goals and practices to particular classes of students? On one hand, there is evidence that direct instruction in cognitive processes and knowledge structures can be more effective than indirect methods of teaching for lower-ability students.[31] There is also evidence that heterogeneous grouping is conducive to learning among both high- and low-ability students, or at least that homogeneous grouping is not preferable.[32] Thus if teachers were following closely the research evidence, they might adapt instruction to individuals within a class, by providing scaffolding for low-achieving students, but would not be highly influenced by class composition in defining instructional goals.

Quite apart from student ability is the issue of students' exposure to particular facts and skills in a subject area and how this might shape instructional choices. In particular, might teachers not reject TFU goals and practices because students have not mastered the basics? Educational psychology is much less ambivalent on this issue. Cognitive psychologists have challenged the sequential view of learning that places simple facts and basic skills prior to problem solving and complex understanding. In fact, research suggests that "basic" and "higher-order" instructional tasks each have their own inherent demands and that mastery of one type of task does not necessarily lead to proficiency on the other type of task.[33] Moreover, proponents of TFU argue that this instructional goal is equally appropriate for high- and low-achieving students. Research demonstrates that low-ability students can master higher-level knowledge structures and strategies if teachers adapt to include more direct instruction.[34]

Nevertheless, research in high schools indicates that teachers often hold the view that low-achieving students are "behind" and need to catch up before going on to the material and skills being mastered by high-achieving peers.[35] Field and ethnographic studies comparing high- and low-track classes document that instruction in low-track classes emphasizes rote memory and highly structured assignments, while in higher-track classes more emphasis is placed on complex tasks that require analytic thinking.[36] These findings appear to derive from two sources: teachers' adaptations to students with different achievement and motivation levels[37] and the knowledge and beliefs of teachers assigned to different classes.

Assorted evidence on patterns of teacher assignment to tracked high school classes suggests that teachers of low-track classes are relatively weaker in subject matter and pedagogical content knowledge than their higher-track counterparts, and that these differences in teachers' technical knowledge, rather than beliefs about adapting to students, may account for the differences in teaching practices across tracks in high schools.

The notion that most capable teachers are assigned to high-track versus low-track classes comes from evidence that most teachers prefer high or average classes, that teachers compete to avoid low-track classes, and that teachers' track assignment is regarded as a sign of their relative competence.[38] On average, teachers prefer highly motivated students in high-track classes or cooperative students in general-track classes to disinterested or defiant students in low-track classes. Additional data consistent with this argument

indicate that teachers assigned to low-track classes have more limited access to professional support and development opportunities
than do their colleagues.[39]

Research on classroom teaching suggests that student composition may be a powerful context for high school teaching but
much less so for elementary school teaching, at least as distinct from
the school and community context. On average, tracking of high
school classes yields different educational goals across tracked
classes and a lower tendency for teachers to embrace TFU standards
in their low-track classes, particularly in mathematics and science.[40]
And, insofar as TFU is committed to constructing knowledge
within a community of diverse learners, homogeneous grouping
which classifies students on the basis of performance standards is
inconsistent with the principles of TFU. Nevertheless, detracking
and heterogeneous grouping is not likely to promote TFU either
unless teachers are able to successfully challenge the operation of
academic status characteristics in the classroom[41] so that the level
of trust is sufficient for the development of a community of learners.

This line of work has gone further than others to specify
qualitative differences in educational outcomes of teaching and to
assess the effects of student context, on average, on teachers' goals
and practices. However, as both scholarship and policy research it
falls short of explaining more than the crudest level of effects and
policy levers. We do not understand from this research why high
school teachers have lower academic expectations for low-achieving
students—understanding essential to designing policies or programs to change expectations and practice. Our interviews with
teachers over the past few years suggest that their adaptations to
low-achieving, nontraditional high school students vary substantially—from maintaining strict standards and failing most students,
to lowering academic standards and supporting students as persons,
to adapting practice to meet student needs within high academic
standards.[42] The last adaptation is rare and should be the critical
focus of policy research aiming to improve practice.

In short, while tracking research reveals that, *on average,*
teachers set goals and practices for their classes according to the
students' prior academic achievement and motivation, it does not
explain this tendency nor the important deviations from the pat-

tern. The research evidence does not, in our view, warrant the conclusion that detracking, for example—a local policy strategy based on the evidence reviewed—will improve the educational experiences of low-achieving high school students. The intervention is likely to have a range of unanticipated consequences and highly variable effects on teaching and learning across classrooms and schools. Extrapolating from such main-effects findings to policy is highly risky when mechanisms and divergent patterns are not understood.

Finally, these lines of research take a much narrower view of the student context of teaching than do teachers and thus miss important ways in which students set the frame for teaching practice. Indeed, students are the most salient and powerful context of teaching. Students' needs, as teachers perceive them, and the constraints and opportunities they present for instructional choices shape teachers' goals, conceptions of practice, and roles in myriad ways.[43] In the next section we broaden our perspective to include some of the features of student context neglected in the context-effects research traditions.

Broader Social and Institutional Contexts of Teaching

Largely ignored in the literature are the broader social and institutional contexts of teaching that permeate each layer of the school organization context. The closer we come to understanding how high school teachers frame their instructional goals and tasks, the more we see the power of contexts outside school administrative boundaries to shape teachers' judgments about practice. Here we highlight a few such contexts that seem to matter a great deal to teachers and teaching and that can overshadow, or interact with, the organization variables analyzed in the major lines of research.

Institutional Routines and Controls from Higher Education

A consistent finding of research in high schools is that the kind of teaching called for by new standards is highly rare, even among high-track secondary-level classes; several researchers call attention to the routine character of teaching in high school classrooms.[44] Their description of schooling—as highly institutionalized, wat-

ered-down subject matter curricula and routine, transmission-
oriented pedagogy—challenges researchers to examine conditions
that constrain teaching for understanding in *most* contexts. Put
differently, we need to analyze the contexts and conditions that
enforce this teaching tradition. This understanding seems indis-
pensable to formulating strategies to enable TFU.

Interviews with teachers and observations of classes in nu-
merous high schools prompt us and other field researchers before
us to conclude that many educators conceive their work as fundamentally a matter of "implementing texts." Teachers can engage in
major battles over the selection of texts for a course or subject; the
text has become, to a significant degree, the locus for control over
the content of subject matter and pedagogy and the focus of professional debate over such matters.[45] The conception of teaching as
transmitting codified knowledge is not simply a matter of tradition,
of individuals' routines, or of public school bureaucracy, as analysts
have alternately posited. Rather, it is enforced by standards for student performance in the institutional environment of primary-
secondary education.

Dominant standards for teaching and learning in higher education are consistent with the "text delivery" model of education
and thus, on the whole, constrain instructional choices among
teachers at lower levels of the system. Teaching practices, particularly in high schools, need to be understood in the broader context
of U.S. schooling. While teachers, parents, and students aiming for
higher education may regard critical thinking, analytic tasks, and
problem solving as important,[46] their concerns over access to preferred colleges and preparation for success in terms of college grading standards may enforce traditional transmission standards for
teaching and learning. Since college entrance exams and advance
placement tests emphasize coverage of course topics,[47] they press
teachers of college-oriented high school students to embrace a
transmission-oriented pedagogy.[48]

One might note, however, that higher education institutions
are highly diverse in terms of their specific expectations for students' roles and learning. Thus they differ as well in the nature of
explicit and tacit controls they exert on primary-secondary education. A substantial literature on the cultures of higher education

institutions[49] reveals qualitative differences in their institutional mandates for primary-secondary education. We know, for example, that large state universities, Ivy League colleges, and small liberal arts colleges have rather different expectations for students' and teachers' roles and success standards. Yet this kind of diversity is largely at the margins, and most students who go on to college will be taught in large lecture classes and evaluated according to how well they master facts and knowledge transmitted. The teachers in our typical high schools and even college-preparatory private schools see their mission as preparing students to do well in such typical college contexts.[50]

Our interviews with high school teachers in a wide variety of educational contexts have taught us about the power of perceived student needs for success in college to define high school teaching standards. And with rare exceptions, higher education institutions place a premium on students' mastery of facts and reproduction of transmitted knowledge as the definition and measure of learning. These criteria of educational success are signaled and supported by college admissions standards, scale of classes and pedagogical norms, and student assessment practices common among higher-education institutions. The success of any initiative for reform of primary-secondary education will, in our view, be heavily conditioned by standards enforced in higher education. Reform in this context thus may be a key lever for advancing TFU in primary-secondary education.

Social Class and Peer Cultures

Another key context of teaching and learning is students', parents', and teachers' perceptions of the value and nature of education. These understandings apparently vary substantially by social class cultures and shape "tastes" for particular educational goals and classroom teaching strategies. For example, in a study of fifth grade instruction in five schools serving families of different occupational strata, Jean Anyon[51] found substantial differences between the schools in parents' and teachers' views about how to prepare children for later schooling and life. In schools serving students from middle- and working-class backgrounds, teachers emphasized knowledge as "received," whereas instruction in a school serving students from professional families prized creativity, and instruction in a school serving the executive elite stressed analysis of classic materials and scientific reasoning.

This research suggests that social-cultural differences in parents' and teachers' expectations for students' educational and occupational futures can substantially influence preferred content and strategies of teaching. That such differences appeared as early as the fifth grade in Anyon's study suggests that community social class is a powerful context of teachers' content-pedagogical choices. Indeed, Anyon's evidence suggests that few parents and teachers in most working- and middle-class communities would choose teaching for understanding.[52]

The role played by parents' social class and educational values in shaping teachers' choices of instructional content and pedagogy should receive much more attention by researchers and policymakers, in our view. Particularly when increased parental choice is a major direction of education policy, we need to know better how this may play out in terms of the new teaching standards. The evidence on social class "tastes" for education suggests that a specialized market for TFU may already exist among professional families, but that teachers will be constrained from learning and practicing TFU in the majority of schools of choice. This proposition suggests that an important role of policy aiming to promote the new teaching standards will be to generate a demand for this form of teaching by educating the public on the benefits and means of deeper student understanding of subject matter.

The peer culture of schools, particularly at the secondary level, is also a powerful context of teaching that can influence teachers' judgments about practice in myriad ways. This context is often thought of in organization terms, as "student discipline" or "school order." However, as with other context conditions we have discussed, the quantitative conception of student culture misses the substance of its meaning for teachers and students and therefore its effect on teaching practice. A serious analysis of the contours and variations of student context is beyond the scope of this chapter. But, suffice it to say, the substance of student cultures is a critical context for teachers who spend their days interacting with students who draw their sense of identity and frame their involvements in terms of peer relationships quite apart from their academic capacities. This domain of context has been largely ignored in the literature and we only illustrate its facets and some ways it shapes teaching.

One key facet of student culture crucial to teaching is norms about class attendance. One way of thinking about this variable is in terms of school attendance policy; another way is in terms of family and peer values regarding attendance and the value of school, more generally. We have seen in our research that attendance mandates do not create the same classroom ambience as does a peer culture that supports class attendance and that, in either case, high school students and teachers co-construct the meaning of attending a particular class. At the extreme end, student disengagement and high rates of class-cutting seriously constrain teachers' instructional choices, especially in a subject like mathematics, which assumes linear progress. In schools where neither student culture nor administrative policy enforce class attendance, teachers need to devote considerable attention and energy to developing a class culture conducive to student commitment.

Changes in student culture over recent decades are salient to most high school teachers and constitute an important historical context of teaching. Teachers in all CRC sites, including an elite academic independent school, complained that today's students simply do not read as much or as broadly as did students in the past. As a consequence, students may bring less to the classroom in terms of understandings and knowledge, and they also may be less willing to complete lengthy reading assignments. A theme common to our interviews with teachers of English and social studies was the shrinking reading list and reduced expectations for students' out-of-classroom work.

Teachers in all school settings also have said that today's students are distracted by nonschool demands to a degree that significantly affects their classroom practices. Teens from all social classes hold after-school jobs, for reasons of economic necessity or interest in keeping at the front of the adolescent fashion parade. Students from families stressed by financial concerns or by insufficient child care or other domestic supports find themselves assuming roles and responsibilities filled in previous generations of students by the nuclear or the extended family. In fact, "changed family circumstances" was the explanation offered with greatest force and frequency by teachers in urban secondary schools for the inadequate attention and insufficient interest and engagement they observe in many students. These changed family circumstances are compounded for many students by the daily pressures of community violence, gangs, drugs, or other threats to their well-being.

These conditions of today's students have fundamental consequences on teachers' decisions about what and how to teach. In many classrooms, homework undone leads to homework no longer assigned. Teachers, in sum, talk not about generic "teaching" when they discuss their conceptions of practice. They reference the values, interests, competencies, and energy students bring into a particular classroom and the implications of these student characteristics for their teaching. And their responses to similar student characteristics vary within and between schools. In some settings, apparent student indifference begets teachers' indifference or frustration and teachers' decisions either to "just flunk them" or "dumb down" the curriculum to make it easy for everyone. In others, it precipitates teacher or faculty reconsideration of practice in ways that promote teaching for understanding.[53] Teachers' responses are largely a product of the norms of practice and the nature of their up-close context, or salient professional community.[54]

Subject Matter Cultures

In many ways subject matter frames the work of teachers, particularly in secondary schools, where teachers' preparation and assignment are likely to be in a single subject, and thus represents a powerful context of teaching. As we have mentioned already, subject area departments are important workplaces for high school teachers and can become strong professional communities that support teacher learning. However, apart from defining boundaries for high school units, subject matter is a powerful context for teaching in both elementary and secondary classrooms.[55] We mention a few ways in which subject matter defines teaching contexts that can constrain or enable TFU:

- As traditions of content and pedagogy—the "stuff" of teaching
- As domains of educational policies and politics and, thus, mediators of centralization effects
- As loci for discourse communities

In our interviews and survey of high school teachers over the past three years, we have observed subject differences in conceptions of knowledge and pedagogy that have important implications for TFU. For example, mathematics teachers are more likely than teachers of other academic subjects to see their subject matter as "given," learning as "hierarchical," and their day-to-day teaching as routine. Both CRC and national survey data show that math teachers feel they have less control over the content of their classes. Further, they are less likely (and English teachers are more likely) than their colleagues to place high priority on students' personal growth as an educational goal. In short, common conceptions of subject matter, student learning, and pedagogy among mathematics teachers may generally constrain the choice and practice of TFU in this subject context.

Further, subject areas are differentially affected, both directly and indirectly, by the development of centralized educational policies. For instance, state and district reforms of student graduation requirements during the 1980s have shifted emphasis toward math and science and, indirectly, away from vocational education and other elective subjects. We have seen a variety of subject-specific effects of this shift, among them more tracking of math and science classes, declines in vocational education courses, and assignment of out-of-subject teachers to (low-track) math classes.[56] In addition, state and district curriculum frameworks are specified for subject areas, and thus their very existence, their content, and their effects on teaching are entirely mediated by the subject context. For example, mathematics teaching at primary and secondary levels may be highly regulated in a district but social science teaching may be entirely controlled by teachers. District curriculum experts and instructional support staff also are defined along subject lines; and the quality of professional support provided in a particular district can be highly variable by subject. Subjects are important media for policy effects and for teachers' instructional support, making them strategic contexts for analyzing policy and system effects on teaching.

Finally, subject areas are important contexts for the development of discourse communities within which TFU, or other forms of teaching, can be defined and sustained. The ongoing collaborations between university researchers and primary school teachers that are the subject of previous chapters are constructed in the context of subject matter. Indeed, this is the most vital context for developing professional communities capable of enabling and sustaining TFU, given the focal point of subject matter in this form of practice. Just as students and teachers construct subject matter in TFU classes, teachers construct together the meaning of teaching in the context of specific subject matter and classes, like how to guide the learning of longitude and latitude. We regard subject matter as a critical context—as source and substance—for discourse communities capable of diffusing, realizing, and enforcing the new teaching standards.

Embedded Contexts of Teaching

Our journey through the literature and three years of research with teachers in highly diverse settings has led us to a view of teaching as permeated by multiple layers of context, each of which has the capacity to significantly shape educational practice. We conclude that the important contexts of teaching are much more varied, embedded, and interactive in their effects on teaching practice than assumed by relevant lines of research. The schema summarizes the multiple and embedded educational contexts that together shape teaching goals and practices in secondary and elementary schools.

Because our research systematically pursued the perspective of classroom teachers, rather than hypotheses derived from the discipline-framed research, we were able to isolate factors previously neglected in prior research. Our bottom–up strategy of analysis revealed the salience and power for teachers of taken-for-granted contexts, such as success standards in higher education, and taught us limits of social science research routines for understanding context effects on teaching.

Figure 6.1. Multiple and Embedded Contexts of Teaching.

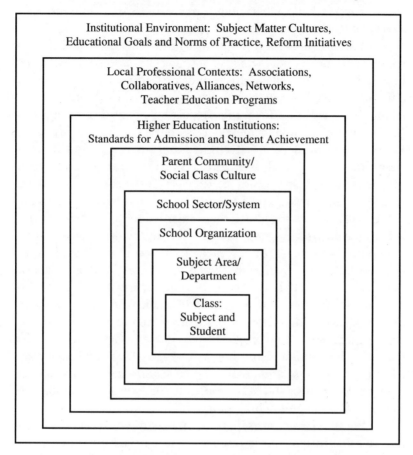

The teacher's-eye view allowed us to see multiple contexts of teaching simultaneously—as a symphony or cacophony of directives toward any particular goals and standards for teaching. By designing our research to capture important contrasts and commonalities across teaching contexts—systematically varying school sector and state policy, district resources, school mission, and student composition—we were able to see the interplay of multiple contexts in teachers' day-to-day work lives and conceptions of practice. Through the multiple lens provided by teachers in distinctly different classes, subjects, departments, schools, districts, and states and with different levels and kinds of professional ties outside the job, we came to see that context conditions are highly interactive in their effects on teaching practice.

The main-effects findings of context-effects research fail to specify conditions under which an average effect is observed and can thus misrepresent context effects and mislead policy. The average effect of a context variable may, for example, conceal radically different effects within different (embedded) contexts. For example, a CRC analysis of school context effects on teacher community using High School and Beyond (HS&B) national survey data revealed opposite effects of school and district size in suburban and urban school contexts.[57] In a study of teachers' instructional objectives, Raudenbush, Rowan, and Cheong[58] found that math teachers are much more likely to adjust their instruction to students' prior achievement, with less emphasis on TFU in low-level classes, than are English and social studies teachers (subject by class/student interaction). Further, we find that teachers in strong, collegial departments are less likely than their colleagues in weak departments to view low-achieving students as problematic and more likely to maintain strong commitment to teaching, even to reject traditional teaching methods in favor of TFU to enable students' success (department by class/student interaction). In short, understanding context effects on teaching requires a view of the conditional nature of any context effect and of the multiple contexts that combine and interact to influence teaching practice.[59]

Put differently, the salience or power of one or another context variable in affecting a teacher's instructional goals and practices depends on conditions in which it is embedded. Extending the earlier example, the power of a strong department or a principal leader to affect teaching may be much greater in a school or class setting in which students are not succeeding under traditional education routines. To understand teaching in context is to understand the interplay of the multiple, embedded contexts of education in the daily lives of teachers.

Implications for Policy Research

The centrality of context to teachers' conception of their work, to the development of classroom practices, and to TFU together with the limits of "average effects" findings for formulating policy suggest several implications for policy research.

First, refined conceptions and measures of context variables that correspond with teachers' realities and that matter to TFU are needed to provide valid representations of conditions of teaching and their effects on educational outcomes. As illustrated for the school community and bureaucratization variables, qualitative differences are as important as quantitative variation in specifying context conditions. Field-based understandings of diverse meanings and manifestations of a particular context variable such as faculty goal consensus will be essential in meeting this challenge.

Second, policy researchers need to think strategically about the contributions and limits of survey research and field-based research. In the past, policy research has focused too much (and sometimes mistakenly) on estimating average effects of particular variables across widely diverse settings and too little on examining and understanding the conditions and processes whereby the multiple contexts of teaching influence teaching and learning for better or worse.

Survey research, with refined measures of both outcomes and context conditions, can provide important information on the *distributions* of key teaching and learning variables and their context correlates in particular *historical* periods. Further, breakdowns of large survey samples into particular *kinds of settings,* such as subject contexts of teachers or metropolitan status of schools, can be helpful in assessing conditional relations. In addition, we have found that survey data on school and department culture, leadership, and educational goals and processes are useful for developing summary institutional "profiles" of secondary schools that depict diversity in educational environments and suggest strategic differences and similarities among schools with common clientele, goals, or management issues. And, by linking such case profiles to national survey measures of teaching conditions, it is possible to further locate field sites in relation to national distributions and norms.

Field-based research can provide important interpretative analysis and identify why and how diverse aspects of school context influence teaching and learning. Research of this order provides critical complement and explanation to survey findings. Field-based research attends to the ways in which broader influences such as state or local curriculum policies, policies concerning student assignment and promotion, or shifts in the broader political economy work through and within the school context to shape classroom activities and outcomes.

These important questions are beyond the reach of survey methods and essential to policymakers' and practitioners' understanding of context effects on teaching. For example, case studies of classrooms, teachers, schools and school systems are needed to obtain evidence on the co-occurrence of, and *complex interactions* among, context conditions that support or undermine particular educational outcomes such as teaching for understanding. Qualitative, field-based research can illuminate the everyday meanings of context that are most salient to teachers as they construct practice in particular educational settings. Qualitative research also can reveal the *processes* through which context conditions enable or constrain teachers' learning and practice of TFU.

The importance of context to practice also underscores the potential of research to help policymakers and practitioners to gain a better conception of what teaching for understanding in fact *is,* and to learn about the conditions that enable or constrain it. While many policymakers acknowledge the value of TFU and the need to develop higher-order thinking skills for students,[60] they also struggle with what these notions mean in practice and the ways in which policy can support them. Policy research that provides contextualized understanding and interpretation can contribute to policymakers' understanding of how this form of education is learned and adopted by teachers and students and begin to identify levers for change.

Likewise for practitioners, policy research that attends to context can support efforts to rethink or reform practice. Practitioners benefited little from policy studies that presented only aggregate statistics and decontextualized summary findings. Teachers and administrators learn best from the experience of other practitioners or opportunities to understand practice in context.[61] Field-based studies of teaching for understanding in context can facilitate practitioners' learning about alternatives to existing practices and their understanding of how such practices might be carried out in their own settings.

However, to fulfill this potential, policy research itself must be sensitive to context. Most lines of research on promising practice or on school effects have ignored those contexts that teachers say are most critical to their practices and beliefs—subject area and students. Research needs to address the ways in which TFU is constructed of and in context. We are coming to see, for example, how teaching for understanding in English departs in some elemental ways from TFU in mathematics. [62] And the challenges and substance of TFU in classes filled with academically motivated and successful students are quite different from those in classes where student mobility is high, where English skills are limited, or where academic motivation is low. Teaching does not take place in generic classrooms stripped of subject matter concerns or mindless of the backgrounds, needs, and interests of the students who make up a class. Teachers need to understand alternatives to existing practices not just in context generally but in contexts specific to their schools and classrooms.

Similarly, both teachers and administrators ask for evidence that new practices "can work here" and concrete information about how to transform their practices in ways that are consistent with teaching and learning for understanding. Policy research carried out in "boutique" schools with special resources or advantages, as opposed to "typical" or difficult school settings, does little to convince educators that the promising practices or reforms reported can be implemented or will "work" in their settings. Likewise, policy research that focuses on outcomes but fails to describe and interpret the processes of transformation—how the teachers and administrators under study were able to change their practices and accomplish the positive outcomes reported—gives practitioners little explicit help in planning their own changes or confidence that they could in fact "get there from here."

In the absence of such information, practitioners' decisions to stick with known practice are understandable. Yet without support from policy research that attends to specific salient contexts, the kinds of learning assumed by teaching for understanding are attenuated or confined to settings where practitioners are able to observe TFU directly. Policy research thus can play a strategic role in supporting systemic change in practice by describing, interpreting, and broadcasting contextualized examples of the teaching and learning activities reformers pursue.

Without strategies to describe, analyze, and circulate contextualized examples of effective practices, it is likely that many policymakers and practitioners still "won't get it," and efforts at reform will continue to produce islands of excellence while most classrooms, schools, and districts continue with the questionably effective but familiar strategies of the past.

To be most useful, policy research also must attend to the *embedded* character of the multiple contexts that shape practice and educational outcomes. As our discussion highlights, the attitudes and practices of actors in any one level of the system—classroom, school, district, as examples—are conditioned by the activities and attitudes of actors in other parts of the system. Policy research that takes a *systemic perspective* can help identify the different levers and resources available in different parts of the system and the ways in which they can work together to enable teaching for understanding (or, conversely, the ways in which actions in one component of the system constrain actors in other system segments).

Finally, research that informs policies to support more productive learning environments—teaching for understanding—can exploit the necessarily indirect relationship between policy and practice that long has frustrated reformers.[63] Policies work through and within the contexts in which they are carried out;[64] policy research, by extension, could aim to understand and influence those contexts as a way to influence practice. Policy research of this stripe moves away from sole focus on questions of "what works" or efforts to influence policy directly to examine aspects of the contexts of practice that constrain or enable desired policy outcomes, or in this case, teaching for understanding.

Notes

1. The CRC began its research program in October 1987. Its study design integrates three years of field research in sixteen public and private high schools in two states and analyses of

national survey data from the High School & Beyond (HS & B) and the NELS: 88 programs.

2. The notion of "context effect" implies that conditions in a particular context—for example, the policies, resources, course structures, shared goals, norms, routines, and social relations in the school context—influence teaching and learning outcomes. Since much of this research is quantitative, context conditions are generally conceived as variables that describe differences among teaching settings, and their effects on variation in educational outcomes are estimated. As we discuss later, however, conditions in American education that *do not* vary across settings can have powerful effects on teaching and learning; the quantitative traditions of much of the context-effects research has meant that taken-for-granted, invariant conditions of teaching often remain unanalyzed.

3. See Chapter One and the works listed in the references for discussion of the new standards for instruction. Here we only highlight key features of this form of practice.

4. Cohen & Spillane, 1992.

5. See Chubb & Moe (1990); Coleman & Hoffer (1987); and Coleman, Hoffer, & Kilgore (1982).

6. For critiques of the early studies see *Sociology of Education* (1982, 1983); Haertel & Levin (1987); and James & Levin (1988). See Glass, G. V. (1991) and Witte (1990) for critiques of Chubb and Moe's recent study.

7. Chubb & Moe, 1990.

8. See, for example, Darling-Hammond & Wise (1985); McNeil (1983); and McNeil (1987).

9. For a review, see Rowan (1990); also see Talbert, McLaughlin, & Rowan (1992) for further discussion of the literature and arguments regarding bureaucracy in U.S. education.

10. Darling-Hammond & Wise, 1985.

11. Rosenholtz, 1987, 534–562.

12. Darling-Hammond & Wise, 1985.

13. Darling-Hammond & Wise, 1985.

14. Cf. Cohen, 1990.

15. As Cohen and Barnes note in Chapter Seven, the back-to-basics movement of the 1980s was successful, in part, because

it was consistent with traditional standards for teaching practice. It is not at all clear that instructional practices changed in qualitative ways under these policies, as some researchers have argued, even though teachers experienced pressure from bureaucratic regulation.

16. Weber, 1924/1947.

17. Holmes Group, 1990.

18. Carnegie Forum on Education and the Economy, 1986.

19. The Interstate Consortium for New Teacher Assessment and Support, founded four years ago by California and Connecticut with NGA funding and now housed with the CCSSO, is evidence that the new standards for teacher certification are being embraced and gradually adopted by state education authorities. The line between bureaucratic organization and professional control in education is blurry indeed; in fact, one could argue that bureaucracy is a necessary vehicle to enhance professionalism in teaching.

20. Chubb & Moe, 1990.

21. For example, we find in our research that public school teachers vary substantially between high schools and departments within schools in their perceptions of bureaucratic controls within the same state and district. The differences are substantially a matter of principal leadership and the extent to which the department or school functions as a professional community.

22. See Purkey & Smith (1983) for review and discussion of this tradition.

23. In addition to Purkey & Smith (1983), see Bryk & Driscoll (1988); McLaughlin, Talbert, Kahne, & Powell (1990); Newmann (1990); and Rutter, Maughan, Mortimore, Outson, & Smith (1979).

24. U.S. General Accounting Office, 1989.

25. See McLaughlin (1990) and Talbert, Eaton, Ennis, Fletcher, & Tsai (1990); see Anyon (1981) for evidence of diverse instructional cultures among elementary schools.

26. See Talbert (1991). Four out of eight regular public schools in the CRC sample had departments scoring in both the top and

the bottom quartiles of a national distribution of school averages on an index of faculty collegiality.

27. Lichtenstein, McLaughlin, & Knudsen, 1991; Lieberman & McLaughlin, in press.

28. See Garet & DeLany (1988) for evidence of the messiness of high schools' tracking practices.

29. Cf. Alexander, Cook, & McDill (1978); Hallinan (1990); Jencks and others (1972); and Rosenbaum (1976).

30. Cf. Gamoran (1986; 1987); Hallinan (1990); and Oakes (1985).

31. Cf. Cronbach & Snow (1977); Doyle (1983); and Snow (1989). One explanation for this effect is that lower-ability students and novices in a particular subject area lack general command of the independent learning skills and strategies needed to formulate their own solutions to tasks presented under conditions of indirect instruction.

32. See Slavin (1990) for extensive review of this literature.

33. See Becker & Gerstein (1982); Brown & Campione (1977, 1980); Greeno (1991a); Greeno, Smith, & Moore (1991); and Mayer & Greeno (1972).

34. See Brown & Campione (1977); Carnine & Stein (1981); Hansen (1981); Lloyd (1980); Rubin (1980); and Scardamalia, Bereiter, & Woodruff (1982).

35. See Oakes (1985); Rosenbaum (1976); and Wilson & Schmits (1978).

36. See Hargreaves (1967); Metz (1978); and Oakes (1985).

37. Metz (1978, pp. 103–106) analyzed rationales for teachers' emphasis on simplified and slow-paced instruction for low-track classes that focused entirely on student motivation. Some teachers regarded this instructional approach as a way to maintain classroom order, especially because routine work often kept unruly students busy. Some said that routine work responded to students' preferences for undemanding and private work.

38. See Finley (1984) and Rosenbaum (1976) for evidence in U.S. schools; see Ball (1981), Burgess (1983), Hargreaves (1967), and Lacey (1970) for data from British schools.

39. See Finley (1984) and Talbert (1990).

40. Raudenbush, Rowan, & Cheong, in press.

41. Cf. Rosenholtz (1984); Rosenholtz & Simpson (1984); and Webb & Kenderski (1983).

42. McLaughlin, Talbert, & Phelan, 1990.

43. McLaughlin, in press.

44. See Goodlad (1984); McNeil (1986); Oakes (1985); and Powell, Farrar, & Cohen (1985).

45. The power of curricular materials to constrain teaching and thus to engender significant professional struggles among teachers has surfaced in our research. In one CRC school, the foreign language department split into two warring factions over approaches and preferable texts for language learning. Likewise, physics teachers in a district came to blows over decisions on text adoption, pitting texts consistent with a transmission model of subject instruction against one more consistent with TFU. (The latter lost, by the way.) Decisions about the goals and content of instruction are framed significantly by text publishers' sense of demand and by administrators' or teacher committees' preferences for alternative instructional approaches.

46. Hargreaves, 1967, and Oakes, 1985.

47. Burgess, 1983, and Oakes, 1985.

48. Although teachers in the academically selective girls' school in our field sample were most articulate about this constraint on TFU, teachers of high-track classes in public schools also complained of pressure to cover content tested on AP exams.

49. Cf. Clark (1970) & Clark (1983).

50. A social studies teacher in a typical California high school, for example, proudly described a "good class session" as one in which all the students are taking notes in good outline form. This, he saw, would be a critical skill for their success in their [large lecture] college classes.

51. Anyon, 1981.

52. See also Hemmings & Metz (1990) and Metz (1990, 1991).

53. McLaughlin, Talbert, & Phelan, 1990.

54. McLaughlin, 1990; and Talbert, in press.

55. Susan Stodolsky, University of Chicago, and Pamela Grossman, University of Washington, have been conducting focused research on subject matter as context with funding from

CRC and the Spencer Foundation. See Stodolsky & Grossman (1992) for initial findings from this research.

56. This effect is especially apparent in comparisons between CRC schools in California and Michigan. In the latter state, where educational reform has been slower and less ambitious, the demand for subjects has been relatively stable in recent years and we have not seen the mass reassignment of teachers out of vocational and other subjects into math and science.
57. Hannaway & Talbert, 1991.
58. Raudenbush, Rowan, & Cheong, in press.
59. See Ragin (1987) for systematic discussion of differences between variable-based and case-based strategies of research and theory development. The latter approach, relatively rare in the social sciences, examines effects of coincident context conditions on outcomes of interest and promises to be more fruitful for formulating teaching policy than traditional research assumptions and methods.
60. See America 2000 (1991), for example.
61. Shedd & Bacharach, 1991.
62. See Grossman (in press) and Stodolsky (in press).
63. Cohen, 1988.
64. Fullan, 1990; McLaughlin, 1987.

References

Alexander, K. L., Cook M. A., & McDill, E. L. (1978). Curriculum tracking and educational stratification. *American Sociological Review, 43*, 47–66.

America 2000. (1991). *An educational strategy to move the American educational system ahead to meet the needs of the 21st century.* Washington, DC: U.S. Department of Education.

Anyon, J. (1981). Social class and school knowledge. *Curriculum Inquiry, 11*, 3–41.

Ball, S. J. (1981). *Beachside comprehensive: A case-study of secondary schooling.* Cambridge: Cambridge University Press.

Becker, W. C., & Gerstein, R. (1982). A follow-up of follow through: The later effects of the direct instruction model on children in fifth and sixth grades. *American Educational Research Journal, 19*, 75–92.

Brown, A. L., & Campione, J. C. (1977). *Memory strategies in learning: Training children to study strategically* (Tech. Rep. No. 22). Urbana: University of Illinois, Center for the Study of Reading.

Brown, A. L., & Campione, J. C. (1980). *Inducing flexible thinking: Problem of access* (Tech. Rep. No. 156). Urbana: University of Illinois, Center for the Study of Reading.

Brown, J. S., Collins, A., & Duguid, P. (1989). Situated cognition and the culture of learning. *Educational Researcher, 18*(1), 32–42.

Bryk, A., & Driscoll, M. E. (1988). *An empirical investigation of the school as community.* Chicago: University of Chicago, School of Education.

Burgess, R. G. (1983). *Experiencing comprehensive education: A study of Bishop McGregor School.* London: Methuen.

Carnegie Forum on Education and the Economy. (1986). *A nation prepared: Teachers for the twenty-first century.* New York: Carnegie Corporation.

Carnine, D. W., & Stein, M. (1981). Strategy and organizational practice procedures for teaching basic facts. *Journal for Research in Mathematics Education, 12,* 65–69.

Chubb, J. E., & Moe, T. E. (1990). *Politics, markets and America's schools.* Washington, DC: The Brookings Institution.

Clark, B. R. (1970). *The distinctive college: Antioch, Reed, and Swarthmore.* Chicago: Aldine.

Clark, B. R. (1983). *The higher education system.* Berkeley: University of California Press.

Cohen, D. K. (1988). Teaching practice, Plus ça change. . . . In P. W. Jackson (Ed.), *Contributing to educational change* (pp. 27–84). Berkeley, CA: McCutchan Publishing Corporation.

Cohen, D. K. (1990). *Policy and practice: The classroom impact of state and federal education policy.* East Lansing: Michigan State University.

Cohen, D. K., & Spillane, J. P. (1992, April). Policy and practice: The relations between governance and instruction. Review of Research in Education. Washington, DC: American Educational Research Association.

Coleman, J. S., & Hoffer, T. (1987). *Public and private high schools: The impact of communities.* New York: Basic Books.

Coleman, J. S., Hoffer, T., & Kilgore, S. D. (1982). *High school achievement: Public, private, and Catholic schools compared.* New York: Basic Books.

Cronbach, L. J., & Snow, R. E. (1977). *Aptitudes and instructional methods: A handbook for research on interactions.* New York: Irvington.

Darling-Hammond, L., & Wise, A. E. (1985). Beyond standardization: State standards and school improvement. *The Elementary School Journal, 85*(3), 315–356.

Doyle, W. (1983). Academic work. *Review of Educational Research, 53*(2), 159–199.

Finley, M. K. (1984). Teachers and tracking in a comprehensive high school. *Sociology of Education, 57,* 233–243.

Fullan, M. (1990). *The new meaning of educational change.* New York: Teachers College Press.

Gamoran, A. (1986). Instructional and institutional effects of ability grouping. *Sociology of Education, 59,* 185–198.

Gamoran, A. (1987). The stratification of high school. *Sociology of Education, 60,* 135–155.

Garet, M., & DeLany, B. (1988). Students, courses, and stratification. *Sociology of Education, 61,* 661–677.

Glass, G. V. (1991). Are data enough? *Educational Researcher, 20*(3), 24–27.

Glass, J. S., Collins, A., & Duguid, P. (1989). Situated cognition and the culture of learning. *Educational Researcher, 18*(1), 32–42.

Goodlad, J. I. (1984). *A place called school.* New York: McGraw-Hill.

Greeno, J. G. (1991a). Mathematical and scientific thinking in classrooms and other situations. In D. Halpern (Ed.), *Enhancement of higher-order thinking in science and mathematics education.* Hillsdale, NJ: Erlbaum.

Greeno, J. G. (1991b). Number sense as situated knowing in a conceptual domain. *Journal for Research in Mathematics Education, 22,* 170–218.

Greeno, J. G., Smith, D. R., & Moore, J. L. (1991). Transfer of situated learning. In D. Detterman & R. Sternberg (Eds.), *Transfer on trial.* Hillsdale, NJ: Erlbaum.

Grossman, P. L. (1992). English as context: English in context (Series paper). In M. W. McLaughlin, J. Knudsen, & J. Talbert (Eds.), *Content as context*. Stanford, CA: Stanford University, Center for Research on the Context of Secondary School Teaching.

Haertel, E. H., & Levin, H. M. (Eds.). (1987). *Comparing public and private schools: School achievement*. New York: Falmer Press.

Hallinan, M. T. (1990). The effects of ability grouping in secondary schools: A response to Slavin's best-evidence synthesis. *Review of Educational Research, 60,* 501–504.

Hannaway, J., & Talbert, J. E. (1991). *Bringing context into effective schools research: Urban-suburban differences* (Paper no. 91–137). Stanford, CA: Stanford University: Center for Research on the Context of Secondary School Teaching.

Hansen, J. (1981). The effects of inference framing and practice on young children's reading comprehension. *Reading Research Quarterly, 16,* 391–417.

Hargreaves, D. H. (1967). *Social relations in a secondary school.* London: C. Tinling.

Hemmings, A., & Metz, M. H. (1990). Real teaching: How high school teachers negotiate societal, local community, and student pressures when they define their work. In R. Page & L. Valli (Eds.), *Curriculum differentiation* (pp. 91–111). Albany: State University of New York Press.

Holmes Group. (1990). *Restructuring schools.* San Francisco: Jossey-Bass.

James, T., & Levin, H. M. (Eds.). (1988). *Comparing public and private schools: Institutions and organizations.* New York: Falmer Press.

Jencks, C. S., Smith, M., Acland, H., Bane, M. J., Cohen, D., Gintis, H., Heynes, B., & Michelson, S. (1972). *Inequality: A reassessment of the effect of family and schooling in America.* New York: Basic Books.

Lacey, C. (1970). *Hightown Grammar.* Manchester, NH: Manchester University Press.

Lampert, M. (1988). What can research on teacher education tell us about improving quality in mathematics education? *Teacher and Teacher Education, 4*(2), 157–170.

Lichtenstein, G., McLaughlin, M., & Knudsen, J. (1991). *Teacher empowerment and professional knowledge.* Stanford, CA: Department of Education, Stanford University.

Lieberman, A., & McLaughlin, M. (in press). Networks for educational change: Powerful and problematic. *Phi Delta Kappan.*

Lloyd, J. (1980). Academic instruction and cognitive behavior modification: The need for attack strategy training. *Exceptional Education Quarterly, 1,* 53–63.

Mayer, R. E., & Greeno, J. G. (1972). Structural differences between learning outcomes produced by different instructional methods. *Journal of Educational Psychology, 63,* 165–173.

McLaughlin, M. (1987). Learning from experience: Lessons from policy implementation. *Educational Evaluation and Policy Analysis, 9,* 171–178.

McLaughlin, M. W. (1990). *Strategic dimensions of teachers' workplace context* (Paper no. 90-119). Stanford, CA: Stanford University, Center for Research on the Context of Secondary School Teaching.

McLaughlin, M. W. (1991). *Strategic sites for teachers' professional development* (Paper no. 91-132). Stanford, CA: Stanford University, Center for Research on the Context of Secondary School Teaching.

McLaughlin, M. W. (in press). What matters most in teachers' workplace context. In J. W. Little & M. W. McLaughlin (Ed.), *Teachers, communities, and contexts.* New York: Teachers College Press.

McLaughlin, M. W., Talbert, J. E., Kahne, J., & Powell, J. (1990). *Constructing a personalized school environment* (Paper no. 90-115). Stanford, CA: Stanford University, Center for Research on the Context of Secondary School Teaching.

McLaughlin, M. W., Talbert, J. E., & Phelan, P. (1990). *1990 CRC report to field sites.* Stanford, CA: Stanford University, Center for Research on the Context of Secondary School Teaching.

McNeil, L. (1983). Defensive teaching and classroom control. In M. Apple & L. Weis (Eds.), *Ideology and practice in schooling.* (pp. 114–142). Philadelphia: Temple University Press.

McNeil, L. M. (1986). *Contradictions of control: School structure and school knowledge.* New York: Routledge & Kegan Paul.

McNeil, L. (1987). Exit, voice and community: Magnet teachers' responses to standardization. *Educational Policy, 1*(1), 93–113.

Metz, M. H. (1978). *Classrooms and corridors: The crisis of author-*

ity in desegregated secondary schools. Berkeley: University of California Press.

Metz, M. H. (1990). How social class differences shape teachers' work. In M. McLaughlin, J. E. Talbert, & N. Bascia (Eds.), *The contexts of teaching in secondary schools* (pp. 40–107). New York: Teachers College Press.

Metz, M. H. (1991). Real school: A universal drama amid disparate experience. In D. Mitchell & M. Goertz (Eds.), *Education politics for the new century: The twentieth anniversary yearbook of the politics of education association.* Philadelphia: Falmer Press.

Newmann, F. M. (1990). Higher-order thinking in teaching social studies: A rationale for the assessment of classroom thoughtfulness. *Journal of Curriculum Studies, 89,* 541–554.

Oakes, J. (1985). *Keeping track: How schools structure inequality.* New Haven: Yale University Press.

Peterson, P. L., Fennema, E., & Carpenter, T. (1991). Using children's mathematical knowledge. In B. Means, C. Chelemer, & M. S. Knapp (Eds.), *Models for teaching advanced skills to disadvantaged students* (pp. 68–101). San Francisco: Jossey-Bass.

Powell, A., Farrar, E., & Cohen, D. (1985). *The shopping mall high school.* Boston: Houghton Mifflin.

Purkey, S. C., & Smith, M. S. (1983). Effective schools: A review. *Elementary School Journal, 83*(4), 427–452.

Ragin, C. C. (1987). *The comparative method: Moving beyond qualitative and quantitative strategies.* Berkeley: University of California Press.

Raudenbush, S. W., Rowan, B., & Cheong, Y. F. (in press). *Teaching for higher-order thinking in secondary schools: Effects of curriculum, teacher preparation, and school organization.* Stanford, CA: Stanford University, Center for Research on the Context of Secondary School Teaching.

Rosenbaum, J. E. (1976). *Making inequality.* New York: Wiley.

Rosenholtz, S. J. (1984). Treating problems of academic status. In J. Berger & M. Zelditch (Eds.), *Studies in expectation states theory.* San Francisco: Jossey-Bass.

Rosenholtz, S. J. (1987). Education reform strategies: Will they increase teacher commitment? *American Journal of Education, 95*(4), 534–562.

Rosenholtz, S. J., & Simpson, C. (1984). The formation of ability conceptions: Developmental trend or social construction? *Review of Educational Research, 54,* 31–63.

Rowan, B. (1990). Commitment and control: Alternative strategies for the organizational design of schools. In C. B. Cazden (Ed.), *Review of Research in Education* (Vol. 16, pp. 353–389). Washington, DC: American Educational Research Association.

Rubin, A. (1980). *Making stories, making sense* (Reading Education Rep. No. 14). Urbana: University of Illinois, Center for the Study of Reading.

Rutter, M., Maughan, B., Mortimore, P., Outson, J., & Smith, A. (1979). *Fifteen thousand hours: Secondary schools and their effects on children.* Cambridge: Harvard University Press.

Scardamalia, M., Bereiter, C., & Woodruff, E. (1982). *Functional and stylistic choices in computer-assisted instruction.* Washington, DC: American Educational Research Association.

Shavelson, R. J., McDonnell, L. M., Oakes, J., & Carey, N. (1987). *Indicator systems for monitoring mathematics and science education.* Santa Monica, CA: RAND Corporation.

Shedd, J. B., & Bacharach, S. B. (1991). *Tangled hierarchies.* San Francisco: Jossey-Bass.

Slavin, R. E. (1990). Achievement effects of ability grouping in secondary schools: A best-evidence synthesis. *Review of Educational Research, 60,* 471–500.

Snow, R. E. (1989). Aptitude-treatment interaction as a framework for research on learning and individual differences. In P. L. Ackerman (Ed.), *Learning and individual differences.* New York: W. H. Freeman.

Sociology of Education. (1982). *55*(2/3).

Sociology of Education. (1983). *56*(4).

Stodolsky, S. S. (1992). A framework for subject matter comparisons in high schools (Series paper). In M. W. McLaughlin, J. Knudsen, & J. E. Talbert (Eds.), *Content as context.* Stanford, CA: Stanford University, Center for Research on the Context of Secondary School Teaching.

Stodolsky, S. S., & Grossman, P. (1992, April). *Subject matter as content.* Paper presented at the annual meeting of the American Educational Research Association, San Francisco.

Talbert, J. E. (1990). *Teacher tracking: Exacerbating inequalities in the high school* (Paper no. 90–121). Stanford, CA: Stanford University, Center for Research on the Context of Secondary School Teaching.

Talbert, J. E. (1991). *Boundaries of teachers' professional communities in U.S. high schools* (Paper no. 91–130). Stanford, CA; Stanford University, Center for Research on the Context of Secondary School Teaching.

Talbert, J. (in press). Constructing a school-wide professional community: The negotiated order of a performing arts school. In J. W. Little & M. W. McLaughlin (Eds.), *Teachers' cultures and contexts.* New York: Teachers College Press.

Talbert, J. E., Eaton, M., Ennis, M., Fletcher, S., & Tsai, C. S. (1990). *Goal diversity among U.S. high schools: Trade-offs with academic excellence* (Paper no. 90–2). Stanford, CA: Stanford University, Center for Research on the Context of Secondary School Teaching.

Talbert, J. E., McLaughlin, M. W., & Rowan, B. (1993). *Understanding context effects on secondary school teaching.* Stanford, CA: Stanford University, Center for Research on the Context of Secondary School Teaching.

U.S. General Accounting Office. (1989). *Effective schools programs: Their extent and characteristics.* (GAO/HRD-89-132BR)

Webb, N., & Kenderski, C. M. (1983). Student interaction and learning in small-group and whole-class settings. In P. L. Peterson, L. C. Wildinson, & M. Hallinan (Eds.), *The social context of instruction: Group organization and group processes.* San Diego, CA: Academic Press.

Weber, M. (1947). *The theory of social and economic organization.* New York: Free Press. (Original work published 1924.)

Wilson, D., & Schmits, P. (1978). What's new in ability grouping? *Phi Delta Kappan, 59,* 535–536.

Witte, J. F. (1990, September). Understanding high school achievement: After a decade of research, do we have any confident policy recommendations? Paper presented at the meeting of the American Political Science Association, San Francisco.

7

Pedagogy and Policy

David K. Cohen
Carol A. Barnes

Much has been written about educational policy, but little has been written about how policy educates. That is curious, for nearly any policy must be educative for those who enact it.[1] Policymakers may not intend such education, and in fact often are blissfully ignorant of the learning that their creations entail for enactors. But policies and programs regularly propose novel purposes. If they did not, they would be completely redundant.[2] Some learning is required to achieve any new purpose, and that would be impossible without some education, even if it is only hasty self-education on the job.

These points hold for policies of all sorts. It is relatively easy to see that very innovative policies would require considerable education for enactors. For example, recent efforts to transform mathematics instruction from rote memorization to deep understanding would require extraordinary learning for most elementary school teachers. After all, they know only a little mathematics and seem to understand less. More important, the math that these teachers know usually is routine and algorithmic rather than deeply understood. The recent policies seek to remedy the consequences for children of teachers' weak knowledge. But teachers could hardly help children to cultivate a much deeper and more complex understanding of mathematics unless they learned a different version of math themselves. And few could learn something so different without considerable education.

Even much more prosaic policies require learning. When states reduced the speed limit to 55 miles per hour, motorists who had been in the habit of driving much faster had to learn to keep their speed down. Such learning was required even though drivers already knew, as a technical matter, how to slow a car down. Theirs may not have been very complex learning. Perhaps they had only to teach themselves to monitor the speedometer more carefully, or to begin their trips earlier. Simple though such things may be, each entails a bit of learning. And as many ticketed speeders can attest, such simple learning can be quite difficult. States and localities increasingly have organized driver reeducation programs to encourage the requisite learning.

Hence learning for enactors is essential, whether or not policies and programs recognize the need for it. Most policies and programs at least tacitly recognize an educational need, as they offer regulations, guidelines, and the like. We might regard these as the most rudimentary curricula of policy. They sometimes include step-by-step manuals for learning; they typically explicate the meaning of key terms; and they often define acceptable interpretations. In some cases the need for instruction is quite explicitly recognized, as when policymakers offer enactors formal "training" or "technical assistance."

But that sort of education may be only a beginning. The ambitious changes in mathematics instruction mentioned above would require much more extensive teacher learning. In contrast, many other policies are thought to have no educational requirements because they demand only "compliance." Title VI of the 1964 Civil Rights Act required that federal funds be cut off if public agencies practiced discrimination, a provision that proved to be a potent tool in southern school desegregation. Regulations, guidelines, and other technical guides to learning played a key role in enacting this policy. But as it happened, legal and administrative compliance required considerable learning of rather different sorts, and often quite extraordinary education as well. For example, federal officials had to learn how to use Title VI to produce desegregation rather than die-hard resistance, damaging political explosions, and enforcement failures.[3] Many local officials also had to learn their own version of these things if they wished to defuse local political dynamite. In those troubled years, when few white Americans had any experience with the enforcement of constitutional guarantees for African-Americans, such learning was no simple matter. Compliance with Title VI also required that many students of both races learn to go to school together, for if schools collapsed in race riots compliance would be impossible. Many local educators also had to learn how to tolerate biracial schooling, and even how to encourage and support it. At a time when few Americans had any experience with equal-status contact between the races, such learning was an extraordinary task for Americans of all sorts. Yet it was essential for the enactment of a policy that seemed only to seek legal compliance.[4]

Our examples suggest that if the education of enactors is nearly always an element in policy, it can be a more or less important element. It has been increasingly important in education since the end of World War II, for policies and programs have made progressively greater demands for educators' learning. The 1950s curriculum reforms sought to improve teaching, as did Head Start and Title I of the Elementary and Secondary Education Act (ESEA) of 1965 and the "back to basics" movement of the 1970s and early 1980s. Each required that teachers learn a good deal in order to make the improvements that policymakers proposed, though these requirements often seemed to go unnoticed by policymakers. The postwar policies and programs were educative in the general sense that is common to any policy. But they also were educative in a very specific sense: they sought to promote new pedagogies for pedagogues.[5] That point holds with a vengeance for recent efforts to promote "higher-order thinking," "teaching for understanding," and much deeper knowledge of academic subjects.

To say that most policies and programs entail learning and thus some education is only to make a logical or psychological claim. It tells us nothing about the education that actually was provided. That is our subject here: what kind of education has educational policy offered to enactors? What has been the pedagogy of policy? To answer these questions we must inquire about how policymakers actually tried to teach teachers to teach differently, and to do that we must consider policy as a sort of instruction. Such a reading of policy is of course more suitable in some cases than others, but it seems marvelously suitable for post–World War II education.

In considering the pedagogy of policy, we employ a scheme that is familiar to students of instruction. We begin with purposes: what pedagogical aims have state and federal policymakers pressed on teachers? Then we turn to methods: what educational approaches have policymakers used as they have sought to teach teachers to teach differently? We also inquire about consistency: how do the pedagogies that policies enact compare with those that they press teachers to adopt?

One thread in our answers to those questions is paradoxical. Though policymakers have developed extraordinarily rich ambitions for schools, educational policies and programs have not been richly educative for enactors. The pedagogy of educational policy generally has been didactic, much as teaching often is didactic. Policymakers are practiced at telling teachers what to do, but they rarely have done much more than lecture. Like many teachers they focus more on broadcasting their message and covering the material than on figuring out what learners make of it and framing instruction accordingly. Cases in which policymakers or program managers engaged educators in extended instructional conversations that were designed to encourage the desired learning are even more scarce than cases in which teachers engage students in such conversations.

Most troubling, policymakers seem to have learned little from experience. The pedagogy of policy remains quite undeveloped even though policymakers' ambitions for classroom pedagogy have developed quite dramatically. In the last five or six years policymakers have advanced a new and much more ambitious agenda for improving pedagogy, as they press schools to offer "higher-order thinking," "teaching for understanding," and the like. Yet for the most part these policies break little new ground in efforts to educate enactors. Though policymakers now seek dramatic revisions in classroom instruction, they make few such revisions in their own efforts to help teachers make those instructional changes. Even that disjunction is only dimly and occasionally noticed by those who

make policies and manage programs. Hence, we conclude by probing another issue: why has the pedagogy of education policy been
so weakly educative?

Policy and Pedagogy

What educational aims have policymakers embraced as they have
tried to teach teachers to improve their teaching? The answers vary,
depending on the policies in question. We consider three of the
great episodes in post–World War II education policy. The 1950s
curriculum reforms sought intellectually ambitious instruction for
America. Students were to become little scientists and mathematicians, "doing" mathematics and "messing about" with
science. These were heady plans, especially in view of American
educators' previous efforts to do just the opposite. Since the beginning of the twentieth century, most educators and reformers had
tried to concoct a "practical" education for most students on the
grounds that few young Americans either wanted or needed anything more intellectually ambitious and that only a few could manage it in any event. If we view the fifties curriculum reforms against
the background of such sad ambitions, it is probably unavoidable
that they should seem elitist. Whether or not reformers intended
improvement only for an elite, they did embrace a sort of academic
seriousness that self-styled democratic reformers had been denounc-
ing as elitist since 1900.[6]

Head Start and Title I of the 1965 ESEA were the leading
programs in the second great postwar policy episode, and they were
hardly elitist: both proposed to improve education for the poor.
Their approach was quite plain in one sense—to provide more
resources for schools, teachers, and families. But in another sense
the approach was quite unclear, for initially both programs were
agnostic about instructional content and pedagogy. How the resources were to be used was not an issue at the outset. For example,
the Head Start and Follow Through Planned Variation experiments in the late 1960s and early 1970s included everything from
open education on one end to highly structured behavior modification programs on the other.[7]

The "back to basics" movement of the 1970s and 1980s was

the third postwar policy episode that we consider, and these reformers were not at all agnostic about curriculum and instruction.
They believed that education had badly deteriorated for most students, including those from disadvantaged circumstances. They
argued that students should at least be required to master the rudiments of knowledge, and pressed a largely traditional concept of the
basics. Though some interpreted the basics as a traditional academic curriculum, most reformers adopted quite a different and
much more narrow view of the ends of education, one that was
light-years from the earlier curriculum reforms. Indeed, this movement was notable for didactic concepts of teaching and formulaic
approaches to improvement. Reform and research abounded with
lists and other tidy formulae, including the elements of "effective"
schools and the steps in teaching with Madeline Hunter's ITIP.

A fourth great episode may be in the making, though it is too
soon to tell. In the last five or six years another group of reformers
has taken off in yet another direction. They demand more thoughtful and intellectually ambitious instruction. They argue that students must become independent thinkers and enterprising problem
solvers, and that schools should offer intellectually challenging instruction that is deeply rooted in the academic disciplines. These
reformers envision instruction that is in some respects reminiscent
of the Sputnik era. It certainly is much more thoughtful, adventurous, and demanding than was proposed by most advocates of back
to basics. And it is a far cry from the rudimentary instruction that
is found in most educational programs for the disadvantaged.

In just forty years, then, policymakers have embraced several
different and sometimes divergent educational purposes. In fact, the
aims of state and national education policy have changed so often
since World War II that we can see no consistent vision of educational improvement in them. Yet these varied purposes have accumulated in schools and school systems. The ambitions for learning
that policymakers pressed on teachers in the 1950s were only partly
displaced by the new lessons that policymakers sought to teach in
the 1960s. For instance, the innovative texts born in the 1950s continued in use in many high schools—especially in the top tracks—
throughout subsequent decades. And the 1960s lessons were only
partly displaced by the newer purposes that policymakers pressed

in the 1970s and 1980s. Chapter I and Head Start still thrive,[8] and back to basics is alive and well in U.S. classrooms today, despite previous reforms and the subsequent turn toward teaching for understanding.

Education policy has been an inconsistent teacher. Americans have tried to solve many different problems with formal schooling, but we have been divided about what education is good, what it is good for, and how best to educate. We also have been politically fickle, giving only brief attention to one great problem before turning to another. Policymakers have tried to teach teachers several different and sometimes divergent lessons in quick succession.

What have teachers learned from this? They often say that whatever policy tells them today, it will tell them something different tomorrow. Upon hearing of a new policy or program, teachers often remind reformers and observers that they have been through something like this before. Though such evidence is important, it is only a beginning. To learn more about the educative character and effects of education policy, one also must investigate the specific instructional approaches that were employed and how they turned out. Those approaches varied, depending on how policy problems were framed and what policy instruments were used.

The 1950s Curriculum Reforms

The 1950s reformers, nearly all gifted researchers who taught at leading universities, saw the problems of education chiefly in curricular terms. They believed that the schools' fare was a largely outmoded pabulum and proposed to replace it with radically new versions of academic subjects. In an early memorandum proposing the reform of science instruction in the schools, Jerrold Zacharias likened education to making good records. To do it well, he wrote, one needs good performers, good equipment, and the like. But " . . . most important of all is the composition itself; without a great composition everything else is pointless."[9]

Zacharias was a distinguished MIT physicist, the chief author of PSSC Physics, and a leader in the reform movement. His comment caught the spirit of the thing: professors would write new symphonies for schools. Ideas would be the chief instruments of change.[10] Zacharias and his fellow academic crusaders composed novel texts and other materials. They enthusiastically promoted plans for reform. And they invented opportunities for teachers to learn much more at universities. The 1950s reforms stand out in the broad sweep of post–World War II education policy partly because the key instruments of policy were those of education itself, and partly because the ambitions for change were so deeply and exuberantly intellectual.

American public education was hardly notable for its intellectuality, its exuberance, or its well-educated teachers. Despite that, educating teachers was not the reformers' top priority. They worked much harder to produce exciting new materials from which students could learn, irrespective of what teachers knew.[11] They did so in part because they thought poorly of teachers, but in much larger part because they thought well of students' independent learning. The reformers worked in the early years of the "cognitive revolution," when psychologists had begun to portray learning as a process of active sense-making and to reject earlier views of it as passive absorption. Jerome Bruner was one of the leading figures in this movement of psychological thought, and he was a prominent curriculum reformer as well. He and others saw learning as a process that required judgment, reflection, and decision making, and they wanted schools to encourage childrens' intelligence and intellectual independence. Additionally, many of the curriculum reformers were scientists who had worked in or near the great scientific revolutions of the twentieth century. They believed that students should learn science by doing the sorts of things that scientists do—"discovering" big ideas, investigating crucial scientific issues, and using authentic methods of scientific inquiry—not learning masses of dead facts and dry formulae. The reformers were convinced that students of all ages could "do" science if only the issues and materials were presented honestly and engagingly. They saw themselves as champions of intellectual independence and excitement in education and as enemies of the drab and mind-numbing instruction that they thought professional educators imposed on students.

Zacharias, Bruner, and many others invested enormous energy, money, and inventiveness in devising lively and novel materials, especially independent investigations, "hands on" work, and films.[12] They assumed that students should learn largely on their own as they "discovered" ideas, "did" mathematics, "messed about in science," and the like.[13] But these eminent professors knew as little of schools, classrooms, and teachers as they imagined most teachers knew of science. They were particularly ignorant of how classroom teachers might apprehend and use novel materials. As it turned out, few teachers gave students much chance to independently use the new curricula. For while few teachers were deeply familiar with the new subject matter, most felt that it would be irresponsible to let students learn with little or no guidance. Hence when teachers used the materials, they did so in ways that made sense to them. Since few knew much of the new science, that meant that their use of the curricula typically was guided both by the inherited knowledge and pedagogy that reformers wanted to circumvent[14] and by teachers' struggles with problems that reformers had never considered, like classroom management and local politics. The curriculum reformers' passion for active learning led them to overestimate the materials' independent power, and their ignorance about schools and teaching led them to underestimate teachers' influence on the use of the materials.[15]

For all that, reformers did not ignore teachers' learning. Federal policymakers created the National Defense Education Act (NDEA) and other fellowships to attract talented new people to teaching. Many able recruits began with the help of such fellowships, and some have become America's educational leaders. But they were only a tiny fraction of a much less select army of new teachers then entering the profession. Most of those other recruits entered in more conventional ways, and got much less elegant education. The National Science Foundation also sponsored summer institutes to help experienced teachers learn more science, math, and the new curricula. While many teachers found the institutes useful, they were voluntary, costly, and mostly oriented to high school teaching. Hence they reached only a modest and relatively committed fraction of teachers. Additionally, few of the institutes were of much help when teachers tried to use the new curricula in their schools, for the institutes and workshops were conducted chiefly by faculty members in university arts and sciences depart

ments. Their chief aim was to "cover" the new subject matter, and
their grasp of the reformers' pedagogical demands on schoolteachers seems to have been rather limited.[16]

Many of the new curricula were marvelously inventive and
an improvement on extant materials, but reformers did not appreciate the learning that they would demand of teachers, students, and
parents. Because they greatly overestimated the materials' independent educative power, reformers failed to frame an adequate pedagogy of change.[17] Many teachers nonetheless learned from them, but
because they lacked appropriate help, most of that learning seems
to have been halting and fragmentary. And because the civil rights
movement soon changed educational priorities, much of what
teachers learned also was ephemeral.

Education for the Disadvantaged

Head Start and Title I of the 1965 ESEA were intended to improve
instruction, but their task was not framed in curricular terms. The
policy problem was instead viewed as one of insufficient resources,
incorrect incentives, and inappropriate teacher behavior. The reformers who devised and managed these programs believed that one
chief problem was inadequate resources to educate disadvantaged
students. Money and materials were one sort of resource, and
teachers' knowledge and attitudes were others. Many reformers believed that another problem was lack of rewards for teaching well
and lack of punishments for teaching badly.

On this view, no one needed to write new symphonies for
schools. The chief tasks of reform were to direct additional resources
to the education of poor children, to offer guidance in the use of
those resources, and to mobilize incentives for educators to do a
good job. Reformers believed that conventional instruments of policy such as regulation and resource allocation would change incentives and professional behavior, and thereby improve instruction.

Resource allocation initially was the chief policy instrument.
Head Start provided meals for children from poor families, screened
and treated them for health problems, and offered an array of educational activities. Title I made grants to states and localities for
schools that enrolled many children from poor families. The mon-

ies would allow schools to beef up instruction by adding teachers, materials, and more instructional assistance.

This seemingly straightforward approach turned out to have major educational requirements. One reason was that the programs were new. Nothing like them had been done before, outside of a handful of small foundation-funded projects. Hence, educators and program administrators had to learn an enormous amount as they started national programs and thousands of local projects. Washington managers offered locals some help, but they could not offer much. For starting new national programs with small staffs meant that national managers' attention was chiefly focused on such rudiments as getting the money out.

Another reason that extensive education was needed was that few of those involved knew much about improving education for disadvantaged students. Initially this lack of knowledge had not seemed to be a problem, for both Head Start and Title I were informed by the assumption that students who had more teachers and books would learn more. Mere exposure to educational resources was thought to be educationally powerful.[18] The assumption helps to explain how reformers could propose sweeping changes in education without considering that educators might have to learn a great deal to make the changes work. Policymakers could ignore instructional design for Head Start and Title I while still believing that classroom learning would improve, for they saw teachers, books, and other resources as instructionally potent in themselves— as a kind of curriculum quite apart from any specific instructional design. Like earlier ideas about the potency of new symphonies for schools, these assumptions about the power of added money, materials, and staff made it easy for policymakers to believe that the Great Society educational programs would have dramatic effects without requiring much education for those who would enact them.

That belief soon was called into question. In the late 1960s researchers began to report that students in Title I and Head Start projects learned no more than similarly situated students who had not been in such projects. Had there been only a few of these studies, they probably would not have taken on such importance, but the reports multiplied. While most reports raised questions only about one particular project, taken together they cast doubt on the entire rationale for Head Start and Title I, and policy analysts took them together. They asked: if students did not learn more when they had more educational resources, why increase resources to improve education?

One response to the query was to assume that more resources would work if they were better focused. Regulation began to play a much larger role as managers sought to ensure that resources were used in educationally productive ways. The first and perhaps largest issue was to make sure that money was concentrated rather than thinly spread.[19] Title I managers used regulation especially assiduously in efforts to require local schools to use federal funds to enrich instruction by adding them to local and state monies, rather than using them to substitute for local and state funds, or to purchase noneducational equipment.

Incentives soon became another focus of regulation. Title I officials began to press state and local educators to attend to instructional results, which in most cases meant test scores. Officials strongly encouraged testing of students as one means to this end, and mandatory evaluation of projects' effects on test scores as another. Federal officials believed that publishing such evaluations would provide valid evidence about projects' success or failure and would show whether teachers and administrators needed to work harder. They also believed that the evidence would give parents and others some leverage to press for better performance where it was indicated.[20] Poor evaluations would produce public pressure for local educators to do a better job in the classroom. As time passed, federal efforts to improve student performance through testing and evaluation increased.

Regulation was educative.[21] For instance, state and local officials learned to organize "pull out" classes, partly because shifting students from regular classes to exclusive Title I offerings seemed a safe way to comply with federal pressure to concentrate resources. State and local officials also learned to use standardized tests, to report results in terms of test scores, and to evaluate projects as national program managers wished. In fact, Title I staffers learned so well that recent reformers, who are promoting more intellectually ambitious teaching, see Chapter I as a major barrier, because standardized testing and pull-out classes are so ingrained in program operations.

Did regulation improve students' learning? The evidence is mixed. If the question is taken to refer to the specific classroom organization that federal officials urged on state and local educators, it seems that it did not. Brian Rowan and his colleagues studied a range of Title I projects and reported that their organizational formats were unrelated to learning. Pull-out classes neither enhanced nor impeded learning. What made a difference to students' learning was the instructional design of projects. The Title I projects that improved achievement over what might otherwise have been expected were those that focused attention on academic instruction, whether or not they were pull-outs.[22]

From one perspective that was reassuring, for it meant that Title I and similar programs could make a difference if they focused on academic learning. From another angle it was troublesome, for it meant that such programs would not make a difference unless they attended closely to curriculum, and organizing federal regulation of curriculum would be very difficult for program managers and policymakers. There were, after all, long-standing political taboos on national curricula. And taboos aside, there would be many practical problems of design and implementation if managers tried to organize a single curricular focus in a vast national program, for that would require extraordinary political muscle and equally extraordinary intergovernmental coordination. No less difficult, learning to enact such a curriculum would require much more education for program staff and teachers than had ever been contemplated.[23]

Back to Basics

As it happened, Title I managers never had to directly face that large instructional problem. Instead, it was partly solved for them during the back to basics movement of the 1970s and early 1980s. Back to basics was a broad tendency in education that comprised many state and local programs and policies. Though these initiatives varied, they were animated by a common sense that American schools were in trouble. The well-publicized decline in SAT scores was one worry. Another was the lagging school achievement of poor children. Still another was the sense that schools were not "accountable," that educators had abused a public trust by failing to sufficiently promote achievement. Other concerns included the seeming collapse of academic standards, the rise of "permissiveness" in the 1960s, and the lack of respect for adult authority in schools.

This was not a tidily defined policy problem of the sort one sometimes finds in textbooks. Back to basics was a collection of discontents and a shared mood, but not a single-minded approach to remedy. Some reformers defined the problem as a matter of standards. Others saw it as a matter of politics and incentives. Still others saw it as a curriculum problem. Some reformers focused on tightening up educational standards, others on reasserting adult authority, and still others on making schools more "accountable." As a slogan, "back to basics" nicely captured a vision of history and a public mood, but it did not focus on a single major intervention like curriculum reform or revised resource allocation. Reformers instead used several policy instruments.

One favorite was regulation, and ideas were another. Stiffened high school graduation requirements was an especially popular regulatory approach. In the early 1980s many state legislatures and executive agencies rushed to add high school graduation course requirements, perhaps on the assumption that adding to the courses that students took would add to what they learned. Another regulatory favorite was minimum competency tests. Between the mid-1970s and the mid-1980s many states and localities adopted such tests in efforts to increase "accountability" for schools. State and local school systems were pressed to specify the results for which they would strive, to measure them with tests, and to publicize students' scores. The tests often were required for high school graduation or for grade promotion, or both. The notion was that plain standards, published evidence on performance, and required passing marks would create incentives for teachers to teach effectively and for students to study hard. The tests were far from perfect. Many were hastily contrived under political pressure and even adapted from standardized norm-referenced instruments that had been designed for radically different purposes. But legislators and others believed that the tests would focus teachers' and students' attention on key learning requirements and encourage them to take school more seriously.

A related regulatory approach was the "alignment" of tests and curricula. Between the mid-1970s and the mid-1980s many districts adopted "basic skills" or "essential skills" curricula. Cities that had large minority group school enrollments and many children of poverty were especially likely to take this step. Many of these districts also adopted tests that were referenced to those curriula and took steps to align teaching and learning to the tests and curricula. Some retrained teachers in "effective" teaching. Others monitored students' performance on tests and encouraged teachers to reteach material on which there were poor scores. Others published test results by school. And still others retrained principals to become "instructional leaders," which included such things as devising common instructional goals for the school and learning how to evaluate teachers on their success in effective teaching or in covering the aligned curriculum, or both.

If regulation was a highly visible feature of the back to basics movement, ideas were no less important an instrument of policy.[24] In fact, one might regard ideas about how to improve teaching and learning as the campaign's curriculum. Beginning in the mid-1970s, American education began to bubble with notions about how teachers and administrators could create "effective schools," how they could make teaching and schools more "accountable," and how they could teach and evaluate teaching according to one checklist of effectiveness or another. One source of these ideas was researchers' dismay about the reports on schools' relative ineffectiveness that had issued from James Coleman, Christopher Jencks, and others. In response to the dismal news, several researchers began looking for unusually effective and ineffective schools, hoping to show that schools could make a difference and to figure out how they did. Another source of the ideas was reformers who had been disappointed with extant efforts to improve education for disadvantaged children and were searching for ways to do better. Still another source was professional educators, who were disturbed about the reports that "schools didn't make a differ-

ence" and were trying to devise schemes that would make it clear
that they did, or could.

These efforts soon created a growing sense that schools did
make a difference, previous dismal reports to the contrary notwith-
standing. Researchers and educators announced that they were discovering the elements of good teaching and instructional
management, and their reports quickly became a curriculum for
school reform. Though these reports issued from several streams of
inquiry, they seemed to have a good deal in common. One crucial
common element was a sonata-form conception of instruction. Effective teachers stated the purpose of every lesson in ways that students could easily comprehend. Then they presented each lesson's
material clearly. As students dug into the material, teachers checked
for students' understanding, evaluated their performance, "re-
taught" material that had not been learned, and the like. As it
developed in these accounts, effective teaching was didactic and
tightly designed. It had clear goals, methods that were directly tied
to the goals, and close systems of monitoring and evaluation. Or-
derliness, step-by-step rationality, and a commitment to direct instruction all were crucial to this instructional approach.
Improvisation around large themes and indirect instruction were
entirely foreign to it.

Another key element in the curriculum of this reform movement was a skills-and-facts view of knowledge. Effective teachers
focused on definable skills that students could master. They taught
in ways that could be assessed on standardized tests. Hence they
presented knowledge in manageable bits and pieces, rather than
dealing with large and loose themes. Effective teachers also held
center stage in their classes, presenting, regulating, monitoring, and
evaluating instruction. These teachers also agreed with others in
their school on the purposes of instruction. And they taught in ways
that allowed "accountability" to parents and higher authorities.[25]

Perhaps the most important feature of this curriculum for
reform was that it existed. Previous reform efforts had offered little
or no such detailed guidance for teachers. Another important feature was the reform curriculum's practicality. The ideas about
teaching that we just sketched above were presented in ways that
seemed usable in classrooms. Still another unique feature of the

reform curriculum was its extraordinary coverage. Reformers blanketed American education, spreading their proposals from every imaginable source—state education agencies, local districts, professional associations, trade magazines, universities, consulting firms, and intermediate school districts. The back to basics curriculum achieved an extraordinary presence in U.S. education in a rather short time. The ideas became very popular in continuing professional education for teachers and administrators, as well as in the education of new teachers. Educators at all levels embraced the ideas, in part because they offered a clear focus for administrative as well as classroom work. By the early 1980s staff evaluation procedures in many local districts were suffused with the rhetoric of effective schools and Madeline Hunter's ITIP. The ideas also caught on within Title I and almost seemed to become its curriculum in many states and localities.

One additional reason that the ideas spread so quickly was that they did not have to be taught deeply. The back to basics reform curriculum generally was conveyed in quick, how-to-do-it formats in stolen hours during afternoon, evening, and weekend meetings. The pedagogy matched the reform ideas. Instruction was didactic and teacher-centered. Many instructors modeled, in their own presentations, the sort of classroom instruction that they proposed for teachers. They presented lessons in easy steps, with flip charts and overheads. Another reason that the ideas spread quickly was that reformers devised a message that could be useful in more than one way. Administrators could learn how to teach teachers to be effective. Some teachers could learn how to teach others. Administrators could learn how to evaluate teachers' classroom performance, using checklists of "effective" instructional methods. [26]

There is no general, direct evidence on how much teachers learned from these reforms or on how extensively the ideas were incorporated into classroom practice. But there is some general indirect evidence of considerable learning and broad incorporation: achievement disparities between African-American and white students narrowed appreciably between 1971 and 1988. Black-white reading score differences in the National Assessment of Educational Progress (NAEP) were cut in half for thirteen-year-olds by 1988, and they were cut by a third for nine-year-olds by 1988. The black-white disparity in mathematics achievement also was reduced by nearly half for thirteen-year-olds by 1988 and by slightly less than one-third for nine-year-olds.[27] These dramatic increases in NAEP reading and math scores for black and Hispanic students all occurred in basic skills, not in "higher-order" knowledge and skills. If, as reformers argued, teachers should be working much harder on basic skills, one would expect such a result.

These results seem to support the idea that there was appreciable incorporation of the back to basics curriculum in American elementary school classrooms.[28] That view gains additional support from observational studies, which show that many teachers adopted at least portions of the back to basics curriculum.[29] It also fits with the curriculum of reform itself, which was framed and promulgated with the notion of application clearly in mind. The ideas were kept simple. They were delivered in easy-listening formats. And they were broadcast to teachers and administrators from a remarkable variety of sources.

But the evidence is equivocal. For one thing, social policy may have played a large role in the NAEP gains. The 1960s and 1970s saw many social changes that would have been likely to improve childrens' school performance. One was greater educational attainment for African-American and Hispanic young adults who would have had children in school between 1971 and 1988. Another was reduced poverty, better housing, and improved welfare assistance.[30] All these things would be highly likely to improve student achievement; they are elements of the "family background" that has a strong influence on school achievement.

For another thing, much of the direct evidence on the effects of the back to basics crusade is equivocal. There are quite a few studies that show good results from small-scale, carefully controlled direct-instruction-oriented interventions.[31] But there also is some evidence that in ordinary districts that have less carefully controlled interventions, teaching reverts to prior form and student achievement falls off once the interventions end.[32] Additionally, several secondary analyses of research and evaluation reports from many effective schools projects raise grave doubts about the quality of the data and analyses.[33] And one careful reanalysis of the performance in unusually effective schools casts doubt on the persistence of achievement gains.[34]

Most important, evidence on the impact of the large-scale regulatory efforts of the 1970s and 1980s is very mixed. The most careful study of graduation requirements concludes that high school course offerings did change and that there may have been a modest effect on students' achievement. But there did not seem to be a strong general effect on either teaching or learning.[35] Nor is there evidence that American teachers learned broadly from minimum competency tests. Several researchers assert that the tests have had a broad and powerful effect on teaching.[36] They report that competency tests drove instruction in a mechanical and simplistic direction, that teachers oriented instruction to the test items, and if students did poorly on the tests, remediation consisted of drill on the items they did not know.[37] Similarly, a recent U.S. Department of Education report claimed that ". . . accountability systems . . . are very powerful policy tools that have changed school-level planning and teaching activities."[38] But for every research claim that testing has such effects, there is another that teachers rarely take testing into account in instruction.[39] And even the reports that argue for powerful effects contain evidence to the contrary.[40]

But competency tests did not need to be salient for most teachers in order to support gains in basic skills. They needed only be salient for the teachers of low-performing African-American and Hispanic students. The evidence suggests that competency testing affected instruction chiefly in "high stakes" situations—that is, when the tests counted for students' academic progress, or for schools or teachers. Many minimum competency testing programs were not in the "high stakes" category and were much more likely to enroll poor and minority group children, since advantaged students typically pass with little effort. Hence, the teachers of poor and minority group children were most likely to have learned from the tests, which fits with the NAEP test results.

As with most large-scale social change endeavors, we will never know exactly what the effects of back to basics were, let alone which feature of the effort was responsible for which effect. We are inclined to believe that the crusade did help to change teaching and learning in many U.S. classrooms and that the movement was responsible for some of the achievement gains that African-American and Hispanic students made in the 1970s and 1980s. But the evidence reveals very partial, spotty, and inconsistent classroom implementation of the reform. The movement's success probably owed a good deal to a combination of educational ideas, political and administrative regulation, broad changes in social policy, and the legacies of previous reform. It was essential that reformers blanketed American education with a curriculum that was relatively easy to understand, that seemed timely and practical, and that appealed to educators of many different sorts for many different reasons. But it also helped that state and local school systems were pushing regulatory reforms that stressed the same ideas, that seemed to offer teachers and administrators significant reasons to follow along, and that were especially salient in schools in low-income neighborhoods. Finally, it helped that Title I of the 1965 ESEA had established a national system of program administration by the mid-1970s and that strong professional networks of Title I administrators, teachers, and consultants were beginning to grow. For with those administrative and professional systems in place, Title I officials at the state, national, and local levels could embrace back to basics as their curriculum. The curriculum of this reform was a convenient answer to the problems of program effectiveness that had dogged the Great Society programs. By themselves, no one of these policy instruments would have had much effect, but together they seemed to have an influenced instruction.

Conclusion

The pedagogy of educational policy has been didactic and inconsistent. Policymakers have told teachers to do many different, hugely important things in a short time. And in each case policymakers have acted as though their assignment was to dispense answers, not to provoke thought, ask questions, or generate discussion. The pedagogy of policy has been teacher-centered. As policymakers taught, they created few opportunities to listen as schoolteachers and other educators tried to make sense of new demands. Nor have policymakers cast policy as something that might be revised in light of what they learned from teachers' experience.

These features of policy seem ubiquitous. The curriculum reformers of the late 1950s and early 1960s were distinguished academics from great universities, yet they addressed teachers in quite didactic fashion. The reformers did not consider teachers as thoughtful learners and seemed largely unaware of vast problems that most would have in learning from the reforms. A didactic orientation is not peculiar to professors. The reformers who planned and operated Head Start and Title I of the 1965 ESEA were hardly professorial; they were cabinet officers, legislators, program managers, bureaucrats, and advocates for the poor. Yet they addressed teachers no less didactically than the professors, and they seemed similarly unaware of great problems of teacher learning. Nor is didactic orientation peculiar to certain types of policies. The advocates of back to basics pressed relatively simple ideas about instruction on teachers, while the 1950s curriculum reformers pressed very complex ideas on them. But like other reformers, the advocates of basics acted as though teaching was active "telling" and learning was passive accumulation.

How can we account for this uniformly didactic pedagogy of policy? In the back to basics crusade reformers urged a set of changes in classrooms that fit relatively well with established practice, which itself was didactic, teacher-centered, and oriented to skills and facts. They presented the reform ideas in practical, easy-to-adopt formats, and blanketed American education relatively effectively. The pedagogy of the reform fit quite nicely with the pedagogy that reformers urged on teachers.

The 1950s curriculum reforms urged a very different sort of instruction that would have required immense changes in teaching. But while these reforms were pedagogically very ambitious, they were much less effective in reaching teachers. Reformers only weakly understood practice and the problems their ideas posed for practitioners. The changes that they urged would have been extraordinarily difficult to pull off even if reformers had been exquisitely sensitive to teaching and extraordinarily thoughful in the education of teachers. In policy as in classrooms, learners ordinarily find it much easier to grasp material that is familiar and consistent with what they already know than material that is unfamiliar and inconsistent with extant knowledge.

Another reason for the generally didactic pedagogy of policy lies in American politics and political organization. This is a vast nation, in which several states are larger than many foreign countries. Local control is a tradition of school governance that is dearly held in states large and small. American government is extraordinarily fragmented at all levels and Americans are deeply divided about many matters of education policy.[41] Under these circumstances it often is very difficult for state or national governments to do more than formulate policy and announce it. Given these circumstances and the political, administrative, and educational resources that a more ambitious pedagogy of policy would entail, a simple and spare approach has been all that state and federal policymakers could manage in most cases.

Most local school boards and administrators have not cultivated a more sophisticated pedagogy in dealing with teachers, so politics alone cannot explain the prevalent pedagogy of policy. Americans' expansive belief in the power of education is another explanation for the very limited pedagogy of policy that we have described. The 1950s curriculum reformers urged fundamental change on schools without considering that teachers might have to relearn their practice. Reformers believed students would learn quite nicely on their own if only they had good materials. The 1960s advocates of Head Start and Title I pressed sweeping changes in the education of disadvantaged children without much attention to what teachers would have to learn, in part because they believed students would learn much more if only they had more teachers and better materials.

These reformers shared a characteristic American faith in the power of education. That faith allowed them to avoid careful consideration of instructional design, for if teaching and learning were as easily shaped as Americans have been inclined to believe, why spend lots of time carefully designing instruction? If learning and teaching were not difficult practices, reformers could easily imagine that students would learn independently from exciting materials and that teachers would find it easy to improve their practice. Lacking a sense that learning and teaching were often difficult, why should policymakers include instructional design in framing policy?

A last explanation for the limited pedagogy of policy is rooted in teaching itself. We have argued that policymakers behave little differently than most teachers. Like teachers, reformers have been in the habit of telling learners what they should learn, without much attention to what teachers thought, or already knew, or made of the policy. Like most teachers, policymakers have made few efforts to engage their students in conversations that could illuminate their grasp of the material or their interpretation of policy. Hence policymakers, like most teachers, have not been able to use learners' ideas and understanding to revise instruction and advance learning. Like most teachers, policymakers focus on "putting the material across." They have learned to consult various interested parties as part of the politics of policymaking, but they inquire little about what enactors may have to learn in order to respond constructively to policy, what it may take for them to learn, how they might best learn, and how policy might be redesigned in consequence of learners' experience. Policy generally has been inattentive to learning, much as teachers often are inattentive.

If teachers typically behave in these ways, why should policymakers act differently? If classroom pedagogy is generally didactic and centered on the teacher, where could policymakers have learned to differently conceive the educational entailments of their handiwork? If, as several scholars point out, school is the chief place in which we all learn about teaching and learning as students,[42] how could policymakers have learned a more attentive and adventurous pedagogy? As long as teaching remains didactic and traditional, how can we expect policymakers to learn to address teachers in ways that are better calculated to change teaching?

Notes

1. We use the terms "policy" and "program" interchangeably to refer to large-scale change efforts. To avoid repetition of the two terms we often simply use the term "policy."

2. We include even such modestly novel purposes as the reaffirmation of older purposes that had not been achieved. Since policy often deals with the same issue at different times, or with different aspects of the same issue at different times, the combination of novelty and continuity is a regular feature of policy. For instance, the civil rights statutes and judicial decisions of the 1960s and 1970s were in a sense reaffirmations of Reconstruction-era policies. As such they should have required no new learning. Yet in another sense the 1960s and 1970s policies were radically new, for the policies that they reaffirmed had fallen into disuse, or had been contradicted by subsequent practice. Hence, the later civil rights policies required extensive learning.

3. See Orfield (1969).

4. The 1964 Civil Rights Act recognized some of these educational entailments in Title IV, which provided education for those concerned with desegregation.

5. This subject is familiar to policy researchers in one sense, for they have increasingly probed the implementation of policies and programs since the 1960s. Investigators have studied the actions of those who enact policies, the regulations with which they deal, the relations among governments, and the design of policy. But in another sense our subject is unfamiliar to policy researchers, for in all the attention to implementation the educative character of policies and programs has been little noticed. For instance, the curricula of policy have been analyzed under the heading of regulation, not teaching and learning (see, for example, Bardach & Kagan, 1982). Only a few students of implementation have considered what enactors had to learn in order to respond to policies. Fewer still have probed how enactors were taught (see especially Elmore & McLaughlin, 1989).

6. On the history of these matters, see Cremin (1961); Dow (1991); Powell, Farrar, & Cohen (1985, chapter 5); and Ravitch (1983). Some of the 1950s reformers did seem to embrace elitist approaches to reform while others did not. Hyman Rickover (1959) appeared to be an unabashed meritocratic elitist in *Ed-*

ucation for Freedom. In contrast, Arthur Bestor (1953) seemed much more Jeffersonian in *Educational Wastelands.* But both argued for high academic seriousness, in opposition to "life adjustment education" and other intellectually flabby doctrines of the interwar decades.

7. These experiments were designed to teach educators and policymakers more about the strengths and weaknesses of various instructional approaches, so they could select those that were best.

8. Chapter 1 was pressed toward basics in the 1970s and 1980s, and is now being pressed back the other way. Head Start seems to have been much more consistent in its embrace of general principles of preschool and nursery education.

9. Silberman, 1970.

10. On ideas as policy instruments see Weiss (1990).

11. See Dow (1991), especially chaps. 3 and 4.

12. Dow, 1991.

13. Though some of the curriculum reformers deliberately tried to "teacher-proof" materials, their focus on materials that would be independently educational had much deeper roots. One key assumption was that learning was or should be active sense-making, and the other was that if new curricular "scores" allowed students to be active sense-makers, they would be powerful. See Bruner (1961) for one participant's view of these notions. See Dow (1991) for a lucid discussion of the issues. Though Dow was a staff member in the Education Development Center (EDC) project that produced *Man A Course of Study (MACOS),* and a close associate of Jerome Bruner in that project, he presents an admirably balanced account of that curriculum development effort.

14. Dow (1991) argues that *MACOS* sought to become an exception to this generalization and presents some evidence on that point. But *MACOS* was killed before its plans for teacher education were fairly tried. See Dow (1991), chap. 4.

15. Some of this ignorance arose from the reformers' arrogant disdain for professional educators, but ignorance would have

been a great problem even if the reformers had been models
of humility.

16. For example, the new science and mathematics educators
tended to see teachers' scientific knowledge as "misconceptions" that needed correction, rather than as efforts to make
sense of complex material that offered opportunities for learning, revision, and extension.

17. For an extended account of this view, see Sarason (1971).

18. Under some circumstances, the idea is correct. In less developed nations, in which some children have no schools to attend, children who attend school learn more school subjects.
Among those who attend school, those who have teachers and
books learn more than those who do not. But in nations like
the United States, in which nearly all children in school have
comparatively rich educational resources, marginal or even
large differences in gross resources are unrelated to students'
achievement. One must define educational resources in more
discriminating ways in order to observe instructional effects.

19. Concentration included focusing on academic year projects in
both programs, on elementary schools in Title I, as well as on
limiting the number of projects.

20. See McLaughlin (1975).

21. The education was not necessarily easy. The 1970s vintage
Chapter 1 guidelines that advised standardized testing for students in state and local projects created a considerable list of
things for state, federal, and local officials to learn about tests
and testing. And the federal regulations typically offered a
spare and often quite arcane pedagogy. In this case they were
so spare that the government soon established agencies that
were intended to offer state and local educators various sorts
of instruction, including technical assistance, in testing.

22. Rowan & Guthrie, 1989.

23. Both Title I and Head Start did use so-called conventional
education in efforts to improve teaching. Program managers
produced and distributed materials on effective approaches to
instruction. They created systems to "disseminate" knowledge
about instruction and sponsored efforts to offer technical as-

sistance in a variety of matters related to instruction. They organized meetings in which program participants exchanged ideas and otherwise instructed one another. But such education nonetheless seems to have occupied a minor part in the two programs' efforts to instruct local educators.

24. Some of the ideas derived from regulation itself, for no policy instrument is pure. Much of the regulatory work was carried out with a great deal of political fanfare and public attention. The pressure for minimum competency testing and stiffened graduation requirements helped to create a political climate that further increased incentives for teachers' and students' performance and focused political pressures on schools and teachers to improve.

25. For a summary of these ideas see Purkey & Smith (1983).

26. Resource allocation played only an indirect role in this policy episode. Though few of the back to basics programs and policies had large amounts of money attached, they were part of a big political trade: If schools would offer better performance and more "accountability," public officials would support more revenues for education. Analysts report that education expenditures increased nationally by about 30 percent during the 1970s, and by about the same percentage during the 1980s. Most of these increases were absorbed in higher teacher salaries.

27. National Assessment of Educational Progress (1990), Table 3.1. More modest reductions in the gap were reported for Hispanic students. These changes occur against a background of belief that students' performance has been declining. There may have been a decline in test scores between the early 1960s and the 1970s, but there is reason to believe that students who attended school since World War II have higher achievement than students who attended in 1900, or the 1930s. When tests that were used in earlier decades are readministered, today's students do better than their colleagues in the past (Farr & Fay, 1982).

28. See Smith & O'Day (1991) for a brief discussion of this point.

29. Guthrie, 1990.

30. Smith & O'Day, 1991.

31. Brophy, 1986; and Brophy & Good, 1986.

32. Stallings & Krasavage, 1986.

33. Purkey & Smith, 1983; and Rowan, Bossert, & Dwyer, 1983.

34. Rowan, Bossert, & Dwyer, 1983.

35. We see no grounds for expecting significant teacher learning in this case, since for the most part they were simply being required to teach courses that were already on the books. See Clune, White, & Patterson (1989).

36. Darling-Hammond & Wise, 1989; Resnick & Resnick, 1985; Romberg, Zarinnia, & Williams, 1989; and Wise, 1979.

37. Madaus, 1988; and Kreitzer, Madaus, & Haney (n.d.).

38. Office of Educational Research and Improvement (OERI) State Accountability Study Group (1988, September).

39. Moreover, the evidence adduced for an effect of testing consists nearly exclusively of interviews and self-reports. See, for example, Floden, Porter, Schmidt, & Freeman (1978); Ruddell (1985); Salmon-Cox (1981); and MacRury, Nagy, & Traub (1987). There seems to be not a single U.S. study in which teaching was directly and independently observed over time in order to investigate the impact of testing (Madaus, 1988). Since no teaching was independently observed in these studies, the claim that state competency tests were "powerful" and "changed . . . teaching" is as difficult to assess as claims that testing has no significant effect. Both claims must be treated with caution. Even a group of researchers who believe that testing has a powerful effect on teaching report that there is " . . . a paucity of definitive information" (Romberg, Zarinnia, & Williams, 1989, p. 16).

40. Teachers also regularly presented evidence that was at variance from the conclusions that researchers drew about the effects of testing. For example, teachers' reports on their behavior often are solicited in a highly simplified form. A recent national survey of eighth grade mathematics teachers was one of the most extensive studies in which teachers were queried about their responses to local and state testing programs. Teachers were asked whether they took test results into ac-

count in making decisions—about student placement in ability groups, the content of instruction, test preparation, and the like. But teachers were not queried about how they took test information into account in these decisions. And in only a few instances were they even queried about how much they took test information into account. On the basis of quite simplified evidence about whether testing plays any role in teachers' decisions, the authors concluded that "testing does have an effect on teaching. . . . The majority of teachers change their allocation of instructional time. They gave practice [on tests] and set aside time to prepare" (Romberg, Zarinnia, & Williams, 1989, p. 88).

But unlike some others, this study offers a few bits of evidence on the extent of use. That evidence belies the categorical reports. The authors write that " . . . just over half . . . " of the teachers in their survey reported that they "set aside time to prepare for the test"—that is, slightly less than half did no test preparation whatever. And of the half that did set aside time for preparation, just under half (45 percent) set aside only " . . . several days a year" (Romberg, Zarinnia, & Williams, 1989, p. 80). Since the study concerned only one school subject which is ordinarily taught no more than an hour a day, the report of "several days'" preparation does not convey a sense of overwhelming impact. Quite the contrary. The report shows that only about a quarter of the teachers spent more than a few class periods on test preparation, and that roughly half spent no time at all.

An OERI report offers a similar picture. In its only discussion of how much teachers take tests into account, the authors present an example drawn from a school that deliberately tried to improve, apparently in response to earlier, poorer test scores. An informant reported that "we spend 30 minutes a week on skills" (Romberg, Zarinnia, & Williams). Averaged over a five-day school week, that comes out to six minutes a day. While six minutes is a noticeable period of time, it hardly seems a major change in instruction.

Similarly, the OERI study cited above reports that "a

majority" of teachers interviewed were " . . . concerned about their students' test performance and are willing to change their teaching to improve it" (OERI, 1988, p. 33). But at the same time, the study notes that teachers expressed " . . . substantial ambivalence" about teaching to the test (p. 33). Apparently many teachers were simply unwilling to even consider changing their teaching in light of the test. Additionally, of the majority who were willing to change their teaching, many were "ambivalent" about whether a competency test was the proper instrument for change (p. 33). This does not suggest that testing was a powerful policy intervention.

41.　On these matters, see Cohen & Spillane (1992).

42.　Lortie, 1975.

References

Bardach, G., & Kagan, R. (1982). *Going by the book: The problem of regulatory unreasonableness.* Philadelphia: Temple University Press.

Bestor, A. (1953). *Educational wastelands.* Urbana: University of Illinois Press.

Brophy, J. (1986). Teacher influences on student achievement. *American Psychologist, 41*(10), 1069–1077.

Brophy J. E., & Good T. L. (1986). Teacher behavior and student achievement. In Merlin C. Wittrock (Ed.), *Handbook of research on teaching* (3rd ed.) Washington, DC: American Educational Research Association.

Bruner, J. (1961). *The process of education.* Cambridge: Harvard University Press.

Clune, W., White, P., & Patterson, J. (1989). *The implementation and effects of high school graduation requirements.* New Brunswick, NJ: Rutgers University, Center for Policy Research in Education.

Cohen, D. K., & Spillane, J. P. (1992, April). Policy and practice: The relations between governance and instruction. *Review of Research in Education.* Washington, DC: American Educational Research Association.

Cremin, L. (1961). *The transformation of the school.* New York: Random House.

Darling-Hammond, L., & Wise, A. E. (1989). Beyond standardization: State standards and school improvement. *The Elementary School Journal, 85* (3), 315–356.

Dow, P. (1991). *Schoolhouse politics: Lessons from the Sputnik era.* Cambridge: Harvard University Press.

Elmore, R. F., & McLaughlin, M. W. (1989). *Steady work: Policy, practice, and the reform of American education.* Santa Monica, CA: RAND Corporation.

Farr, R., & Fay, L. (1982). Reading trend data in the United States: A mandate for caveats and caution. In G. R. Austin & H. Garber (Eds.), *The rise and fall of national test scores* (pp. 83–137). New York: Academic Press.

Floden, R. E., Porter, A. C., Schmidt, W. H., & Freeman, D. J. (1978). *Don't they all measure the same thing? Consequences of selecting standardized tests* (Research Series No. 25). East Lansing: Michigan State University, Institute for Research on Teaching.

Guthrie, J. W. (Ed.). (1990). *Educational evaluation and policy analysis, 12*(3).

Kreitzer, A. E., Madaus, G. F., & Haney, W. (n.d.). *Competency testing and dropouts* (pp. 1–28). Unpublished paper. Boston: Boston College.

Lortie, D. (1975). *Schoolteacher: A sociological study.* Chicago: University of Chicago Press.

McLaughlin, M. (1975). *Evaluation and reform.* Cambridge, MA: Ballinger.

MacRury, K., Nagy, P., & Traub, R. E. (1987). *Reflections on large-scale assessments of study achievement.* Toronto: The Ontario Institute for Studies in Education.

Madaus, G. F. (1988). *The influence of testing on the curriculum.* Unpublished paper. Boston: Boston College.

National Assessment of Educational Progress. (1990). *America's challenge: Accelerating academic achievement.* Princeton, NJ: Educational Testing Service.

OERI State Accountability Study Group. (September, 1988). *Creat-*

ing responsible and responsive accountability systems. Washington, DC: U.S. Department of Education.

Orfield, G. (1969). *The reconstruction of southern education.* Chicago: University of Chicago Press.

Powell, A., Farrar, E., & Cohen, D. (1985). *The shopping mall high school.* Boston: Houghton Mifflin.

Purkey, S. C., & Smith, M. S. (1983). Effective schools: A review. *Elementary School Journal, 83*(4), 427–452.

Ravitch, D. (1983). *The troubled crusade.* New York: Basic Books.

Resnick, D. P., & Resnick, L. B. (1985, April). Standards, curriculum, and performance: A historical and comparative perspective. *Educational Researcher, 14,* 5–20.

Rickover, H. (1959). *Education for freedom.* New York: Dutton.

Romberg, T. A., Zarinnia, E. A., & Williams, S. R. (1989, March). *The influence of mandated testing on mathematics instruction: Grade 8 teachers' perceptions.* Unpublished paper. Madison: University of Wisconsin.

Rowan, B., Bossert, S., & Dwyer, D. (1983). Research on effective schools: A cautionary note. *Educational Researcher, 12*(4), 24–31.

Rowan, B., & Guthrie, L. F. (1989). The quality of Chapter 1 instruction: Results from a study of twenty-four schools. In R. Slavin, N. L. Karweit, & N. A. Madden (Eds.), *Effective programs for students at risk* (pp. 195–219). Needham Heights, MA: Allyn & Bacon.

Ruddell, R. B. (1985). Knowledge and attitude toward testing: Field educators and legislators. *The Reading Teacher, 38*(6), 538–543.

Salmon-Cox, L. (1981). Teachers and standardized achievement tests: What's really happening? *Phi Delta Kappan, 62*(9), 631–633.

Sarason, S. (1971). *The culture of schools and the problem of change.* Needham Heights, MA: Allyn & Bacon.

Silberman, C. (1970). *Crisis in the classroom.* New York: Random House.

Smith, M., & O'Day, J. (1991). Systemic school reform. In S. H. Fuhrman & B. Malen (Eds.), *The politics of curriculum and testing* (pp. 233–268). New York: Falmer.

Stallings, J., & Krasavage, E. (1986, January). *Peaks, valleys, and plateaus in program implementation: A longitudinal study of a Madeline Hunter follow through project.* Paper presented at the Family and Research Action V Conference, Lubbock, Texas.

Weiss, J. (1990). Ideas and inducements in mental health policy. *Journal of Policy Analysis and Management, 9,* 178–200.

Wise, A. (1979). *Legislated learning.* Berkeley: University of California Press.

8

Conclusion:
A New Pedagogy for Policy?

David K. Cohen
Carol A. Barnes

Educational reformers now press for radical changes in American classrooms. Leaders in politics and business demand "critical thinking" and "teaching for understanding." They insist on "world-class standards" for schools. They argue that students must become independent thinkers and enterprising problem solvers. Educators say that schools must offer intellectually challenging instruction that is deeply rooted in the academic disciplines. These proposals come from many different sources. The California State Department of Education has been urging such ideas on schools since 1985, and several other states are taking similar steps. The National Council of Teachers of Mathematics (NCTM) has launched a campaign to replace rote memorization of facts and procedures with deep understanding of mathematical ideas in all American schools. Researchers and reformers concerned with reading and writing are pressing a parallel approach in schools across the country. Several other professional associations and disciplinary groups are writing new curricula and instructional standards. Publishers have begun to climb on the bandwagon, and new tests and texts are being proposed, designed, and written.

These reform efforts differ from one another in some important ways, but they all differ vastly from most current practice. For many reformers envision an active, constructivist sort of learning and an intellectually adventurous approach to teaching. They believe that instruction should be rooted in a thorough knowledge of academic disciplines and that students should grapple with deep issues in those disciplines as a regular part of their classwork. In contrast, most teaching in U.S. classrooms is rather didactic. Teachers and students spend most of their time with lectures, or formal recitations, or worksheets, or some combination thereof. Intellectual demands generally are relaxed, and a great deal of the work strikes observers as dull. Only a modest fraction of public school teachers have deep knowledge of any academic subject.

What are the prospects for efforts to reform teaching in American schools? The question is as old as public education, though reformers rarely seem aware of it. In the 1840s Horace Mann and other advocates of more thoughtful and humane instruction proposed several of the ideas that enthrall today's reformers and exhorted teachers to embrace them. In the 1890s John Dewey and many allies refined and expanded the ideas and launched a campaign to get teachers to adopt them. Some of the same ideas were revived or discovered anew by reformers in the Sputnik era and sent sailing toward teachers with federal financial and political support. A decade or so later some of the same ideas were again discovered and urged on teachers in the Open Education and Free School movements. Several elements in these reform programs have been broadly adopted, but only at the price of accommodation to many persistently traditional features of prior practice.[1] If John Dewey or Horace Mann were suddenly transported to classrooms today, they would find both startling changes and many sadly familiar practices.

One reason for such mixed and slow progress has been the great difficulty of teaching as many reformers wish—a point that generally has escaped most of those who propose it. Another reason is the great difficulty of learning to teach very differently, which also has escaped most reformers. The progress of reform also has been slowed by Americans' chronic ambivalence about serious intellectual work. One additional reason for slow progress is that educational policies have only occasionally and weakly promoted the sorts of teaching that reformers now propose. As we argued in Chapter Seven, policymakers have not earned high marks in pedagogy. The policies that are most simplistic intellectually have been most effective pedagogically, while the policies that are most ambitious intellectually have been least effective pedagogically.

New Designs for Policy

Despite this mixed and disappointing record, policymakers now urge much more challenging instruction on schools. In what follows we explore what it might take for them to succeed. We begin with a sketch of the sort of teaching that many current reformers envision, in part to suggest some of the things that most teachers would have to learn. With that in mind we turn to how teachers might learn a new approach to instruction and how policy might promote it. We sketch some proposals for a more educational approach to educational policy, but we note that it would be very different from current arrangements. Hence we also ask whether such a novel approach could reasonably be expected to work, given politics and education as we know them. Our aim in all this is exploratory: we want to probe unfamiliar terrain, not to issue a five-point program.

One thing that is missing in most reform proposals is a sense of what the new teaching might look like and what teachers would have to know and do in order to carry it off.[2] Several of the chapters in this book help in this department, for they sketch a few portraits of new pedagogies.[3] The portraits are unusual; in them teachers try to help students to learn to think and work in something like the ways that historians, mathematicians, and scientists think and work. These teachers treat the terrain of teaching as intellectual practices, that is, as history or mathematics or science. They see instruction in history or biology as a matter of getting students to engage significant problems in these practices, rather than simply transmitting the finished knowledge. Teachers invite students to try out ideas about how to set the problems, to discuss alternative ways to solve them, to test their arguments against evidence, and the like. Rather than acting as though students were empty vessels to be filled, teachers act as though students were active and interesting thinkers. Students must of course learn many finished products of these practices, but they do so while working as apprentice historians, mathematicians, and biologists work, rather than learning the finished products in isolation.

In order to do such work, teachers must find ways to provoke students' performance within the practices they teach. Hence they try to frame classroom tasks that are intellectually authentic yet accessible to apprentices. They try to set these tasks in ways that will stimulate students' interest and evoke lively work. They try to cultivate deep thought and rich discourse by devising appropriate activities, coaching, and conducting rather than didactically "telling knowledge" to students.[4] And teachers try to organize all of this so that members of the class will have access to one another's thinking.

Teaching of this sort defies many inherited ideological categories. It is not conventionally child-centered, for it is rooted in intellectual practices instead of childish activities. Yet it also is rooted in students' performance in those practices, and in their understanding of what makes a good performance. Similarly, though much teaching is done by learners in such classrooms, teaching is much more difficult than in conventional "knowledge telling." Finally, while teachers must be much more knowledgeable and active than their conventional colleagues in order to carry off such teaching, they must do so while finding ways to be much less prominent in the class's work.

When such teaching works, it greatly enriches instruction; but whether it works or not, it greatly complicates instruction. For teachers open up classroom communication to many more voices and much more independent and thoughtful speech. They revise the discourse structure of classrooms so that authority is diffused from teachers and texts to anyone who makes persuasive arguments. Students assume much larger instructional roles and responsibilities. The social organization of classrooms grows much more lively and rich, but teachers' intellectual and managerial responsibilities grow as well.

Learning and teaching as we have sketched them are much more social activities than ordinarily is the case in U.S. classrooms.

Deborah Ball writes that " . . . the GROUP is a focus of attention, even a sort of crucible for learning. Teaching in this way is not just some way to enhance each student's thinking and knowledge. It is also about interaction and community—as both means and goal. I keep thinking of how struck visitors to my class are (especially non-academics) when they see the . . . interactions and sense of community. [One visitor] . . . recently . . . was amazed to find that the girl he was sitting next to had an explicit record of what different issues had come up and what different kids had said during the previous class. She drew on these notes to extend the conversation during the class he was observing (she wrote 'Yesterday, T. said that 3/3 would be equal to 1 and I agree with that, but I also agree with what D. was saying. Let me try something up on the overhead?'). The kids build on one another's work, and they are working TOGETHER . . . playing off one another and . . . mov[ing] . . . collective understandings, assumptions, agreements along."[5]

To work in such ways teachers try to create classroom cultures that support disciplined inquiry. To do so they must respect and understand students' efforts to make sense of material. That is no mean feat, since students' ideas can be as puzzling and oblique as they are inventive and insightful. Their efforts to make sense of things sometimes parallel deep disputes and significant historical developments within fields, but they are expressed in the words and ideas of young beginners rather than experienced professionals. Teachers cannot make much sense of students' efforts to learn unless they understand the fields and know something of their development, as well as understand how children think about particular subjects and how they develop intellectually. Uncommon as such understanding is, it is still not enough, for teachers work with little crowds in classrooms. To create classroom cultures in which disciplined inquiry thrives, teachers also must encourage students to be both tolerant and critical—to respect others' views but also to subject those views to the intellectual discipline of historical or mathematical thought.[6] Teachers must cultivate students' respect for one another's ideas and their capacities for disciplined argument, for probing one another's ideas, and for thoughtful listening. These qualities can be encouraged among young children, but not easily.

No one knows if the sort of teaching and learning that we

have been describing is exactly what most reformers have in mind, for the rhetoric of reform is largely a paper and pencil matter. Few reformers have spent much time in classrooms of any description, and few have written in detail about teaching or referred to specific examples of instruction in their reports, speeches, and proposals.[7] But the pedagogies sketched above do have much in common with recent reform rhetoric. Unlike arguments for reform, though, examples of ambitious pedagogy are quite rare, for most schoolteachers and students see instruction as a matter of giving and getting the right answers. The combination of intellectual tolerance and intellectual discipline that our colleagues have written about in this book is unusual even in college and university classrooms, where most teachers are quite knowledgeable and most students are easy to manage. American education offers few examples that suggest what might be possible, and from which teachers might learn.

But even if teachers had many examples from which to learn, they would find that teaching of this sort is very difficult. Academic work is much more complex and demanding when students try to make sense of biology or literature than when they simply memorize the frog's anatomy or the sentence's structure. Teachers need to know a great deal to understand and appreciate students' ideas, and they must be able to manage complex social interactions about the ideas. Still another reason such teaching is rare is that it is uncertain. Instruction is much less predictable when students discuss and debate their interpretations of a story, or their conception of vertebrate anatomy, than when they memorize facts in isolated silence at their desks and disgorge them in recitation. Teachers must cope with much greater uncertainty when students present ideas that are difficult to understand, when they offer unpredictable insights in discussions, and when they get into complicated disagreements. It is unsettling to confront such uncertainties and difficult to manage them without closing down discussion. Much modern social and psychological research converges on the notion that the mind typically deals with uncertainty by reducing or eliminating it.[8] If so, teaching of the sort that we discuss here cuts across the grain of some deep psychic dispositions or cognitive structures.

Another reason that teaching of this sort is rare is that it is risky. When teachers construct classroom work so that it turns on extensive student participation, they enhance their dependence on students. Teachers are the professionals in charge, but if students do not do the work, have good ideas, and engage in lively discussions, the class will fall flat and the teacher will have failed publicly. Teachers who try to work in the ways we have sketched must manage greater vulnerability to students than if they taught in a more closed and traditional manner.[9]

The teaching that reformers seem to envision thus would require vast changes in what most teachers know and believe. Teachers would have to revise their conception of learning, to treat it as an active process of constructing ideas rather than a passive process of absorbing information. They would have to rediscover knowledge as something that is constructed and contested rather than handed down by authorities.[10] They would have to see that learning sometimes flourishes better in groups than alone at one's desk with a worksheet. And in order to learn, teachers would have to unlearn much deeply held knowledge and many fond beliefs. Such learning and unlearning would require a revolution in thought, and scholars in several fields have shown that such revolutions are very difficult to foment.[11] Moreover, once teachers' academic knowledge and conceptions of learning changed, they would have to learn how to teach differently.

The reform of teaching therefore would entail an extraordinary agenda for teachers' learning. We wonder if it could be accomplished, and if it could, by what means. Several of our colleagues in this book doubt that teachers would learn a new pedagogy from conventional teacher education, and they suggest some elements of an alternative. One is that teachers would have extended opportunities to "practice" in ways that enabled them to gradually contrive a very different pedagogy, rather than the usual quick-hit "inservice" workshops.[12] Another is that thoughtful colleagues would observe teachers' work, report on it, and make the observations part of a sustained conversation about teaching and learning to teach. Teachers then would have opportunities to see their teaching from other perspectives, perhaps would learn how to adopt such perspectives themselves, and thus would become more reflective about their work. Another element still is that teachers would have opportunities to reflect on the content of the conversations, to try out revisions in their work, and to weigh the results.

These ideas imply another: as they learned a new pedagogy, teachers would profit from working in protected situations. Protection would be useful in part because teachers would have so much to learn and unlearn. Unlearning is a difficult and little-explored feature of learning that would be especially troublesome in this case, for teachers would have to become novices after many years of thinking they had been accomplished professionals. They would have to cast aside much that they had known and done confidently, yet they would still have to carry on as professionals in their classrooms. Protection also would be useful because teachers would be learning to work in ways that were much more uncertain, and that made them quite vulnerable. Teachers also would profit from protection against the many mistakes they would make as they abandoned old practices and acquired new ones. There is, after all, the possibility that their novice efforts would impede students' learning, or would become unduly painful, or would damage them professionally. Many arrangements could afford some such protection, including special schools, classes, institutes, support groups, and networks for professional development. But one key feature of any such arrangement would be work with more accomplished professionals in relationships that combined trust and critical reflection.[13] Finally, teachers would profit from protection against the typically frantic press for reform-in-a-minute, so that their time to learn would be commensurate with the scale and scope of the learning.[14]

How could policy promote this unusual agenda for teachers' learning? The simplest course of action for policymakers would be to declare the matter an important priority, set goals or standards, and turn operations over to colleges, universities, and other agencies that educate teachers. But those institutions have little capacity to support the sorts of teaching or teacher learning described here. To begin with, inadequate preparation still is no barrier to becoming a teacher. Most colleges and universities grant degrees to intending elementary teachers despite their thin knowledge of the subjects they will teach, and they grant degrees to intending secondary teachers despite their thin knowledge of pedagogy and learning. School systems readily hire those teachers. In a sense the schools have little choice, for undergraduates who declare an intention to teach elementary school cannot major in an academic subject in most institutions of higher education; they must instead major in teaching, learning, and other aspects of education. In contrast, those who declare an intention to teach secondary school must major in an academic subject, and study learning and pedagogy only quite superficially. But the schools have made few efforts to change things. Many state and local school systems make it exceedingly difficult for applicants to get elementary school teaching jobs if they have majored in an academic subject rather than elementary education, and they offer no incentives for secondary teachers to acquire strong pedagogical preparation. One would think that universities could easily repair the situation by opening academic majors to intending elementary school teachers so they could more adequately study the subjects they will teach and by requiring much deeper study of pedagogy and learning for intending secondary school teachers. But those seemingly simple steps would be very difficult. Efforts to replace the elementary education major with academic fields, or to create joint majors, have been resisted by disciplinarians as well as by educationists, as have efforts to deepen the education of intending secondary school teachers by including more attention to learning and pedagogy. [15]

Even if these problems of curriculum and course offerings were miraculously solved tomorrow, teachers still would find it very difficult to learn the pedagogy that recent reformers propose. One reason is that few college and university professors teach that way. Most intending teachers get most of their undergraduate education in departments of humanities, science, and social sciences. Even those who major in elementary education do two-thirds or three-quarters of their studies in such departments, and instruction there generally is as traditional and didactic as most schoolteaching. Professors know their subjects much more deeply than most schoolteachers, but more sophisticated teaching does not follow necessarily or even frequently from greater academic knowledge. [16] Another reason it would be very difficult for teachers to learn the pedagogy that recent reformers propose is that most teachers are educated at public universities and colleges in which large classes, multiple-choice tests, and little student contact with faculty are the order of the day. Like most other undergraduates, intending teachers' education often is in the hands of graduate students who are beginners in their subjects, inexperienced at teaching, and unwilling or unable to invest much in learning to teach well. Still another reason it would be very difficult for teachers to learn the pedagogy that recent reformers propose is that most academic departments would neither permit intending elementary school teachers to take the regular sequence of disciplinary courses for majors, nor offer an alternative sequence of intellectually sound courses for those who wished to major but did not intend graduate work in the field. It also would be very difficult for teachers to learn the pedagogy that recent reformers propose, because most education schools and departments could not now offer professionally sound and intellectually defensible studies in pedagogy and learning in academic subjects for teachers at any level. Much of what these schools and departments currently offer is notoriously thin, and little of it is deeply grounded in knowledge of academic subjects.[17] Hence even if colleges and universities did greatly increase intending teachers' opportunities to study academic subjects, learning, and pedagogy, that would be unlikely to produce the teaching that reformers now envision.

To reform schoolteaching by revising college and university instruction would entail much more than revamping undergraduate curricula and course requirements. Great changes in the culture and educational priorities of higher-education institutions also would be required. Few members of the academy exhibit any taste for such work, and signs of inducements that could alter their inclinations are scarce. Recent efforts to reform teacher education have been launched with much fanfare, but they have made only a little progress at best. Moreover, many institutions of higher education have been in a serious revenue squeeze for years, and it is getting worse. The likelihood that colleges and universities will take up major reforms of curriculum and instruction diminishes as money grows shorter, administrative discretion is reduced, and faculty positions are lost. If state and federal policymakers relied on higher education to fundamentally revise instruction in the public schools, they would almost certainly be disappointed.

Reformers could instead turn to continuing professional education, in hope of reeducating teachers while they are at work. But while state and local school systems and universities spend heavily for such education every year, most of it has a dismal reputation. Various professional agencies sponsor a blizzard of workshops, but most are short, simple, and superficial. Universities and colleges also offer much continuing professional education, but most of that is commonly regarded as either irrelevant or thin. Challenging content is almost as rare as the continuing professional contact that can sustain new ideas and practices in classrooms. Some professors and professional development agencies do a better job, but they tend to be few in number and to have modest capacity. Many subsist on external grants from one year to the next, and regularly must change their agendas to accommodate shifting governmental and philanthropic fashions. Few work with teachers for the time or with the intensity that would be required to make and sustain basic change in practice.

Schools also offer extensive continuing education, and policymakers might hope to turn it toward reform. But most of the schools' education for teachers is reported to be a pabulum of brief, superficial, and unconnected workshops. They are rarely inspired by a larger vision of instruction, nor are they tied to deeper issues in curriculum, assessment, or learning. Additionally, few schools offer teachers extended or well-designed opportunities to learn on the job, nor do they create powerful inducements for it.[18] Thoughtful observers argue that schools would become places for teachers to learn only if there were major changes in the institutional culture, in teachers' conceptions of their work, and perhaps in their jobs as well.[19] Such changes would take a great deal of time and energy in any circumstances, but they would be especially demanding when educators were struggling with shrinking budgets and rising social problems, as they do today.

If our analysis is roughly correct, policymakers would not dramatically change pedagogy by simply passing that assignment to the existing agencies of teacher education, for those agencies have neither the capacity to carry most of the educational load themselves nor the disposition to build that capacity. Policymakers and analysts committed to reform, therefore, would have to find other ways to enable teachers to learn. Schools, universities, and professional development agencies would almost surely play an important part in any such effort, but simple delegation is not indicated.

What might policymakers do instead? They could make policy itself much more educational for educators. Educational policy continues to grow: reformers in and out of government are devising more demanding standards, designing more challenging assessments, writing more thoughtful instructional frameworks, and developing more intelligent curricula. Each of these endeavors increases the things that teachers would have to learn if they were to succeed, but few are well enough designed to promote such learning. To make such policies much more educational for educators, the processes in which policy is made and enacted would have to be opened up so that they created many more opportunities to learn. And those opportunities would have to be designed so that they embodied the sorts of teaching and learning that reformers wish to promote for classrooms.[20]

This approach would give an entirely new meaning to the term "educational policy." The idea has a certain appeal; if policymakers want to promote reform, should they not organize policy so that teachers could learn what they needed to know in order to succeed? But Americans have little experience with endeavors of this sort, and we know little about what may be entailed. To probe those entailments, we consider a few examples of how educational policy could become more educational for those who enact it.

Take the case of creating a new instructional framework in any academic subject. Framework design opens up fundamental questions about the nature and purposes of instruction, and thus presents many educational opportunities. Perhaps the most direct way to make framework design more educational for educators would be to create an accompanying design for learning—in effect, a curriculum of framework creation. If such a curriculum were tightly tied to framework development, the very act of constructing new instructional goals and standards would be embedded in an educational scheme. The formation of instructional policy would become a simultaneous venture in adult education. But a curriculum of framework design also could be more loosely tied to actual framework construction. Educators could be engaged in learning activities that simulated or paralleled framework construction, but on a separate track. In this case the formation of instructional policy would be accompanied at a distance by related educational endeavors. A given venture in framework design could, of course, have some tight and some loose links to a curriculum for learning from the activity.

However these links were set, the aim would be to undertake framework design so that it also presented a rich set of occasions for educators to learn. One key element in any such curriculum would be strategies to help educators think about the scope and structure of instructional frameworks. Such things are largely unknown to Americans, and it would be important to cultivate familiarity with a new approach to instructional purposes and content. Reading and analyzing frameworks from other nations and the few U.S. states that have them would be one fruitful way to begin. In that connection the curriculum also could invite teachers to draft, justify, and criticize their own framework proposals, or to comment on draft proposals for state or national frameworks. An important part of such work would include helping teachers to identify themes for a proposed framework, to consider relations among themes, to analyze the advantages and disadvantages of particular themes, and to cultivate ways to discuss these matters. None of this could be done well without knowledge of the disciplinary fields involved, and given the state of most teachers' knowledge, any such curriculum would have to offer ways for many of them to learn much more. A curriculum could, for example, suggest how teachers could develop the themes that they proposed by identifying and investigating sample topics within one, and planning a few lessons. Such activities would offer a way of learning more about the content of a field and teaching and learning in it, as well as about what remained to be learned.

Another crucial element in any curriculum of framework design would be the identification of materials. Teachers could read books, original sources, experiments, and the like and discuss their suitability. Such work would be an extraordinary opportunity to learn about the intellectual terrain of a field, about the various approaches to mapping it, and about the many different ways in which a single set of instructional goals could be realized in classrooms. A curriculum of this sort also could invite teachers to imagine how they might deal with a particular theme in a series of lessons. Teachers could teach the lessons to colleagues, and, in light of that experience, discuss how they could revise readings, lesson formats, and even framework designs. A proper curriculum would suggest ways to go about such work, including guides to help teachers in scrutinizing the instructional properties of materials, advice about how to weigh their value for teaching and learning, assistance in developing and teaching sample lessons, and guidance in the revision of frameworks in light of discussions and classroom trials.

The same sort of curriculum could be created for the design of new assessments, for, like framework construction, assessment raises fundamental questions: what has been learned? What should be? How is learning best investigated? Here again, the key point would be to frame reform as a set of educational opportunities. One key element in any such curriculum would be guidance in writing blueprints for new assessment, including examples from other school systems, suggested ways to compare blueprints, and exercises that help educators and interested officials or members of the public to learn something of the genre. A curriculum of assessment design could also suggest ways in which teachers might draft blueprints, or comment on drafts already circulating in their state or region. In that connection a curriculum also could suggest ways to use the drafts and comments as a basis for investigating the strengths and weaknesses of proposed blueprints—that is, comparing them to extant assessments and instructional frameworks, exchanging analyses, inviting comments from assessment specialists, and the like.

All of this would in a sense be preliminary to creating assessments. A curriculum of assessment design could offer teachers guidance in the definition of domains, in the composition of questions and other assessment tasks, and in developing rubrics for evaluating answers. It could suggest how teachers might analyze the quality of the questions they wrote and improve on them. Such a curriculum also could organize ways in which teachers could study the topics that they wrote questions about, as they wrote and discussed the questions. That sort of work would both deepen teachers' knowledge of the matters assessed and improve their understanding of the strengths and limitations of assessment within specific subject matter fields. Finally, with work of this sort en route, a curriculum of assessment design could help to guide teachers' study of the relations among assessment, frameworks, and curricula.

One notion behind these ideas is that the education of educators could flower if it were tied to certain crucial practical tasks that also were intellectually fundamental.[21] The short list of such tasks certainly would include much of the program of the current reform movement: devising new academic standards, designing new assessments, writing new instructional frameworks, and developing new curricula. In that sense the present moment in American education offers unparalleled educational opportunities. While it would be no mean feat to develop curricula for reform that could realize those opportunities, if it were done well, many teachers could gain enormously. Since framework and assessment revision would be continuing tasks in any vital educational system, teachers would be able to contribute to reform and learn from it on a continuing basis. Several states have edged a bit in these directions recently, as they have begun to devise new frameworks and revamp curriculum and testing;[22] but state officials have neither envisioned nor designed such work as a major project in the education of educators. That is not surprising, for the agenda that we have outlined could hardly be done well in the ways that most education agencies now approach continuing professional education—that is, in a few stolen hours after school, on weekends, or in isolated bursts of summer activity.

What would this sort of scheme entail for policy? Most generally, policy would be reconceived as an educational endeavor, and many opportunities to learn would be designed into policymaking processes. Such work would take extraordinary imagination as well as instructional design capacities that now barely exist either in government or in public education. Yet those changes would be for naught if teachers did not capitalize on them, and most teachers already are quite busy, and few have any sense that the sorts of activities that we have sketched should be part of their assignments.[23] Hence teachers' work, or their ideas about their work, also would have to be substantially revised. Additionally, teachers could not do it alone. An educational approach to educational policy also would require learning and teaching on a broader scale, including specialists in assessment, experts in pedagogy, and subject matter specialists from universities and other agencies. They would have much to contribute as teachers and much to learn as participants in a novel sort of educational policy. None of these things would be likely to occur without other changes: in the way teachers' work was understood and treated by administrators, politicians, and the public, in the mobilization of potent inducements to learn, in the provision of money and other resources to support learning, and hence in the quality of political and educational leadership.

But we are getting ahead of our story. Consider one more example of the approach we have discussed—the development of new curricula for students. Curriculum could be one of the most intimate connections between policymakers and classroom practitioners, for curriculum standards and materials play a large role in the work that teachers and students do together every day. The recent reform movement has produced a small avalanche of proposals to revise that work by fundamentally changing the substance and structure of academic subjects. The projects include those of NCTM, Project 2061, several in the National Academy of Sciences, several others in state governments, as well as others. Like the 1950s curriculum reforms, though, these endeavors often are discussed and carried out as though their authors were unaware of the enormous agenda for educators' learning that they entail.

It is not difficult to envision an alternative: reformers could design new curricula for students so that they were deeply educational for teachers. For example, an innovative unit on fractions for fourth graders could be accompanied by a teachers' fractions curriculum. The teachers' curriculum could offer an array of approaches to teaching and learning fractions and weave discussion of the mathematical ideas into those approaches. The curriculum also could discuss different ways to present each topic and analyze the strengths and limitations of various presentations. Each alternative could include examples of how to frame the mathematics, reports on the sorts of things that students said and did when material was presented to them in that way, and discussion of the mathematical content both of the material presented and students' responses. Such a curriculum also could discuss the ways in which teachers could interpret students' responses and how they could probe students' ideas to get a better idea of their thinking. In these ways and others, a teachers' fractions curriculum could offer teachers extended discussion of mathematics in the context of considering various ways to teach and learn mathematics. It could be accompanied by additional reading or other supporting material on the mathematical content of fractions, on how students think about this domain of mathematics, and on how accomplished teachers have handled both the material and students' responses to it.

We have not proposed a teacher's guide or classroom scripts. This sort of curriculum would be pointless if it did not influence teaching, but it would be equally pointless if it were mechanically conceived or executed. Our intention is to tie a program for teachers' learning to improved curriculum for students. The teachers' curriculum would be focused on mathematical pedagogy, that is, on the interactions among mathematics, representations of mathematical ideas, teaching, and learning. It could be organized around instructional issues that teachers would face every day as they sought to use the new curriculum with students. Our reasoning in this is straightforward. If recent efforts to reform education do entail the extraordinary learning for teachers that we suggest, new policies could not work unless ways were found to enable that learning. Since most teachers would have to continue to teach even as they learned to teach differently, much of that learning should be situated in or near classrooms. The curricula that teachers and students use every day would be one such situation.[24]

Curricula of this sort would substantially increase teachers' chances to learn the things that recent instructional policies entail, but they would not be easy to create. Curriculum design and publishing would have to be sharply reoriented so that they attended as much to teachers' as to students' learning. Teachers also would need opportunities to learn from the new curricula that were similar to the learning that reformers intend for students, for few American adults have experienced such learning, and teachers could hardly be expected to competently guide students through intricate processes of which they were ignorant. In addition to a new approach to curriculum design for teachers, such curricula also would require that teachers have time to read the new materials, chances to discuss them, helpful and knowledgeable people with whom to discuss them, opportunities to try out new approaches in their classes or elsewhere, and assistance in such tryouts. Changes of these sorts would add greatly to the time and other resources required to design and enact new curricula. They could not occur without thoughtful action by policymakers, publishers, schools, colleges, and universities, and a variety of professional and disciplinary organizations.[25]

These examples throw a little more light on what it may take to weave a suitable education for educators into educational policy. Policymakers would have to create opportunities for teachers to learn practices such as history or biology by engaging in them, conversing about them, articulating ideas, testing them against evidence, and the like. Rather than acting as though teachers were empty vessels to be filled, policymakers would act as though teachers were active and interesting thinkers and central in policymaking. Teachers would have the sort of opportunities to learn that reformers think students should have. Doing these things would not be easy, since few policymakers and managers ever learned that way in school, let alone taught others. We wonder where policymakers could learn. But assume they did, somehow. Rather than considering teachers as the "implementers" of policy, they would treat teachers and administrators as though they were intelligent commentators on policy and significant participants in creating and revising it. Policymakers and managers would eschew more familiar and didactic roles in which they "tell knowledge" to educators, and instead would engage them as active, learning collaborators.

Analysts are familiar with several criteria for effective policy, including political feasibility, leadership, appeal to important constituencies, and the like. Our proposal adds another: educational policy should be deeply educational for those who enact it. That criterion would not be easy to satisfy. Simply to design the sorts of opportunities to learn from policy that we have sketched would be difficult, time-consuming, and costly. To actually integrate teachers' learning into policymaking would be vastly more so. Revising extant conceptions of teachers' work and its organization would further add to the costs and complications.

Moreover, thus far we have focused chiefly on what an educational approach to educational policy would entail for teachers. But such curricula as we have sketched also would complicate pol-

icy formation and enactment. Efforts to incorporate pedagogy as
well as politics and finance would greatly complicate policymaking. Additionally, if learning from policy became crucial, policymakers would have to attend closely to what teachers and other
educators understood. That would greatly complicate what analysts
have called implementation; the activity itself might have to be
reconceived as reinventing policy.[26] Finally, if they did carefully
attend to teachers, policymakers' uncertainty and dependence on
teachers would increase. For discourse about policy would open up,
much as classroom discourse opens up in adventurous teaching.
New voices would be drawn into policymaking, and other voices
long silent or ignored would be raised. Teachers' role in producing
policy would be more plainly recognized and enhanced, but that
could crowd policymakers in unfamiliar and often uncomfortable
ways. As in innovative classrooms, such measures could improve
understanding, but they would increase debate and division. One
expects that results would improve in the long run, but one knows
that difficulties would increase in the meantime.

Conclusion

Though we have only sketched the outline of a new pedagogy for
policy, it conjures up a cloud of questions. One particularly stands
out: could state and national agencies actually devise and enact such
"educational policies" as we have discussed?

It is not difficult to imagine a policy agenda—we already
have sketched some of it. Policies and programs intended to reform
instructional standards and assessment would have to be greatly
expanded in order to enhance their educative power. Curriculum
reform would have to be redefined and broadened to help teachers
learn to teach in unfamiliar and demanding ways. New policies and
programs might be required so that higher education institutions
could offer teachers extensive help in such learning. Agencies of
continuing professional education surely would have to be expanded, reoriented, and strengthened. Schools' organization and
professional culture also would have to change to strongly support
teachers' learning. That would not be easy, for while policymakers
could relatively easily "restructure" schools to offer teachers more

time, autonomy, power, and the like, such things often come to little by themselves. As Sarah McCarthey and Penelope Peterson argue in Chapter Five, when restructuring is unaccompanied by extensive opportunities for teachers to learn, the results are unimpressive.[27] And Joan Talbert and Milbrey McLaughlin point out in Chapter One that professional and institutional cultures are much more potent influences on teaching than most structural arrangements in education.[28] Hence policymakers could find themselves searching for ways to tie change in schools' organization to changes in their culture and educational opportunities for teachers.

One way to make that connection would be to make learning count much more heavily than it now does for teachers. At the moment university course credits count for advanced degrees, and often for salaries as well. But those incentives have not produced many fine courses, nor do they seem to have appreciably advanced teachers' knowledge of pedagogy or academic subjects. As things now stand, serious learning only counts professionally for teachers if they individually choose to make it count. Many teachers are eager to learn, but they are most interested in learning about specific practices that will help them today and tomorrow. They exhibit much less interest either in learning deeply about academic subjects or in learning how to dramatically change their teaching. Yet the current reforms would not take deep root unless teachers were strongly motivated to learn just such things, and to make their teaching much more difficult in the process. Policymakers could decide that they should devise potent incentives for teachers to learn such things and to continue to learn through many difficulties.[29]

Were government to undertake such an agenda, educational policy would greatly expand. State or federal agencies would set dramatically new and higher standards, devise new curricula, create new assessments, build vastly greater capacity for teacher education, and more. As policymaking became more ambitious and complex, government would grow.

Yet the reform agenda that we sketched would not succeed unless educational policymaking also was drastically reduced.[30] A clearer focus on ambitious teaching and learning would require that the accumulated clutter of competing and overlapping programs and policies be cut back and cleaned up. Lacking such action, reforms would only add to conflict and ambiguity in instructional guidance.[31] But such cutbacks would require painful merger or discontinuation of many state and federal initiatives, and of the administrative units tied to them. If they focused on a smaller and more coherent agenda of fundamental change, policymakers also would have to alter many of their present habits—for example, embrace much longer time horizons for policy development and enactment, as well as evaluation. They also would have to abandon their continuing intervention in schools and the associated shifts of direction every few years. That would entail new relationships with local schools in which much stronger guidance for content, standards, and results was mixed with much broader support and much less interference in other areas.

This would be a curious combination: dramatic expansion of government in certain respects and equally dramatically contraction in others. The combination would be difficult in any political system, but it would be especially troublesome in the United States. One reason is the power of short-term incentives. Elected officials crave programs or policies that are identified with their name and for which they can claim quick credit with constituents. Would state, local, and federal policymakers willingly renounce the political benefits of short-term tinkering with schools? We cannot imagine why, short of a major crisis or an extraordinarily powerful reform movement. Another source of trouble would be the interest groups that have grown up around existing policies and programs. It would be unprecedented for them to give up concrete and immediate political benefits in favor of more abstract and distant reform schemes.

Efforts to simultaneously shrink and expand education policy also would require extensive coordination among governments within America's fragmented political system. Only a few federal agencies are concerned with schools, and there are fifty state governments—a modest number as U.S. politics goes. But each of those governments is divided into executive and legislative branches, which have deeply different responsibilities for education and whose incumbents regularly differ about educational policy. The work of both branches also is subject to review by state and federal judiciaries, which have been increasingly active in education and quite willing to overturn the decisions of legislators and governors. There also are more than fifteen thousand autonomous local school governments, and an even larger number of county and municipal governments whose actions bear on local schools through finance and other means. If the reforms sketched above were national or regional in scope, they would require unprecedented coordination among many of these governments. Hundreds or thousands of school agencies at all levels would have to agree on new educational purposes and on new instructional guidance arrangements to achieve those purposes. They also would have to acquiesce in roughly identical reductions of their authority in order to clean up the existing clutter of programs and policies. Yet those same battalions of governments would have to accept an extraordinary expansion in the power both of the state or federal agencies that would guide instruction and of the local schools that would enact a new education. We can imagine such unprecedented intergovernmental coordination, but not without also imagining some extraordinary educational crisis or powerful movement for reform that would compel action.

Political fragmentation would pose one additional problem. A more educational approach to educational policy would require close connections between policy and practice, but the design of American government frustrates such connections. For example, devising and enacting the curricula of framework reform that we sketched earlier would entail close and sustained work among state or federal policymakers, publishers, university faculty, schoolteachers, and administrators, among others. Lacking such collaboration, educators would have few opportunities to learn from new instructional frameworks, and developers and policymakers could not learn from educators' efforts to use the frameworks. Yet making and sustaining such connections would be very difficult, for American government was designed to frustrate such things. Authority in education was divided among state, local, and federal governments in an elaborate federal system, and it was divided within governments by the separation of powers. These divisions were specifically calculated to limit the powers of each branch of government and to inhibit coordinated action across governments. They gained force from the country's great size and diversity. Close relations between policy and practice are difficult to sustain even in much smaller and more coherent systems, but the vast sprawl of internally divided and jurisdictionally distinct state, federal, and local governments has made them nearly impossible to arrange in America.[32] Great gulfs separate state and national policymaking from classroom practice in the United States,[33] and building the infrastructure to span those gulfs would not be easy.

The reforms that we have been discussing would require a paradoxical mixture of political activism and restraint. Government officials would have to make the sort of extraordinary investments in their spheres that adventurous teaching requires from teachers and students. These would include a great expansion of government action and associated outlays of energy, time, money, and effort, but they also would include much less government action in many areas of education, an entirely different way of relating to those who enact policy, and much longer political and educational time horizons. Those who made and managed policy would work harder, face much greater uncertainty, and take many more risks, in return for many fewer short-term political rewards.

One could therefore conclude that the generally weak pedagogies of policy described in Chapter Seven make sense. The fragmented structure of U.S. government and our old diffidence about intellectually demanding education may mean that policymakers should ignore proposals for intellectually more demanding education and for a more educational approach to educational policy. There is, after all, a relatively good fit between recent emphasis on "basics" and traditional pedagogy. There also is a good fit between basics and what the adult population knows about academic work and believes about school. But there is a great difference between traditional pedagogy and the recent reform proposals. Conversely, there is a great gulf between reformers' conceptions of knowledge and instruction and what most adult Americans know and believe about school. The recent reforms would provoke terrific tensions with inherited knowledge and beliefs, and they would demand extraordinary change and learning from most American grown-ups. There are a few signs of a few of these changes, but only a few.[34] We wonder if American governments are well suited to lead the struggle for reform, given the great changes that would be required and the political tensions that would have to be endured.

To share this doubt is not to think that reform is lost. One may only conclude that American governments are presently an unsuitable vehicle for fundamental change in teaching and learning. If so, reformers would need to invent ways to improve instruction in state-sponsored schools without requiring state agencies to bear the chief burden of change. For example, reformers could create nongovernmental agencies with broad charters to improve public education by various "systemic" approaches to reform. The National Board for Professional Teaching Standards is one current case in point, though its charter is restricted to teacher certification. Agencies of this sort could develop the linked instructional frameworks, curricula, and examination systems that many reformers now advocate. The New Standards Project presently has something of that sort under way in several states. Such agencies also could devise and implement the sort of curricula for reform that we sketched above, to create opportunities for teachers to learn in and around the development processes, something that no agency appears to be doing on a large scale. The same agencies could organize field trials that would enable systematic learning from the endeavor and consequent revision and redevelopment.

Nongovernmental agencies of this sort would of course have to work closely with some state and local school systems, or with networks dedicated to local school improvement, or with consortia of individual schools. But they would do that work while keeping sponsorship and development of new approaches to instruction at a healthy distance from government. Given the weak pedagogical record of education governments, building the capacities for instructional change might better be undertaken by agencies that stand outside the official policy apparatus. Whatever their enthusiasm today, precedent suggests that policymakers would be likely to corrupt and distract ambitious instructional reforms tomorrow, rather than support and sustain them. If schooling did change, government might adopt the new system, but in the charged atmosphere of U.S. politics even that could be troublesome. The development work also would have to be scheduled so that it made room for the extraordinary learning that successful enactment would entail. Patience and persistence are not virtues of domestic politics in the United States, and they have been especially unfamiliar in education. Keeping the development work largely outside public political management might protect it from the fickleness of American politics well enough for a new system of instruction to mature. But that would require large infusions of private funds and great managerial tact and skill. It also would be unlikely to succeed without at least modest support from state and federal governments and enthusiastic participation by many schools and school systems.

Nongovernmental agencies would not eliminate the problems of public sponsorship. They would only permit reformers to struggle with those problems from a different and possibly improved vantage point. And even if reformers did well on that score, everything else would remain. The stuff of reform itself would have to be developed—new instructional frameworks, curricula, and examination systems and the links among them. It also would remain to revise schools, teaching, and the incentives that surround schooling, so that much more ambitious approaches to instruction made sense for those working in and around schools. And it would remain to create a new pedagogy of reform, so that teachers and others had ample opportunities to learn, in and around the processes of development and change. Whatever their sponsorship, new pedagogies are unlikely to mature in classrooms unless they also ripen in reform itself.

Notes

1. Cohen, 1989; Cohen & Grant, in press; and Cuban, 1984.
2. Elmore & McLaughlin (1988) frame the problem of changing teacher practice as one of teachers' willingness to learn and their opportunities to learn.
3. Chapters Two, Three, and Four of this book.
4. Duffy & Roehler, 1986; Lampert, 1988a; Newmann, 1988; Sizer, 1984; and Scardamalia, Bereiter, & Steinbach, 1984.
5. Deborah Ball, personal communication, March 23, 1992.
6. Lampert, 1986.
7. One additional reason that we are unsure about reformers' ideas is that they are imprecise about the sorts of teaching they

wish to promote. Everyone argues for intellectually demanding teaching, but agreement often ends there. Some advocate a constructivist approach to knowledge, while others seem to hold more traditional conceptions of knowledge. Some reformers point approvingly to innovative teachers who encourage rich discourse in classrooms, while others admire instruction in nonpublic schools, where most teaching seems to be quite traditional and didactic. For relevant discussions of teaching in nonpublic schools see Powell, Farrar, & Cohen (1985) and Bryk & Lee (in press).

8. Braybrooke & Lindblom, 1963; and Simon, 1976.

9. Lampert, 1988b; Duffy & Roehler, 1986; Newmann, 1988; Cuban, 1984; Cohen, 1988; Cohen, unpublished manuscripts, March 1992.

10. For instance, mathematics is a leading area in the current reforms, but most elementary school teachers have a very modest understanding of this subject (Post, Behr, Harel, Lesh, & Taylor, 1988; Thompson, 1984). Teachers would need to learn a great deal more mathematics and they would have to shed the idea that mathematical knowledge is fixed and given, handed down by authorities in books and other sacred locations.

11. Fiske & Taylor, 1984; Guthrie, 1990; Kuhn, 1962; Lakatos & Musgrave, 1970; Markus & Zajonc, 1985; and Nisbett & Ross, 1980. Teachers' difficulties would not stem only from the intellectual problems of changing well-established ideas and practices. Teachers' efforts to become active inquirers often disturbs their personal and professional lives, as several of the earlier chapters note.

12. Chapters Two and Three of this book.

13. Chapters Two, Three, and Four of this book. The combination of support and criticism here parallels the classroom culture that adventurous teachers try to create with their students. The theme is explored in the earlier chapters just cited, where the authors describe the difficulties they encounter in trying to create a context in which students are encouraged to learn but in which they also will risk trying new ideas and com-

menting thoughtfully on each other's ideas. Peter Elbow (1986) writes about this challenge.

14. Teachers additionally would benefit if they were protected from many of the program mandates that pervade state and federal school policy, for they often produce a compliance orientation that runs counter to the approach to instruction that teachers would be trying to learn.

15. There are many reasons for resistance. One is structural: The undergraduate curriculum has steadily grown as new subjects or subfields were created and old ones grew. Undergraduate requirements also have grown apace, and there is less room to add courses. Many undergraduate majors therefor are now precariously close to an undeclared five-year term. Another reason for resistance is governmental: The education curriculum has grown more packed as state governments have added requirements in reading, mathematics, special education, and other areas. Still another reason is simple self-interest: Most arts and sciences departments are unwilling to give up their academic dominion over intending secondary teachers' coursework, and most education departments are unwilling to cede dominion over intending elementary teachers' coursework. Another reason still is attitudinal: Most faculty members and administrators in arts and sciences departments hold educationists in low regard and prefer not to be associated with their endeavors, while most educationists are defensive about their low standing in academia and avoid contact with those resident on the main line. A final reason for resistance is intellectual: Few educationists are deeply knowledgeable about arts and sciences disciplines, and few members of arts and sciences departments are deeply knowledgeable about pedagogy and learning. Hence few members of either group are well situated to thoughtfully discuss the issues that serious curriculum revision would entail.

16. Boyer, 1983; Cohen, 1988; Cuban, 1984; McKeachie, Pintrich, Lin, & Smith, 1986.

17. The academic quality of education schools and departments has greatly improved in the last three decades, but the improvements all have been in imitation of conventional mainline aca-

demic values. Education schools and departments have recruited more faculty members who are active researchers and who publish in academic journals. Moreover they have added faculty in the more academically respectable subfields of educational psychology, sociology, politics, and the like and have deemphasized practical work in teaching, teacher supervision, and studies of learning in classrooms. Hence these improvements did not increase, and in many cases actually reduced, the capacity of education schools and departments either to undertake thoughtful research on teaching or to offer intellectually and professionally substantial teacher education.

18. There are some counterexamples of well-designed educational activities. One is teacher work and discussion groups that are organized around deepening knowledge and improving practice in specific areas of the curriculum. The Bay Area Writing Project is one case in point. But we know of few examples in which schools have devised and supported such endeavors.

19. Johnson, 1990; Little, 1982.

20. Elmore & McLaughlin deal very thoughtfully with some of these issues. And Milbrey McLaughlin's studies of change in classroom organization found that change in practice occurred when teachers were actively involved in policy development and implementation—that is, in creating materials, solving problems, and interacting with one another as well as with curriculum specialists and other outside consultants around policy issues (McLaughlin, 1978). From this and other accounts of teacher collaboration in reform she concluded that success in changing practice may require an ongoing process of "mutual adaptation" (p. 340) in which teachers are treated as developers of new practices and allowed, over time, to adapt policy goals to the concrete setting of their classrooms. Here again there are some parallels between uncommon cases of policy enactment and the pedagogy of policy that we discuss.

21. In all of these examples we sketch one possible version of a learning community that embraces a variety of associated activities: collaborative projects, frequent personal exchanges, and connections to other professional communities. Some readers will recognize John Dewey's notion of the continuum.

In such educational activities, he argued, accepted distinctions dissolve, and seemingly distinct elements become part of the same practical process: the subject matter and the method of instruction, the policy and its enactment, knowing and doing. The processes themselves might be considered both as means and important goals of education reform. In these cases the means and ends would continually be reinvented (see Deborah Ball's comment on p. 244 about interaction and sense of community in her classroom as "both means and goal.") For a brief discussion of the education change process viewed as both means and goal see Sarason (1982).

22. Education officials in California, Vermont, and several other states recently did something of this sort as they revised assessments and content standards. For example, California state officials have involved some teachers in redesign of the CAP, and teachers there also have been represented on various bodies that have designed reform policies. But with a few exceptions state officials have involved only a few dozen teachers on statewide oversight committees. None of the committees have developed an extensive instructional agenda for other teachers, nor have they involved many teachers. In contrast, the New Standards Project has proposed an examination system that would incoporate many of the education elements discussed here, though the scale and depth of such education-from-reform remains to be seen.

23. These difficulties recently have impeded assessment and curriculum redesign in Vermont.

24. A curriculum of this sort could be offered in print, but it would be much better in a combination of videotape and text. It would be even more powerful in an interactive computer-video environment, especially if teachers also had the capacity for network consultation with each other and more accomplished colleagues.

25. Our discussion reveals that not only teaching but many practices that bear on schools would have to change. For example, during most of this century politicians and businessmen ignored public schools or supported only minimum programs for most students. And most leaders in education long have

been inclined to the view that most students needed basic and practical education, rather than more high-flown and demanding stuff. These tendencies were entirely representative. Though the American people have been enthusiasts for schooling, few have been keen on intellectually ambitious education. This is as true for parents as it is for political and business leaders, which suggests a large task for adult education and political persuasion. Dramatic changes in educational processes and content within schools would require changes in the expectations that parents and politicians have held for schools and students, and in a divided society like that of the United States, in which schools are locally controlled, efforts to make such changes could generate terrific conflict.

26. On that point see the essay by Wildavsky & Majone (1979).

27. For further discussion on the topic of discourse communities, see McCarthy and Peterson (Chapter Five of this book).

28. Chapter Six of this book.

29. There is no plainly best way to rearrange American education so that most teachers and other educators have strong incentives to tackle the difficult sorts of learning sketched above. One possible approach arises from school systems in Europe and Asia. In some of those nations teachers' promotion and other aspects of professional advancement are tied to assessments of their teaching performance by inspectors who conduct extended classroom observations and interviews. The inspectors are themselves experienced teachers who were judged good enough (by other inspectors) to advance to the inspectorate. If some sort of a U.S. inspectorate were established, if successful performance in the classroom were defined as recent reformers have proposed, and if inspectors were both knowledgeable judges and helpful instructors, teachers might have sound professional reasons to want to learn to teach differently. If so, they would have a useful resource in learning— the inspectorate would be a perambulating archive of craft knowledge whose assignment would be to help teachers learn. Under such an arrangement it would be in teachers' professional self-interest to draw on that archive to improve themselves and then to validate the improvement. The link between

good teaching and professional advancement would be one potent incentive to learn, and hence an engine of reform. But one problem with such an approach would be its cost, and another would be the difficulty of establishing a suitable large and expert inspectorate. Still another would be the tendency of such an arrangement to preserve any given pedagogical status quo.

Another approach, more American in flavor, would be to test teachers' knowledge and to tie money rewards and penalties to the results. One version of such tests exists today—the National Teachers Examination, a standardized test published by the Educational Testing Service. One advantage of this approach is its relatively modest cost and ease of operation. But one objection is that such tests would dramatically constrain what could be learned about teachers' knowledge. An alternative would be to condition entry to teaching and advancement within it on teacher performance on complex written and perhaps oral examinations. The difference would be both in the performance criterion—exams versus tests—and in the incentives—professional advancement rather than money. The National Board for Professional Teaching Standards currently is developing the latter approach.

30. One discussion of the rationale for such cutbacks is offered by Smith & O'Day (1991).

31. Cohen & Spillane (1992) report one premise underlying this sort of policy agenda is that guidance for instruction in U.S. education is weak, inconsistent, and diffuse. Many private and public agencies issue advice concerning instructional purposes, content, and methods for teachers and students, but few take account of each other's advice. Hence much of the guidance is unrelated, divergent, or contradictory. Guidance for instruction also has been largely decoupled from government. While public agencies have extensive authority to guide instruction, historically they delegated much of it to private firms or local schools. The influence of U.S. school governments therefore pales when compared to central or provincial agencies elsewhere. The result is paradoxical: public and private agencies here prolifically produce guidance, more than in

societies with much more potent advice for instruction, but it does not press instruction in any consistent direction. When guidance is inconsistent and diffuse, no single test, curriculum, policy, or program is likely to have a broad or marked effect. Many teachers and students are aware of different sorts of advice, but few are keenly aware of most of it. Many know that most guidance is either weakly supported or contradicted by other advice, and that much can safely be ignored. The din of diverse, often inconsistent, and generally weak guidance opens considerable latitude to those who work within it.

Another premise for the policy agenda sketched above is that guidance for instruction might have to be greatly strengthened if teaching is to dramatically improve. In this connection, many reformers recently have embraced proposals for "systemic" change—that is, a linked set of reforms in curriculum, teaching, standards, assessment, and teacher education, all aimed at promoting intellectually demanding instruction (see Smith & O'Day, 1991). Some advocates of this approach argue that close alignment among assessment, curriculum frameworks, and texts and other materials would make it clear to teachers and students what they needed to teach and learn. Advocates also contend that such a system would offer many salient opportunities for educators to learn. For instance, grading students' work on systemwide examinations could be an extraordinary educational opportunity for teachers and administrators, if it were properly organized. That would require the selection of useful papers for discussion, finding adequate time to discuss them, and representing a range of useful perspectives in the discussions, including, for example, university subject matter specialists. Such exam grading also could provide many useful opportunities to consider the links between examinations and curricula, and thus to revise exams and curricula.

32. Cohen & Spillane (1992). Teaching is uncertain anywhere and difficult to influence in any system. It also is a rather different sort of work than administration or policymaking, entailing different sorts of knowledge and skills. All this is true in any system. But in some systems inspection and promotion ar-

rangements mean that no one winds up in administrative or ministry posts unless they have been experienced teachers who were judged to be of high quality. That tends to link policy and administration with practice. But in the United States those links are entirely absent. What professionals need to succeed as policymakers or administrators depends not at all on their performance as classroom practitioners. That greatly attenuates connections between the two worlds.

33. Firestone, 1989.

34. Smith, O'Day, & Cohen (1990) report that the American public and many national leaders have changed their attitudes about education considerably in the last twenty years. In 1971 the U.S. Congress asserted, "No provision of any applicable program shall be construed to authorize any department, agency, officer, or employee of the United States to exercise any direction, supervision, or control over the curriculum . . . of any educational institution" (p. 10). This belief in the local control of curriculum and instruction was consistent with the beliefs of most Americans. But by 1989, public opinion about curriculum was shifting toward support of a national curriculum, national standards, and a testing program to measure progress. A Gallup poll conducted that year showed 70 percent of Americans were in favor of national achievement standards and goals, 69 percent were in favor of a standardized national curriculum, and 77 percent were in favor of a national testing program.

References

Boyer, E. (1983). *American high school: A report on secondary education in America.* New York: HarperCollins.

Braybrooke, D., & Lindblom, C. E. (1963). *A strategy of decision: Policy evaluation as a social process.* New York: Free Press.

Bryk, A., & Lee, V. (in press). *Catholic high schools.* Cambridge: Harvard University Press.

Cohen, D. K. (1989). Practice and policy: Notes on the history of instruction. In D. Warren (Ed.), *American teachers: Histories of a profession at work.* New York: Macmillan.

Cohen, D. K. (1988). Teaching practice: Plus que ça change. . . . In P. W. Jackson (Ed.), *Contributing to educational change: Perspectives on research and practice* (pp. 27–84). Berkeley, CA: McCutchan.

Cohen, D. K., & Grant, S. G. (in press). America's children and their elementary schools. *Daedelus* [Special issue: America's children, age three to eleven].

Cohen, D. K., & Spillane, J. S. (1992, April). Policy and practice: The relations between governance and instruction. *Review of Research in Education, 18.* Washington, DC: American Educational Research Association, 3–50.

Cuban, L. (1984). *How teachers taught: Constancy and change in the American classroom.* New York: Longman.

Dewey, J. (1956). *The child and the curriculum.* Chicago: University of Chicago Press. (Original work published 1902)

Dewey, J. (1966). The nature of method. In *Democracy and education* (pp. 164–179). New York: Free Press. (Original work published 1916)

Duffy, J., & Roehler, L. (1986). *Improving classroom reading instruction: A decision-making approach.* New York: Random House.

Elbow, P. (1986). The teaching process. In *Embracing contraries: Explorations in learning and teaching.* New York: Oxford University Press.

Elmore, R. F., & McLaughlin, M. W. (1988). *Steady work: Policy, practice, and the reform of American education.* Santa Monica, CA: RAND Corporation.

Firestone, W. (1989). Educational policy as an ecology of games, *Educational Researcher, 18*(7), 18–24.

Fiske, S. T., & Taylor, S. E. (1984). *Social cognition.* Reading, MA: Addison-Wesley.

Guthrie, J. W. (Ed.). (1990). *Educational Evaluation and Policy Analysis, 12*(3) [Entire issue].

Johnson, S. M. (1990). *Teachers at work: Achieving success in our schools.* New York: Basic Books.

Kuhn, T. S. (1962). *The structure of scientific revolutions.* Chicago: University of Chicago Press.

Lakatos, I., & Musgrave, A. (Eds.). (1970). Criticism and the growth of knowledge. *Proceedings of the International Colloquium in the Philosophy of Science, 4.* Bedford College, England, 1965.

Lampert, M. (1986). Teachers' strategies for understanding and managing classroom dilemmas. In M. Ben-Peretz, R. Bromme, & R. Halkes (Eds.), *Advances in research on teacher thinking.* Lisse, Netherlands: Swets and Zeitlinger.

Lampert, M. (1988a). Teachers' thinking about students' thinking about geometry: The effects of new teaching tools. Cambridge, MA: Educational Technology Center.

Lampert, M. (1988b). *Teaching that connects students' inquiry with curricular agendas in schools* (Technical Report). Cambridge, MA: Educational Technology Center.

Little, J. (1982). *Norms of collegiality and experimentation: Workplace conditions of school success. American Education Research Journal, 19*(3), 325–340.

March, J. G. (1979). *Ambiguity and choice in organizations* (2nd ed.). Bergen, Norway: Universitetsforlaget.

Markus, H., & Zajonc, R. (1985). The cognitive perspective in social psychology. In G. Lindzey & E. Aaronson (Eds.), *Handbook of social psychology* (3rd ed., *1*). Hillsdale, NJ: Erlbaum.

McLaughlin, M. (1978). Implementation as mutual adaptation: Change in classroom organization. In W. Williams & R. F. Elmore (Eds.), *Social program implementation* (pp. 167–180). New York: Academic Press.

McKeachie, W., Pintrich, P., Lin, Y., & Smith, D. (1986). *Teaching and learning in the college classroom: A review of the research literature.* Ann Arbor, MI: National Center for Research to Improve Postsecondary Teaching and Learning.

Newmann, F. M. (1988). Higher order thinking in the high school curriculum. *NASSP Bulletin, 72,* 58–64.

Nisbett, R. E., & Ross, L. (1980). *Human inference: Strategies and shortcomings of social judgement.* Englewood Cliffs, NJ: Prentice-Hall.

Post, T., Behr, M., Harel, G., Lesh, R., & Taylor, B. R. (1988). *Intermediate teachers' knowledge of rational number concepts.* Unpublished paper. University of Wisconsin, National Center for Research in Mathematical Sciences Education, Madison.

Powell, A., Farrar, E., & Cohen, D. (1985). *The shopping mall high school.* Boston: Houghton Mifflin.

Sarason, S. (1982). *The culture of the school and the problem of change* (2nd ed.). Needham Heights, MA: Allyn & Bacon.

Scardamalia, M., Bereiter, C., & Steinbach, R. (1984). Teachability of reflective processes in written composition. *Cognitive Science, 8*(2), 173-190.

Sizer, T. R. (1984). *Horace's compromise: The dilemma of the American high school.* Boston: Houghton Mifflin.

Smith, M., & O'Day, J. (1991). Systemic school reform. In S. H. Fuhrman & B. Malen (Eds.), *The politics of curriculum and testing* (pp. 233-268). New York: Falmer.

Smith, M., O'Day, J., & Cohen, D. K. (1990, Winter). National curriculum American style. *American Educator, 14*(4), 10-17, 40-47.

Thompson, A. (1984). The relationships of teachers' conceptions of mathematics and mathematics teaching to instructional practice. *Educational Studies in Mathematics, 15,* 105-127.

Wildavsky, A., & Majone, G. (1979). Implementation: Exorcising the ghost in the machine. In J. Pressman, & A. Wildavsky, (Eds.), *Implementation.* Berkeley: University of California Press.

Name Index

Subject Index